# Reasoning from the Scriptures

*with the*

# MUSLIMS

## Ron Rhodes

HARVEST HOUSE™ PUBLISHERS

EUGENE, OREGON

*Cover by Terry Dugan Design, Minneapolis, Minnesota*

**REASONING FROM THE SCRIPTURES WITH MUSLIMS**
Copyright © 2002 by Ron Rhodes
Published by Harvest House Publishers
Eugene, Oregon 97402

Library of Congress Cataloging-in-Publication Data

Rhodes, Ron.
  Reasoning from the scriptures with Muslims / Ron Rhodes.
    p. cm.
  Includes bibliographical references and index.
  ISBN: 0-7369-1010-7
  1. Missions to Muslims. 2. Christianity and other religions—Islam.
  3. Islam—Relations—Christianity. I. Title.

  BV2625 .R46 2002
  266'.0088'2971—dc21                                    2002001754

**Printed in the United States of America.**

02 03 04 05 06 07 08 09 10 / DP-MS / 10 9 8 7 6 5 4 3 2 1

*To Christians everywhere*
*who seek to share the good news of Jesus Christ*
*with Muslim friends and neighbors*

# Acknowledgments

I never tire of thanking my wife, Kerri, and my two children, David and Kylie, for their continued sacrificial commitment to my work of ministry. Kerri is a treasure of a wife, a woman of virtue, and a joy to my heart (Proverbs 31:10). Our two children are without a doubt the two greatest gifts God has ever bestowed on us (Psalm 127:3). I cannot help but revel in the wonder of God's blessing.

# Contents

The Phenomenal Growth of Islam. . . . . . . . . . . . . . . . 7

1. Dialoguing with Muslims . . . . . . . . . . . . . . . . . . . . . 21

2. Muhammad and the Emergence of Islam . . . . . . . . . . 33

3. A Christian Critique of Muhammad . . . . . . . . . . . . . 49

4. The Quran—The Scriptures of Islam . . . . . . . . . . . . 69

5. A Christian Critique of the Quran . . . . . . . . . . . . . . . 79

6. Allah—The God of Islam . . . . . . . . . . . . . . . . . . . . . 95

7. The Biblical View of God . . . . . . . . . . . . . . . . . . . . 105

8. Jesus—A Prophet of Islam . . . . . . . . . . . . . . . . . . . 131

9. The Biblical View of Jesus, Part One . . . . . . . . . . . . 141

10. The Biblical View of Jesus, Part Two . . . . . . . . . . . . 161

11. The Muslim View of the Bible . . . . . . . . . . . . . . . . . 185

12. A Defense of the Bible, Part One . . . . . . . . . . . . . . . 195

13. A Defense of the Bible, Part Two . . . . . . . . . . . . . . . 215

14. Sin and Salvation in Islam. . . . . . . . . . . . . . . . . . . . 233

15. The Muslim View of the Afterlife . . . . . . . . . . . . . . . 255

16. Tips for Evangelizing Among Muslims . . . . . . . . . . . 277

     Postscript . . . . . . . . . . . . . . . . . . . . . . . . . . . . . . . . 291

     Appendix A—The Two Major Sects of Islam . . . . . . . 293

     Appendix B—Jihad—"Holy War" . . . . . . . . . . . . . . 297

     Appendix C—Resources Dealing
          with Bible Difficulties. . . . . . . . . . . . . . . . . . . . 299

     Notes . . . . . . . . . . . . . . . . . . . . . . . . . . . . . . . . . . . 301

     Bibliography . . . . . . . . . . . . . . . . . . . . . . . . . . . . . . 317

     Index to Subjects . . . . . . . . . . . . . . . . . . . . . . . . . . . 321

     Index to Bible Quotations . . . . . . . . . . . . . . . . . . . . 329

     Index to Quran Quotations . . . . . . . . . . . . . . . . . . . 341

If you run into witnessing trouble, feel free to contact Reasoning from the Scriptures Ministries. We will help you if we can.

Phone: 1-214-853-4370
E-mail: rhodes2@pacbell.net
Web site: www.ronrhodes.org

Free newsletter available upon request.

# The Phenomenal Growth of Islam

There are about 1.3 billion Muslims in the world—about 20 percent of the world's population.[1] That is one out of every five persons on Earth! Presently there are more than 3000 Muslim mosques in the United States; in 1990 there were only 30.[2] An average of one new mosque opens each week in the United States. There are presently 165 Islamic schools, 426 Islamic associations, and 90 Islamic publications in the United States.[3]

Islam certainly has some well-known adherents in this country. Pop musician Cat Stevens converted to Islam in 1977 and is now known by the name Yusuf Islam. Basketball star Kareem Abdul-Jabbar is another highly visible convert to Islam. These two individuals alone have generated substantial publicity for the religion.

Islam has enjoyed impressive growth around the world.

- It is presently the world's second largest religion, behind only Christianity.

- Over 65 nations in the world are Islamic.

- It is estimated that Muslims constitute 85 percent of the population in 32 countries.[4]

- There are more Muslims in the United Kingdom than Methodists and Baptists combined.[5]

- Though there was only one mosque in England in 1945, there are now thousands. Hundreds of the buildings used for mosques were originally churches —including the church that sent well-known Christian missionary William Carey to India.[6]

- Muslims are the second largest religious group in France. The number of mosques in France has mushroomed from only one in 1974 to thousands today.[7]

- Saudi Arabia and other Muslim countries are donating many tens of millions of dollars toward the furtherance of Islam in the United States.[8]

In the United States, it has been traditionally estimated that there are between four and eight million Muslims, the most likely figure being around five million. However, recent studies call this figure into question. The American Religious Identification Survey (ARIS) 2001, carried out by the Graduate Center of the City University of New York, did a substantial poll and found the total American Muslim population to be about 1.8 million.[9] Another recent study estimates the Muslim population to be 1,886,000. However, "with a nod toward figures supplied by Islamic organizations," the scholar who oversaw this later study allows that this number could be as high as 2,814,000 Muslims.[10]

I personally wonder whether the actual figure may be higher in view of the fact that some Muslims in the United States may feel trepidation at admitting they are Muslims. Even a survey that simply asks, "What is your religion, if any?" may give some Muslims pause simply because of the horrible press Islam has received over the last few decades because of Islamic terrorists. It is hard to objectively measure such factors, but I would not be surprised if the actual number of Muslims in the U.S. were 3 million or more.

In any event, because of the phenomenal growth of Islam around the world, many Muslims argue that this constitutes proof that Islam is the true religion. After all, how could the religion grow so rapidly without God's blessing?[11]

## Reasons for Islamic Growth

There are a number of reasons for the rapid growth of Islam around the world. Below I summarize only the more pertinent factors that are acknowledged by Muslim leaders:

- *Financial support.* A great deal of money is being poured into Arab missions around the world, especially in the United States. This money is being used to build mosques, Islamic centers at major universities, and for the publication of Islamic literature.[12]

- *A universal religion.* Islam claims to be a universal religion. Though it originated in Mecca, it claims to be for all people everywhere. Islam claims to know no barriers between races.[13] (Interestingly, though, the Shiites and Sunnis and other sects among the Muslims disagree on key issues and divide themselves from one another.)

- *A simple religion.* Islam has few requirements. It is a much simpler religion, Muslims claim, than Christianity. There are no difficult doctrines like the Trinity and the two natures (divine and human) in the one person of Christ. A person who recites the Islamic creed is a Muslim. A person who keeps the five pillars of Islam is a *good* Muslim. A person who emulates the life of Muhammad will be a *successful* Muslim.

- *A comprehensive religion.* Unlike Christianity, which focuses on spiritual matters only, Muslims say that Islam encompasses all spheres of life— political, economic, judicial, social, moral, and religious. (To be fair, though, Christians believe a relationship with Christ affects how one interacts in *all* these realms.)

- *An easier-to-obey religion.* Muslims say that Islam is a much easier religion to obey than Christianity. Many of the requirements laid down by Christ can seem almost impossible to fulfill. By contrast, the commands listed in the Quran are realistic, and the average person can obey them. (To be fair, though,

Christians believe that though Christ's commands are indeed loftier, the Holy Spirit empowers them and enables them to successfully live the Christian life.)

- *A rational religion.* To Muslims, there are certain doctrines in Christianity that do not make sense. For example, the idea that one man can die for another or for many people is nonsensical to them. They also think it is ridiculous that God cannot forgive people without sacrificing someone on a cross. Likewise, they think the idea of Jesus being the Son of God is nonsensical and even blasphemous, because it implies that God has had physical relations with a female. By contrast, Islam is a thinking man's religion. It contains no irrational concepts like Christianity does. (I will address these issues later in the book.)

- *A brotherhood religion.* Because Muslims all over the world follow the Muslim *hadith* (tradition), which contains details on how Muhammad acted in various circumstances, they have a sense of camaraderie and brotherhood known by few other religious groups.

- *Proselytizing*. Muslims proselytize. They actively share their faith. They are commanded in the Quran to "invite (all) to the way of thy Lord with wisdom" (Sura 16:125).[14]

## Introducing Islam

Islam is a monotheistic religion that arose in the seventh century A.D. under the leadership of Muhammad (also spelled *Muhammed* and *Mohammed*). Muhammad was alleged to be the greatest of a long line of prophets that included Moses and Jesus. His primary revelation was that the one true God is Allah. Allah's revelation to Muhammad occurred over a 23-year period and is recorded in the Quran (Islam's holy book, also spelled *Qur'an* and *Koran*). "Quran" means "that which is to be read."

"Islam" literally means "submission to the will of Allah." Members of Islam are called Muslims ("those who submit"). The word "Muslim" expresses the inner attitude of those who have hearkened to the preaching of Muhammad.[15] The word conveys a *perpetual* and *ongoing* submission to God. Scholar Charles J. Adams states,

> By its very form [a verbal noun] it conveys a feeling of action and ongoingness, not of something that is static and finished, once and for all, but of an inward state which is always repeated and renewed....One who thoughtfully declares "I am a Muslim" has done much more than affirm his membership in a community....[He is saying,] "I am one who commits himself to God."[16]

Islam involves both *beliefs* ("The Five Doctrines of Islam") and *obligations* ("The Five Pillars of Islam"). Though I will discuss all these in greater detail later in the book, I will summarize them here to give you an overall understanding of Islam before I discuss the specifics.

## The Five Doctrines of Islam

There are five essential doctrines Muslims subscribe to.

1. *God.* There is only one true God, whose name is Allah. The term "Allah" is probably derived from *al illah,* which means "the god." Allah is said to have seven primary characteristics. First and foremost, he has absolute unity—that is, he is "one" and there is no such thing as a Trinity (God cannot have a "Son," and God cannot have a partner). He

is also all-seeing, all-hearing, all-speaking, all-knowing, all-willing, and all-powerful.

2. *Angels*. There is a hierarchy of angels between Allah and humankind, the chief of whom is Gabriel, the archangel who allegedly gave revelations to Muhammad (Sura 2:97). Each human being is said to have two recording angels who list all of his or her deeds, good or bad (Sura 50:17). These recorded deeds will be brought forth at the coming judgment.

3. *Holy books*. There are four inspired books: the Torah of Moses, the Psalms of David, the Gospel of Jesus Christ, and the Quran (which contains the teachings of Muhammad). The Quran is said to contain Allah's final message to humankind, and it supersedes all previous revelations. The Quran abrogates (abolishes or annuls) any conflicting claims about truth. Only the Quran has been preserved to the present time in an uncorrupted state.

4. *Prophets*. There are allegedly 124,000 prophets who have been sent to human beings throughout history. The most important ones number less than 30—the greatest of whom is Muhammad. Other prominent prophets include Adam, Noah, Abraham, Moses, David, Solomon, Jonah, John the Baptist, and Jesus. Each prophet brought truth for his particular age, but Muhammad is a prophet for all time.

5. *A future judgment.* There will be a Day of Judgment and a resurrection. Allah will be the judge. Depending on how one fares as Allah weighs one's good and bad deeds, one will end up either in paradise (a place of pleasure) or hell (a place of torment).

6. *Fate.* A sixth doctrine that is sometimes taught is that Allah foreordains all things. He is totally sovereign. Nothing can take place without Allah ordaining it to happen. There is no such thing as a random event.

## The Five Pillars of the Faith

There are five religious duties or obligations expected of every good Muslim.

### 1. Creedal Recitation

Muslims are expected to publicly recite the *Shahadah* (literally, "to bear witness"). The creed reads: "There is no god but Allah, and Muhammad is the Prophet of Allah." Muslim literature often affirms that the reciting of this creed makes one a Muslim.

I should note, however, that a mere *mechanical* reciting of the words is not sufficient to make one a Muslim. There are six conditions that must be met: 1) The creed must be repeated aloud; 2) it must be perfectly understood; 3) it must be believed in the heart; 4) it must be professed until one dies; 5) it must be recited correctly; and 6) it must be professed and declared without hesitation.[17]

The creed is the first thing whispered into a baby's ears when he or she is born into the world. If humanly possible, just prior to the moment of death, Muslims seek to have these words upon their lips.[18] If not, then someone close to them may utter the words for them.

Scholar Jamal J. Elias has noted that reciting just the first half of the creed—"There is no God but Allah"—makes one a monotheist, but not necessarily a Muslim. After all, the Arabic word for "God" is "Allah," and a person who says in Arabic that there is one God may just be asserting that he is a monotheist. However, Elias notes, the second half of the recitation— "Muhammad is the Prophet of Allah"—distinguishes Muslims from all other monotheists.[19]

### 2. Prayers

Muslims are expected to perform *salat,* or offer prayers, five times a day: at dawn, noon, afternoon, evening, and night. Such prayers are compulsory for everyone over the age of ten. These prayers involve specific words and a series of postures (standing, kneeling, hands and face on the ground, and so forth) while the believer is facing Mecca, the holy city for Muslims.[20]

In Muslim parts of the world, when it comes time for prayer, a strong-voiced man called a *muezzin* will climb atop a tower— a *minaret*—and cry out that it is time for prayer. This call for prayer is called the *adhan*. Upon hearing the voice of this man, Muslims pause from whatever they are doing—whether relaxing at home or working in an office—and engage in the prescribed prayer.[21] In urban areas, a public-address system often signals the beginning of prayer.[22] It is permissible to pray at home, at work, or even outdoors, so long as the place of prayer is free from distractions and is clean.

Muslims are required to wash themselves (hands, face, and feet) in a prescribed manner before praying. This is called ablution or *wudu*.[23] "This is a ritual purification rather than a matter of hygiene. No soap is used, and when water is unavailable one can simply go through the motions of washing with one's dry hands."[24]

In the modern world, Muslims who work in corporate America—particularly in situations where few others in the office are sympathetic to Muslim religious practices—may find it a challenge to engage in such regular prayer. The traveling businessperson can also find it a challenge. These Muslims often shorten or combine their prayers, depending on their circumstances. They also carry "Mecca Finders," compasses with the coordinates for Mecca.[25]

## 3. Giving Alms

Muslims are expected to give alms *(zakat)* to the Muslim community that amount to one-fortieth (or 2½ percent) of their income. This offering benefits widows, orphans, and the sick, or it can be used toward furthering Islam (for example, building mosques and religious schools). Giving to charity is considered an extremely meritorious act in Islam (see Suras 24:56; 57:18).

Different Muslim communities handle charity in different ways. In some communities it is up to the individual Muslim to make a charitable contribution to the cause of his choice—generally a local charity. Some Muslims give the money to their local mosque, or to a respected Islamic leader, who then applies the funds to good use. In other Muslim communities there is a *zakat* tax collected by the government. The income derived from this tax is then used either for social benefit (building schools, for example) or for religious purposes.

Students of Islam have long noted that Muhammad himself was once poor and was an orphan. It is thus understandable that there would be an emphasis in Islam on giving charitably to the poor.

## 4. Fasting During the Month of Ramadan

Muslims are expected to fast during the month of Ramadan, the ninth month of the Muslim lunar year. During this month Muslims abstain from food, drink, smoking, and sexual relations during the daylight hours. Indeed, as soon as there is enough light to distinguish a white thread from a black thread each morning, the fast begins.[26] At sundown—when there is *not* enough light to distinguish the threads—they are allowed to partake of these things again until sunrise the next morning.

Understandably, it is much easier to engage in this fast if one is wealthy enough to be able to stay home during the day, and perhaps sleep more during the day than the night. But for those who work during the daylight hours, the fast can quickly exhaust one's stamina and mental drive.[27] In any event, the fast is intended to be a time of purifying both body and soul, as well as increase one's self-awareness.[28]

The month of Ramadan is important to Muslims because it is believed Muhammad received the initial revelation of the Quran during this month. Muhammad himself fasted during this sacred time, so in honor of the Prophet, Muslims do so as well.[29] Because the Islamic calendar is based upon a lunar year, the dates of

Ramadan shift from year to year on the Western calendar. For instance, in the year 2003, the first day of Ramadan is October 27; in 2007, it is September 13.

There are some cases in which it is permissible for a Muslim not to engage in this fast. Muslims excused from this requirement include those who are sick, small children, mothers nursing infants, and travelers. Also exempt are old and feeble people, as well as the insane.

Islam scholar William Miller reports that there are some Muslims who are so strict with this fast that they won't even swallow their own saliva during the daylight hours. They also believe that if even a drop of water goes down their throat while they are cleaning their teeth, they are required to atone for this slip by keeping another fast.[30] Other Muslims are not so strict. These Muslims are more concerned about avoiding a *deliberate* breaking of the fast—eating a meal or engaging in sexual relations. Frederick Denny points out that a deliberate breaking of the fast carries a penalty of having to "fast sixty days, to feed sixty people the equivalent of one meal each, or to give charity equal to a meal to sixty persons. This penalty is known as *kaffara*, meaning 'reparation, penance.' "[31]

Practically speaking, most Muslim families get up early enough to eat a substantial breakfast before the sun rises—a breakfast intended to last the day. In Muslim communities, the beginning of the fast is often indicated by the blast of a siren, or perhaps by a man walking through the street beating a drum. During the daytime hours, many restaurants close for business. Some, however, stay open to serve non-Muslims. Some Muslim communities are so strict that there is a law against eating or drinking in public during the fast. At the end of the day, after the sun has gone down, Muslim families often sit down to a rather elaborate meal. Interestingly, more food is sold in Muslim communities during the month of Ramadan than any other month of the year.[32]

## 5. The Pilgrimage to Mecca

Every Muslim is expected to make an official pilgrimage to Mecca *(hajj)* at least once in his or her life. A woman may go on the hajj only with her husband's permission, and even then she must be under the protection of a guardian. It is believed that going on this pilgrimage is meritorious and greatly enhances one's chances for salvation.[33] It is an exciting time for a Muslim, for he has prayed toward Mecca his entire life, and now he has the chance to go there.

The hajj actually begins before the pilgrim leaves for Mecca during the month of the pilgrimage. As Islam scholar Abdulkader Tayob points out,

> The hajj begins at home, where preparations have to be made for the journey….Before the actual departure, a pilgrim visits family and friends and seeks their forgiveness for both known and unintentional acts that may have transpired between them. The pilgrim is getting ready to stand in front of God, and does not want that encounter to be sullied by less than perfect human relations. A perfect pilgrimage leads to complete absolution of sins, and nobody would want to mar such an expectation by neglecting to resolve inter-human friction.[34]

Making the pilgrimage hinges on one's health and financial ability to make the trip. If one is unable to go for health reasons, it is permissible to have another person make the hajj for one as a proxy. Financially, there must be enough money not only to pay for the pilgrimage to Mecca but also to take care of loved ones while one is away. Because the trip is costly, Muslims typically save money for many years to be able to make the trip. Borrowing money to pay for the trip is not wise, since the hajj does not become valid until all debts are paid off.

As Muslims approach Mecca, and throughout the entire pilgrimage, they repeatedly recite the *talbiya:* "I am here, O my God, I am here! I am here, Thou art without any associate, I am here! Praise and blessing belong to Thee, and Power."[35] As the pilgrims make their way to the holy precincts of Mecca, they go through gates or checkpoints—*miqats*—beyond which non-Muslims are not permitted to go.[36] As they enter the sacred mosque in Mecca, they recite verses from the Quran, especially Sura 17:80-81:

> Say: "O my Lord! Let my entry be by the Gate of Truth and Honor, and likewise my exit by the Gate of Truth and Honor; and grant me from Thy Presence an authority to aid (me)." And say: "Truth has (now) arrived, and Falsehood perished: for Falsehood is (by its nature) bound to perish."

Once in Mecca, all pilgrims go through the same basic rituals. They start at the Black Stone, which is embedded in the southeast corner of the *Kaaba* (religious shrine), and then run around the building seven times, three times fast and four times slow, in a counterclockwise direction. According to Muslim tradition, both Abraham and Ishmael circled the Kaaba in this way, as did Muhammad. This event is known as *tawaf.* Each time pilgrims go around the building, they pause at the southeast corner in order to kiss the Black Stone. If there is a huge crowd of Muslims there, it is permissible to simply touch the stone with one's hand, or perhaps with a stick. If even that proves difficult, one can simply observe the stone and meditate upon it.[37] This ritual is believed to yield a blessing from heaven.

The Black Stone is worshiped by Muslims, who believe it fell from heaven in the days of Adam.[38] They also believe it is the site of God's covenant with Abraham and Ishmael, so it carries great religious significance.

One highly relevant factor regarding the hajj is that everyone participating in the rituals is dressed the same way. They all wear white garments called *ihram*. This attire serves to eliminate all class or status distinctions during the pilgrimage. The rich and the poor are on equal footing.

There are other events that take place during the pilgrimage besides just running around the Kaaba. Muslims visit a number of sacred sites, tombs of Muslim saints, and sites containing the relics of Muhammad (this can take a week).[39] Visiting such places is believed to increase one's merit before Allah on the Day of Judgment.[40] Those who successfully complete the pilgrimage are given the title of *hajji*, and they look forward to receiving a reward from Allah for visiting the sacred sites.

Not unexpectedly, it takes massive organization and planning on the part of the Saudi Arabian government to accommodate up to two million pilgrims participating in the same rituals over the space of a few days. These pilgrims pour into the area from Algeria, Afghanistan, Indonesia, Syria, Pakistan, Sudan, Europe, America, Africa, and other places. They come by car, bus, train, ship, and plane. The Saudi Arabian government has invested a fortune in building highways, tunnels, and galleries to make things run as smoothly as possible.[41]

## The Call to Evangelism

More than one Christian missionary has noted that there seem to be very few converts from Islam to Christianity. Yet, as others note, Muslim conversions are few not because Muslims are so hard to convert, but because they have been largely ignored by the Christian church. The current estimates are that a mere two percent of the Protestant missionary force is actively involved in evangelizing among 1.3 billion Muslims.[42] William Miller says that "with some glorious exceptions, the Christians of the world have signally failed to obey Christ by sending laborers to sow and reap a harvest in Muslim lands."[43] Not only are there too few Christian missionaries evangelizing Muslims in other countries, there are far too few Christians seeking to reach Muslims in our own country. This is not as it should be.

Jesus, though not speaking specifically about Muslims, nevertheless made a statement very much needed for this hour: "The harvest is plentiful but the workers are few. Ask the Lord of the harvest, therefore, to send out workers into his harvest field" (Matthew 9:37-38). The apostle Paul also spoke eloquent words needed for our times: "How, then, can they call on the one they have not believed in? And how can they believe in the one of whom they have not heard? And how can they hear without someone preaching to them?" (Romans 10:14). Let us not forget that we are called to be Christ's witnesses to all peoples and all nations (Matthew 24:14; 28:19; Mark 16:15; Luke 24:47)— including Muslims. *And let us not be shy about it.* We must boldly tell the truth about Jesus to our Muslim acquaintances and pray mightily that God would work in the hearts of those we speak to. We can praise the Lord that, even now, there are Muslims coming to know Jesus Christ every day.

# 1

# *Dialoguing with Muslims*

Witnessing to Muslims can be a trying experience. But you can greatly enhance your effectiveness in dialoguing with them by deciding in advance to handle your witnessing encounters in a certain way. Following are some suggestions.

## Always Prepare by Prayer

I urge you to pray regularly in regard to your witnessing opportunities. Remember, only God in His mighty power can lift the veil of spiritual blindness from the human heart (2 Corinthians 4:4; see also 3:16; John 8:32). Pray fervently for the Muslims you witness to and pray often (Matthew 7:7-12; Luke 18:1-8; James 5:16).

A verse I especially appreciate in this regard is Acts 16:14: "One of those listening [to Paul speaking] was a woman named Lydia, a dealer in purple cloth from the city of Thyatira, who was a worshiper of God. *The Lord opened her heart to respond to Paul's message*" (emphasis added). I suggest that, when you are praying for your Muslim friends, pray that the Lord would *open their hearts* to the gospel of Jesus Christ. He has the power to do it.

## Develop Personal Relationships

It may be that the Muslim to whom you want to witness is a friend or family member. In that case, you've already got a lot going for you, because personal relationships are very important to success in witnessing. If, however, the Muslim to whom you want to witness is someone you encounter socially, and you do not yet have a personal relationship, it is important to try to develop one.

A sincere friendship characterized by trust and compassion can earn you the right to be heard.[1] Christian writer Phil Parshall says he has found in his long experience that Muslims typically become attracted to Christianity through the life and witness of a person who takes the time and effort to cultivate a genuine friendship.[2] John Gilchrist agrees, adding that "Muslims are unlikely to become your *brethren* until they first become your *friends*."[3] By building and developing friendships with Muslims, Christians lay a strong foundation for an effective witness.

Muslims sometimes claim Americans are superficial and hollow in their friendships. You should therefore try to dispel this stereotype and not be superficial. Develop a genuine friendship.

As you develop your friendship, do not make it contingent on whether the Muslim responds favorably to the gospel. Be a friend to him or her *regardless* of his or her response. Muslims will definitely notice this, and this may open the door for you to lead them to Christ further on in your relationship.

Keep in mind that Muslims are well known for their generous hospitality. If you ever visit the home of a Muslim family, they will almost certainly offer you food and drink and make you feel right at home. You should try to reciprocate and show hospitality to your Muslim acquaintances. Offer them food and drink when they visit.

Note, however, that Muslims do not drink alcohol or eat any food products containing pork (don't offer them a ham sandwich).

## Meet Only with Individual Muslims

Witnessing to Muslims is best done on a one-to-one basis. I say this because, generally speaking, Muslims are vigorous and dutiful in their defense of Islam in the presence of other Muslims.[4] In a group setting, individual Muslims will not feel the freedom to express any doubts they have about Islam, and they will be fearful of asking questions about Christianity. This makes evangelism nearly impossible. To avoid this problem, speak to a single Muslim at a time.

## Realize Islam Is a Way of Life

Islam is not just a religion, it is a way of life. Especially in Muslim societies, Islam encompasses the cultural, economic, political, social, and religious dimensions of life. In such a society, unlike the United States, "church and state" are essentially united. Islam scholar William Miller notes that the laws of Islam are both civil and religious, and these laws tell the Muslim man and woman what their duties are in all areas of life.[5] Former Muslim Reza F. Safa says that "when Islam takes over a home, family, society or country, it controls everything."[6]

Islam is thus all-encompassing. The Islamic worldview is tightly integrated and cohesive. Segmentation of life into "secular" and "religious" categories is resisted. One's daily activities are governed by the awareness that Allah is involved in every aspect of life.[7] Christian witnesses must understand that growing up in an Islamic society can so thoroughly train, behavioralize, and indoctrinate a person that witnessing to him can prove to be a tremendous challenge.[8] I mention this because this realization can help you to remain patient when it seems like you have come against a "brick wall" in your witnessing. (Remaining patient is *very* important.)

## Beware of Stereotypes

There are stereotypes that Muslims have of Americans *and* stereotypes that Americans have of Muslims. Unless these stereotypes are recognized and dealt with, they can erect unnecessary and troublesome barriers to communication.

Bruce McDowell and Anees Zaka discuss some of these stereotypes in their excellent book *Muslims and Christians at the Table*. Among the stereotypes Muslims have of Westerners are that they are materialistic, immoral (sexually free, drink a lot of alcohol, have racist attitudes), and do not value life (too many abortions). Among the stereotypes Americans have of Muslims is that they are all Arabs, many are rich oil sheiks, most of them are extremists and terrorists, and they are generally sinister and dangerous people. Among the stereotypes we Christians have of ourselves is that we are incapable of reaching them for Christ ("I don't know enough and I'm not qualified"). Among the stereotypes Muslims have of themselves is that they are very religious people following the truth, are enlightened with the true religion, and are peace-loving, tolerant, and reasonable people.[9]

When Christians encounter Muslims who argue for the supremacy of Islam by slamming Christianity—equating it with Western degeneracy—it is important for the Christian to distinguish between Christianity and the vices of the West. Christians must point out that the West has succumbed to so many vices not because the West is "Christian" but because the West has largely *ignored* Christianity.[10] Christians can also point out that such vices illustrate one of the primary teachings of Christianity—that is, that humankind is engulfed in a serious sin problem (more on this later in the book).

Be forewarned that one of the ways Muslims sometimes back Christians into a corner is by asking them, "Are you a Christian?" If the Christian says "yes" without qualifying his answer, the Muslim will likely assume he is a person of low morals. As Sobhi Malek points out, most Muslims use the word "Christian" to mean "someone who comes from a culture which is broadly labeled as 'Christian.'...Muslims often associate with the term 'Christian' the things that born-again believers from the West often associate with the term 'non-Christian'!"[11] Malek suggests handling the discussion in this way:

> MUSLIM: "Are you a Christian?"
>
> MISSIONARY: "What do you mean by 'Christian'?"
>
> MUSLIM: "I mean Westerner, European, non-Muslim, someone who does not follow the teachings of the Quran. I mean someone with low morals like the people I see in the movies and read about in the books that come from Europe and the United States."
>
> MISSIONARY: "If that is what you mean, my answer is 'No.' In fact, I was that kind of person you have described, but I got converted! Now I follow Christ according to the Bible."[12]

## Be Kind but Firm

It is imperative that Christians not develop a hostile attitude when interacting with Muslim acquaintances. Christians should show only kindness. After all, as Scripture says, you are to always be ready "to make a defense to everyone who asks you to give an account for the hope that is in you, *yet with gentleness and reverence*" (1 Peter 3:15 NASB, emphasis added). Colossians 4:6 urges, "Let your conversation be *always full of grace,* seasoned with salt, so that you may know how to answer everyone" (emphasis added). Likewise, 2 Timothy 2:24-25 says, "The Lord's servant must *not quarrel*; instead, he must *be kind to everyone,* able to teach, not resentful. Those who oppose him he must *gently instruct*" (emphasis added).

While being kind and gentle, however, you must also be firm in setting forth and defending the truth of the gospel. Remember, eternal souls are at stake. Just as the first-century Christians were bold in their witness for Christ, so must we be bold witnesses (see Acts 2:32; 3:15; 4:33; 13:30-31).

## Identify with the Muslim

Muslims are people before they are Muslims. They have families, children, needs, frustrations, and fears, and they are brothers and sisters in Adam, though not in Christ. Acts 17:26-28 tells us that all people on earth, by virtue of being created by God, are "offspring" of God. In Adam, then, all of us share a common heritage. In view of this, we should talk to Muslims from the "family-of-Adam perspective," prayerfully hoping to bring them to the "family-of-God perspective."[13]

If you can keep in mind that Muslims are people before they are Muslims—people who have the need for friendship, the need for love and security, people who laugh and cry, and so forth—you will find it much easier to treat them with respect and kindness when you speak with them.

## Do Not Assume That All Muslims Believe the Same Thing

Not all Muslims believe the same thing. There are several reasons for this. One factor has to do with national distinctions—with certain Islamic sects (such as the Sunnis and Shiites) dominating in certain nations. Islam in Africa is not identical to the Islam in the Middle East or in India. Muslims from different nations vary as to their beliefs, practices, and behavior.[14] When Muslims migrate to the United States from their various countries, they bring with them their Islamic distinctions.

Another factor that accounts for divergence among Muslims is that not all of them read the Arabic Quran. Many Muslims believe that since the Quran was *written* in Arabic, it can only be *read* in Arabic. The problem is, Arabic is a foreign language for the majority of the world's Muslims. In fact, scholars believe there are between 140 and 200 million Muslims living in the 22 Arab nations in the world, which means that less than 20 percent of the world's 1.3 billion Muslims are Arabs. This also means that more than 80 percent of the world's Muslims cannot read or write Arabic.[15] Since many American Muslims cannot read Arabic, they cannot read the Quran, and hence their knowledge of the Quran may be quite limited (though some do succumb to reading English translations of the Quran).

Even in Arabic lands, there is a high rate of illiteracy, and hence not even all Arab Muslims can read the Arabic Quran.[16] An additional complicating factor is that the classical Arabic of the Quran is now removed from modern Arabic by 1300 years. For this reason, the meaning of the words and phrases may be partly unclear to even an educated speaker of Arabic.

Despite such factors, the one thing all Muslims have in common is their belief that Allah is the one true God, and Muhammad is his holy prophet. Further, despite their differences, and despite their sense of nationalism and patriotism regarding their individual homelands, Muslims around the world believe they are part of an Islamic community (the *ummah*) and accordingly extend a welcoming hand and a strong sense of kinship to all other Muslims.[17]

## Do Not Assume That All Muslims Are Militant

It is wrong and foolish to conclude that all Muslims are militant and hostile toward Western civilization. The sad reality is that most reports in the media relating to Muslims focus attention on extremists engaged in terrorism. This constitutes unfair "bad press" for mainstream Muslims living in the United States. As Donald S. Tingle points out, "These news stories of extremist activities by a minority of Arabs in one part of the world distort the overall picture of Islam….In a study of any religion we must step beyond the extremist activities of a few and view the religion as a whole."[18]

I recall that just after the terrorist attack against the World Trade Center in New York City on September 11, 2001, a kindly

Muslim family showed up at our church on a Sunday morning to give flowers to the pastoral staff as an act of love and compassion. Their loving act drew a wide line in the sand between them and the Muslim terrorists responsible for the New York tragedy.

Many Muslims in the United States make very good friends and neighbors, are loving and hospitable people, and are open to discussing their faith with you. Indeed, they very well may try to convert you to Islam, which is something you should welcome, since it opens the door for you to share your faith with them.

## Define Your Terms

Muslims often refer to God, Jesus, the Holy Spirit, prayer, the angels, and other terms common to the Bible, but they attach entirely different meanings to these words. This means that when *they* use these terms, you may not understand what they mean by what they are saying. Likewise, when *you* use such terms, they will likely not interpret your words in the way you are intending. This is known as a "terminology block." Unless you define your terms biblically and overcome the terminology block, little true communication will take place. (It is my hope that this book will help you to overcome the terminology block.)

## Ask Leading Questions

You will not be able to force your opinion on a Muslim. But if you can help the Muslim discover problems in the Quran and in Islamic theology for himself, then you have really accomplished a good thing.

One great way of helping a Muslim discover problems in his viewpoint is by asking strategic questions, all the while remaining tactful and kind. Remember, Jesus often asked questions to make a point (for example, Luke 9:20). Christian apologist David Reed notes that "rather than shower his listeners with information, [Jesus] used questions to draw answers out of them. A person can close his ears to facts he doesn't want to hear, but if a pointed question causes him to form the answer in his own mind, he cannot escape the conclusion—because it's a conclusion that he reached himself."[19] We must use this same type of methodology with Muslims.

For example, you might ask your Muslim acquaintance, "Do you know *for sure* you will go to paradise when you die?" (It is well known that Muslims have no assurance of salvation, and hence the Muslim will probably say *no*.) Then you can ask, "Have you considered Jesus' words about how His followers *can* be sure that they are saved? What do you think He meant when He said, 'I give them eternal life, and they shall never perish; no one can snatch them out of my hand'" (John 10:28)?

Another thought-provoking question might be this: "If the Quran is an eternal book, as Muslims claim, then why is it that certain later revelations in the Quran are said to abrogate certain earlier revelations in the Quran? If the book were truly eternal, why would there be a need for a change in revelation?"

By tactfully asking such questions, you can cause the Muslim to think for himself about issues that may open his heart to the truth of the Bible. I will provide examples of helpful questions throughout this book.

## Beware of Satanic Resistance

Many Christians who have engaged in evangelism among Muslims have noted that the religion of Islam is perhaps Satan's greatest masterpiece in leading people astray and holding them in spiritual bondage.[20] It has seemed to many Christian witnesses that Satan expends extra effort in making sure there are few converts from Islam to Christianity. In view of this, Christians must recognize that, when they are witnessing to Muslims, there may be a heightened level of spiritual warfare. Satan will not stand idly by while you lead others out of his dark kingdom. When witnessing to Muslims, then, be sure to put on your spiritual armor (Ephesians 6:10-20), and pray accordingly.

## Beware That Conflict May Develop

If a Muslim converts to Christianity, he can be persecuted, reviled, kicked out of his family, lose his job, and—in certain Islamic countries—be put to death. Since he is fully aware of such factors, it is very difficult for a Muslim to become a Christian, even if he senses Christianity may be true. On the other hand, the danger of *not* turning to the true God is obvious.

God Himself has told us that in terms of priority, we must always obey God above men (Acts 5:29). If there is ever a conflict between what God desires of us and what our family members say or do, we must unhesitatingly yield in obedience to God—even if it leads to disruption in the family. Jesus once said,

> He who loves father or mother more than Me is
> not worthy of Me; and he who loves son or
> daughter more than Me is not worthy of Me. And
> he who does not take his cross and follow after
> Me is not worthy of Me. He who has found his
> life will lose it, and he who has lost his life for
> My sake will find it (Matthew 10:36-39 NASB).

Later in the book, I will talk about the importance of helping the newly converted Muslim gain a new spiritual family by introducing him or her to other Christian friends who can be a support.

## Consider Yourself a Missionary

A Christian leader once said, "Every heart with Christ is a missionary; every heart without Christ is a mission field." Consider yourself a missionary! And consider this book a missionary training manual for reaching Muslims with the wonderful gospel of grace (Ephesians 2:8-9).

## Postscript: A Warning to Christians Witnessing in Arab Lands

I am confident that the great majority of my readers live on American soil, but I want to include a brief warning for those who may visit Arab countries. Be aware that many Arab nations consider Christian missions a crime that is severely punishable. This means that if you share Jesus Christ with Muslims in these countries, and the authorities catch you, you could end up in jail or worse. In fact, the evidence is clear that missionaries and pastors in such countries have been *executed* for the cause of Christ.[21] Exercise extreme caution!

# 2

## *Muhammad and the Emergence of Islam*

One often hears the name of Muhammad upon the lips of Muslims—something that shows the tremendous respect and even veneration they have for him. One hears his name from the lips of worshipers at Muslim mosques, beggars seeking alms, the sick and the dying, and Muslim soldiers under attack. A mother soothes her infant to sleep by singing his name in a cradlesong. Muslim homes often have the name inscribed on the doorpost. Muhammad is quite simply a holy name among Muslims.[1]

### The Prophetic Backdrop

The Quran says Allah has sent a prophet to every nation to let people know there is only one true God. Prophets mentioned in the Quran include Adam, Saleh, Lut (Lot), Hud, Yüacub (Jacob), Ibrahim (Abraham), Yunus (Jonah), Musa (Moses), Daud (David), Al-Yaüsa (Elisha), Zakara (Zachariah), Dhul-Kifl (Ezekiel), Isa (Jesus), Nuhu (Noah), Shuüaib, Ismaiüil (Ishmael),

Yusuf (Joseph), Ishaq (Isaac), Harun (Aaron), Sulaiman (Solomon), Yahya (John the Baptist), Ayyub (Job), Ilyas (Elijah), Idrees, and Muhammad.[2] Islamic tradition claims 124,000 prophets have been sent to humankind, but the actual number of books given to the prophets is said to be just 104. Even prophets like Adam, Noah, and Abraham wrote prophetic books, but they no longer exist.

Most Muslims believe the prophets were sinless or at least free from all major sins (even Adam). In reality, though, only Jesus was sinless. Indeed, even the Quran records the sins of the prophets, including Adam's eating of the forbidden fruit (Sura 7:11-27), Moses' murder of the Egyptian (Sura 28:16), David's adultery with Bathsheba (Sura 38:18-25), Solomon's repentance (Sura 38:31-36), and Muhammad's need for forgiveness (Sura 47:19).[3]

Each prophet's revelation is said to have been appropriate only for the age in which he lived. When God gives a new book to one of the great prophets, he thereby abrogates (abolishes or annuls) the previous books. This means the revelation that came through Muhammad abrogated all previous revelations, including that of the Bible. Each of the great prophets allegedly foretold the coming of the prophet who would succeed him. The last and greatest of the prophets, Muhammad, is called the "Seal of the prophets" (Sura 33:40). Whereas the previous prophets presented revelation only for their age, Muhammad's revelation is said to be for all time.[4]

Islam teaches that human sin emerges not as a result of an active rebellion against God, or because of an inner sin nature, but rather because people have an inherent feebleness and forgetfulness (Sura 4:28). *That* is why we need Allah's laws. If sin emerges as a result of forgetfulness and feebleness, then Allah's laws serve as a constant reminder of what is expected of humankind. The need for prophets is thus apparent, for it is the prophets that deliver Allah's laws to humankind.[5]

Muslims believe that all the prophets raised up by Allah taught the same basic message—that there is only one true God, and that people must submit to his laws and do good works in view of the coming Day of Judgment.[6] Different prophets may *appear* to have delivered different messages, but that is because of peoples' distortions of the prophets' fundamentally identical teachings. Even Jesus' words are said to be hopelessly distorted in the New Testament. Jesus' *original* teachings are said to have been in full agreement with those of Muhammad.

## The Culture into Which Muhammad Was Born

The Arabian Peninsula, where Muhammad was born, was a rather desolate area with barren mountains and a forbidding desert.[7] Prior to his birth, his tribe—the Quraysh—had come into possession of Mecca, a barren valley, and had built a thriving community there. The community flourished as a result of commercial trade, and the Quraysh tribe rapidly emerged as a powerful tribal group to be reckoned with. There was protection to be had by being a member of a tribe like the Quraysh. Should an outsider murder a member, the tribe would avenge him. The fear of blood vengeance served as a powerful deterrent to crime in Arabia.[8]

The culture into which Muhammad was born was polytheistic. The people believed in many gods and goddesses. Some of these deities were strictly tribal, whereas others were believed to preside over certain geographical areas. All who lived within a particular geographical area were obliged to worship the deity affiliated with that area.[9] The people also believed in animism, for in their thinking there were various spirits, demons, and powers associated with rocks, streams, trees, and other parts of nature, which had to be propitiated.

## Muhammad's Birth

Muhammad was born in Mecca in A.D. 570, shortly after the death of his father. After Muhammad's mother died when he was six years old, his grandfather cared for him briefly, and then Muhammad's father's brother, Abu Talib, brought him up.

According to the Quran, Muhammad grew up in poverty (Sura 93:6ff.). At first he shared the religious beliefs of his community. As time passed, however, he grew increasingly dissatisfied with the polytheism and animism that permeated his culture. He became uncomfortable with the fact that 360 gods and idols were worshiped within the walls of the Kaaba (the religious black stone shrine in the heart of Mecca). This dissatisfaction stayed with him into adulthood.

## Muhammad the Merchant

Some records indicate that, as a young man, Muhammad was of medium height and build, had dark and slightly curly hair, and heavy eyebrows. He is also said to have had rather large extremities—head, hands, and feet. He apparently had a black vein that swelled out on his forehead whenever he became angry.[10] We are told that Muhammad was extremely neat, gentle, sincere, amiable and companionable, generous, shrewd, disliked strong odors, had a keen insight into the psychology of human nature, was a good improviser, was undeniably sensual, and could be cruel and vindictive to his enemies.[11]

As an adult, Muhammad became apprenticed as camel-boy to a rich widow named Khadija. While under her employ, he showed himself honest and trustworthy, and he eventually rose to become the manager of all her trading interests, overseeing caravans on her behalf.

As a merchant, Muhammad often went on lengthy caravan journeys, sometimes going as far as Syria and possibly Egypt. These journeys enabled Muhammad to encounter people of different religions and nationalities.[12] Indeed, he met Christians, Jews, and perhaps Zoroastrians on the trade routes he traveled for the next 15 years. At the same time he observed the degenerate state of religion and morals of his own people in Mecca.[13] One idea that apparently stuck with him from his encounters with these three religions is their common teaching that there would be a Judgment Day in which the righteous would be rewarded but the wicked punished and tormented in hell. This teaching would become a central tenet of Islam.

Muhammad also likely encountered representatives of Christianity and Judaism in Mecca, as a result of caravans and merchants visiting the city to do business. Often there would be commercial fairs, at which representatives of Christianity and Judaism would address the crowds. It may be that Muhammad attended some of these events.

Unfortunately, the historical evidence seems to suggest that the version of Christianity Muhammad was exposed to during these years was a particular brand of unorthodox Christianity known as Nestorianism. Scholar Harold J. Berry explains this deviant form of Christianity:

> Throughout the centuries of church history, not all have agreed that Jesus Christ is the God–Man. Nestorius, patriarch of Constantinople for three years (428–431), was such a person. He became the founder of the Nestorian Church, which had many followers in Persia (present-day Iran). Nestorius denied the biblical teaching that Jesus Christ was the God–Man come to earth to redeem fallen mankind. To Nestorius, "Christ was in effect only a perfect man who was morally linked to deity."…Nestorius's views were condemned in 431 at the Council of Nicea at Ephesus, 139 years before Muhammad was born.[14]

The influence of Nestorianism on Muhammad showed itself later when he would teach that Jesus was not God, was not the Son of God, was not a Savior or Redeemer, but rather was just a man who was a prophet of God. During these years, Muhammad's theological views were slowly taking shape.

According to historical sources, Muhammad served Khadija so well that she decided to marry him, even though he was 15 years younger than her. Because Khadija was so wealthy, Muhammad no longer had to work for a living. He could now focus his attention solely on spiritual matters and engage in long periods of seclusion and meditation. By all accounts Muhammad's marriage to Khadija was a happy one.[15]

Of pertinence to our present study is the fact that Khadija had an Ebionite Christian background.[16] Ebionite Christianity denied the deity of Jesus Christ, and held that He was a mere man, a prophet who was the natural son of Joseph and Mary. Jesus allegedly distinguished Himself by strict observance of the Jewish law, and was accordingly chosen to be the Messiah because of His legal piety. The consciousness that God chose Him to be the Messiah came at his baptism, when He received the Holy Spirit. Jesus' mission as the Messiah was not to save humankind, but to call all humanity to obey the law. Here, again, is another distorted view of Christianity that would later surface in the theology of Muhammad.

## Muhammad Receives Revelation

It was commonplace in those days for spiritually minded people to retreat once a year and spend time in a cave in utter solitude. Muhammad engaged in this practice for several years in a cave in Mount Hira. While there, he would ponder the coming Day of Judgment and the idolatry and polytheism of his own people. He increasingly became convinced of the existence and transcendence of one true God.

According to the traditional account, Muhammad was engaged in meditation in a cave when suddenly the angel Gabriel appeared to him and commanded him to "recite" in the name of God. At first Muhammad failed to respond, and the angel seized him by the throat and shook him as he repeated the command to recite. Muhammad again failed to respond, so the angel choked him until he yielded.[17] Muhammad began to recite revelations given to him by the angel.

Muhammad was unsure what to make of this experience. He was concerned that perhaps he might be possessed by an evil spirit. Upon sharing these concerns with his wife Khadija, however, he was assured by her that the source of the revelations was divine, and she encouraged him to be obedient to what the angel said.

Muhammad's concern over the nature of these revelations is understandable. After all, he would receive the revelations from the angel in what can only be described as an altered state of consciousness.[18] Scholar Geoffrey Parrinder explains:

> Although little is known about Muhammad's mental and physical states during the reception of the revelation, it is clear that his normal consciousness and functioning were suspended. The revelation was accompanied by trance-like states in which he was oblivious to his surroundings. These abnormal circumstances were clearly observable to others. Apparently the revelation was an ecstatic experience, during which Muhammad gave every evidence of being under the influence of a power outside himself that overwhelmed him and bore him down. When he emerged from these unusual states, often severely shaken and weakened, especially in the beginning, he would pass on to his companions what had come to him.[19]

Other historical accounts reveal that Muhammad was subject to ecstatic seizures. William Miller reports that when Muhammad received revelation his whole body would become agitated, perspiration would pour down his face, and he would fall to the ground and foam at the mouth.[20] Sometimes when inspiration came upon him, he felt as if it were like the painful sounding of a loud bell.[21] Sometimes Muhammad would actually see the angel Gabriel, while at other times would only hear his voice. Sometimes he might receive messages in a dream.

Eventually, after a period of self-questioning that may have lasted some months, Muhammad finally came to look upon himself as a genuine prophet of Allah. He felt he was a messenger of the one true God already known to Christians and Jews, who had been revealed through such men as Abraham, Moses, Solomon, Jonah, and Jesus. Muhammad also came to believe that the revelations received through these earlier prophets had become corrupted through time, and that he was now called by God to restore God's message to its original purity. Moreover, whereas the former prophets had received only an incomplete revelation of Allah, Muhammad was now called to bring about the complete and final revelation of Allah.[22]

As Allah's prophet, Muhammad was to "recite" revelations delivered through the angel Gabriel. The word translated "recite" is the word that gives the Quran its title; it means "the reciting," or "the reading." These revelations to Muhammad would continue for several decades, and would later be compiled into the Quran, Islam's holy book.

I should note at this juncture that the Quran is often called "the miracle of Muhammad" because of the traditional belief that Muhammad was uneducated and was unable to write. He was known as the "unlettered prophet." I will examine this claim of illiteracy in the next chapter.

Key among the revelations Muhammad received was that Allah is the one true God who created heaven and earth, and that he himself had been specially appointed by Allah to be his messenger. He denounced the local gods in Mecca as false, and worship of them as idolatrous. He said these idolaters were associating partners with the one true God (Allah), and he preached a strict monotheism. He taught that man is to be Allah's slave, and his first duty to Allah is to submit to and obey him. (Remember that "Islam" means "submission," and "Muslim" means "one who submits.") Muhammad spoke of a terrible Day of Judgment in the future, in which the righteous would be rewarded with the pleasures of a sensual paradise, but evildoers would be punished in the fires of hell.

## Resistance in Mecca

Muhammad had very few converts at first. In fact, in the three years after his calling as a prophet, he gained only 13 followers, including his wife Khadija and some close friends. The number eventually grew to around 40, including people mostly from the poorer classes.

The richer classes did not like Muhammad's message because they felt it interfered with their business. After all, the main source of income in the city was the many pilgrims who came from all over the world to worship the 360 idols in the Kaaba. Each tribe in Arabia had handpicked its own deity and traveled to Mecca every year to pay homage to this deity in the Kaaba.[23] If suddenly a prophet branded all these deities "false," the number of visitors to Mecca would drop dramatically, and the business market would crash. Hence, Muhammad made few friends among the businessmen of the city.

As Muhammad was persecuted by such men, he became ever more convinced that he was a true prophet of God, for he was experiencing the same kind of rejection and persecution Moses and Jesus had faced. Fortunately for him, both his wife Khadija and his uncle Abu Talib had prestige and influence and were able to protect Muhammad against attack.

In the year 619, however, Muhammad suffered the loss of Khadija and Abu Talib. After the death of Abu Talib, Muhammad found himself without the protection of his clan, and life suddenly became difficult for him and his followers.

Parenthetically, I want to point out that in the ten years following Khadija's death, Muhammad would marry another 11 women. This is notable only because of the Quranic requirement that limits the number of wives a man can marry to four (Sura

4:3). Many have wondered why Allah's law did not apply to Muhammad.

## Migration to Medina

Following Abu Talib's death, the leaders of some of the various tribes in Mecca vowed to assassinate Muhammad. Muhammad became aware of this plot through a revelation from Gabriel and, along with his 150 followers, fled to Yathrib, a city 280 miles north of Mecca, on September 25, A.D. 622. This escape was so important that it became known as the *hijra* (literally, "emigration"); the year 622 became the first year of the Muslim calendar, and it marks the official beginning of Islam.[24]

The people of Yathrib were much more open to monotheism than those in Mecca because many of the town's residents were monotheistic Jews. This no doubt had a certain appeal to Muhammad.

Muhammad quickly made the best of fulfilling his role as prophet in a new town. He was successful in his leadership, and many of the people in the city became Muslims. He set up a virtual theocracy, combining politics with religion. Muhammad became king *and* prophet.[25] In honor of Muhammad, the name of the town was changed to Medina—"city of the Prophet."

Not *all* went according to Muhammad's plans, however. Muhammad had expected the Jews and Christians to recognize him as one in a long line of prophets and give allegiance to him. With this in mind, Muhammad initially taught, based on revelation from Allah, that people were to turn toward Jerusalem when praying. Muhammad became bitterly disappointed when Jews and Christians rejected him. (They considered him an impostor.) Following this, Muhammad's attitude toward both groups shifted dramatically and hardened as he grew older. Through revelation from Allah, the direction of prayer was promptly changed to be toward Mecca. This shift in the direction of prayer marked Muhammad's abandonment of the Jewish–Christian tradition and the beginning of Islam as an independent religion.[26]

Though things began well at Medina for the most part, life eventually became difficult for those who had migrated from Mecca because they had no money and no valuables. They were on the verge of straining the good graces of the people of Medina, and something needed to be done. Muhammad promptly received a revelation from Allah: "O prophet, contend against the infidels and be rigorous with them" (Sura 9:74). Muhammad gave his followers divine approval for the raiding of caravans en route to Mecca, where his enemies lived. By raiding caravans headed for Mecca, he would greatly aid himself and his followers while at the same time dealing a blow to his enemies.

Muhammad's movement took on the character of religious militarism. He transformed his followers into fanatical fighters by teaching them that if they died fighting for Allah's cause, they would be instantly admitted to paradise. Another motivation for fighting was that the spoils of these caravan raids were divided among Muhammad's men, with Muhammad keeping one-fifth of everything. Not unexpectedly, these caravan raids led to war with the Meccans, for their very livelihood was threatened. Muhammad's Medina years became marked by constant warfare.

## Muhammad Takes Mecca

Eventually, in the year 628, the leaders of the Quraysh tribe in Mecca made a treaty with Muhammad, which stipulated that both sides would not fight and would keep the peace for the next ten years. The treaty also stipulated that Muhammad and his followers would be permitted to make pilgrimages to Mecca. However, just two years after the treaty was signed, in January 630, Muhammad broke the treaty because a Muslim was murdered by a Meccan, and he attacked Mecca with an overwhelming force of 10,000 men.

The leaders of Mecca surrendered with little resistance, and Muhammad quickly took control of the city, destroying all the idols in the Kaaba. Because Muhammad gave a general amnesty and later a generous pardon to his former enemies in Mecca, many of them were won over to his side and followed him in future campaigns. The Kaaba was then made a center for religious pilgrimage. From that point forward, Allah alone would be worshiped in the Kaaba.

## The Death of the Prophet

Muhammad died suddenly in the year 632, a mere two years after his Meccan conquest. The big problem for Muslims was that Muhammad had not designated who would become leader should he die. The process of choosing a new leader caused a conflict. On the one hand were some Muslims who believed the *caliphs* should be elected by the Islamic leadership (a caliph is a "representative," or "delegate"[27]). On the other hand were Muslims who believed the successor should be hereditary. (I'll talk about these two groups—the Sunnis and the Shiites—later in the book.) Abu Bakr, who had been designated by Muhammad to lead prayers when he was absent, was soon elected by the majority to be the new caliph.

## Muhammad—A *Superior* Prophet?

Modern Muslims have gone to great lengths to prove to the world that Muhammad was a superior prophet. They even argue that Muhammad was prophesied in the Christian Bible:

- In *Deuteronomy 18:15,18* we read, "The LORD your God...will raise up a prophet from among their countrymen like you, and I will put My words in his mouth, and he shall speak to them all that I command him" (NASB). Muslims argue that the prophet would come from among the brethren of the Israelites, which would be the Ishmaelites—because Israel (Jacob) and Ishmael both descended from Abraham, and the tribes who descended from Ishmael are therefore "brethren" of the tribes who descended from Israel (Jacob).

- In *Deuteronomy 33:2* we read, "The LORD came from Sinai, and dawned on them from Seir; he shone forth from Mount Paran." Muslims believe this verse predicts three separate visitations of God— one on "Sinai" to Moses, another in "Seir" to Jesus, and a third in "Paran" (Arabia) to Muhammad.

- Muslims cite *Deuteronomy 34:10:* "There arose not a prophet since in Israel like unto Moses…" (KJV), and argue that this proves the predicted prophet could not be an Israelite (like Jesus) but was Muhammad instead.

- Muslims say *Psalm 45:3-5* refers to Muhammad with its mention of one coming with a "sword." Muhammad was known as the "prophet of the sword."

- Muslims also cite *Isaiah 21:7* in regard to Muhammad: "When he sees chariots with teams of horses, riders on donkeys or riders on camels, let him be alert, fully alert." Muslim commentators take the rider on the "donkeys" to be Jesus and the rider on "camels" to be Muhammad, whom they believe supersedes Jesus.

- They further point to *Habakkuk 3:3:* "God came from Teman, the Holy One from Mount Paran. His glory covered the heavens and his praise filled the earth." Muslims say this refers to the prophet Muhammad coming from Arabia (Paran).

- Additionally, they cite *John 14:16:* "And I will ask the Father, and he will give you another Counselor to be with you forever." Muslim scholars see in Jesus' reference to the promised "Counselor" (Greek, *paraclete*) a prediction of Muhammad, because the Quran (Sura 61:6) refers to Muhammad as "Ahmad" *(periclytos),* which they take to be the correct rendering of "paraclete." One Muslim writer argues, "Our doctors contend that *Paracletos* is a corrupt reading for *Periclytos*, and that in their original saying of Jesus there was a prophecy of our holy Prophet Ahmad by name."[28]

Aside from alleged Bible prophecies of Muhammad in the Bible, we are told that the language and teaching of the Quran are without parallel. Since Muhammad was an "unlettered prophet" (that is, illiterate), the beauty of the Quran is all the more miraculous.

Still further, we are told that Muhammad accomplished other miracles, which are recorded not in the Quran but in the *Hadith* (traditions). For example, Muhammad allegedly fed a multitude of people with a handful of dates. He allegedly healed blind eyes and cured the sick of their diseases. He allegedly raised people from the dead and caused barren fields to yield fruit.[29]

Muslims additionally assert that Muhammad's life and character demonstrate that he was the last and greatest of all the prophets. And besides, Muslims say, the geometric growth of Islam around the world proves that Muhammad and his religion had divine approval.

## The Veneration of Muhammad

This chapter would be incomplete without pointing to the great veneration many Muslims around the world give to Muhammad. Though certainly orthodox Islam does not go along with this, the fact remains that many Muslims come close to deifying Muhammad.

Scholars Norman Geisler and Abdul Saleeb point out that there is an abundance of Muslim traditions that speak of Muhammad's preexistence; other traditions affirm that Muhammad was the purpose for God's creation of the universe.[30] Frederick Mathewson Denny points out that among Muslims, Muhammad "takes on some of the attributes of other holy personages, such as...preeminence above all created things, and perfect wisdom."[31] Jamal

J. Elias notes that "devotion to the prophet extends to veneration of his relics. There are several shrines around the world devoted to an individual hair from his beard."[32] Muhammad is truly a most holy and venerated name among Muslims.

# 3

# *A Christian Critique of Muhammad*

From a biblical perspective, revelations from a *new* prophet must be in agreement with the revelations of *former* prophets, assuming all these prophets were genuine spokesmen for the same one true God. We see this principle illustrated in the writings of the apostle Paul, who said that "even if we or an angel from heaven should preach a gospel other than the one we preached to you, let him be eternally condemned!" (Galatians 1:8). Any teaching that contradicts previous authoritative teaching from God is anathema.

The Bereans knew the critical importance of making sure that new claims to truth are measured against what we know to be true from Scripture. They had heard Paul speak in Berea, and they checked everything he said against the Old Testament Scriptures (Acts 17:11). Paul commended them for this practice, for he knew that any revelation communicated through him as an *apostle* of God had to be in agreement with what was previously communicated through the *prophets* of God in Old Testament times.

Since revelations from Muhammad contradict what we know to be revelation from God (which is contained in the Christian Bible)—especially on such central doctrines as God, Jesus Christ, and the gospel of salvation—they do not qualify as revelations from God. Rather, Muhammad falls into the category of a false prophet (Matthew 24:24-25).

## Muhammad's Knowledge of Christianity Was Inaccurate

Muhammad's knowledge of Christian doctrine was inaccurate in many ways. In the previous chapter I noted that the Christians Muhammad came into contact with in his early years were primarily either Nestorians or Ebionites, both of whom held to heretical views of Jesus Christ. Further, Muhammad's knowledge of Christianity was completely *oral* in origin, and was not based on a personal study of the Christian Scriptures, for, indeed, a translation of the New Testament into Arabic did not exist at that time.[1] As scholar William Saal points out, "Though the Bible had been translated into several languages (e.g., Coptic, Ethiopic, Syriac) before the sixth century, the New Testament was probably not translated into Arabic until A.D. 720 (i.e., about a century after the time of Muhammad)."[2] Hence, what Muhammad learned about Christianity was based solely on conversations he had with people during his travels.

As we read the Quran, we find numerous stories of John the Baptist and Jesus, as well as Old Testament characters like Abraham, Joseph, and Moses. Though some of what is in the Quran agrees with the Bible, much of it does not.[3] The sad reality is that Muslims have a defective view of the biblical prophets and apostles, and especially of Jesus Christ.

Even to the end of his life, Muhammad never came to grasp what the true gospel of Jesus Christ is (a serious lack according to Galatians 1:8). He missed the way to God, and as a result ended up leading many others on the wrong path.

## _Ask..._

- Can you tell me what you think the fundamental message of Christianity is?

- Can I share with you what I think the fundamental message of Christianity is?

### Muhammad Was Lacking as a Moral Example

Since Muslims claim Muhammad's life and character demonstrate that he was the last and greatest of all the prophets, it is fair to examine whether the historical data backs up the claim. In my view, and in the view of many others, it does not.[4]

- Whereas the Quran speaks of Jesus as being sinless, no such claims are made about Muhammad. Rather the Quran speaks of Muhammad's need to ask for forgiveness (see Suras 40:55; 48:2).

- The Quran, based on revelation received from Allah through the angel Gabriel, commands that men should have no more than four wives (Sura 4:3). But Muhammad married 11 women after the death of his first wife, Khadija. How can Muhammad qualify as a good moral example for humankind when he does not live up to one of the basic laws he laid down as from Allah?

- Muhammad ordered his men to raid caravans, and allowed them to keep the booty so long as he was given one-fifth of everything. Such piracy hardly seems compatible with claims that Muhammad is a good moral example.

- Unlike Jesus, who taught that we should love our enemies (Matthew 5:44), Muhammad ordered executions of some people in Mecca who had formerly stood against him.

• Whereas Jesus told Peter to put away his sword (Matthew 26:52), Muhammad was well known as the "prophet of the sword," actively using it for the furtherance of Islam. This hardly seems like a good moral example.

Some Muslims may respond to this latter point by bringing up the issue of the Crusades, in which Christians themselves used the sword. This truly was a sad development in the history of Christianity. However, as apologist Robert Morey has pointed out, "It is logically erroneous to set up a parallel between Muslims killing people in *obedience* to the Quran and Christians killing people in *disobedience* to the Bible. While the Quran commands Jihad, the New Testament forbids it."[5] (The interested reader will want to consider Jesus' words on this in Matthew 26:52.)

## _____ *Ask...* _____

*If your Muslim acquaintance brings up the Crusades, ask this question.*

• I agree the Crusades were terrible. But do you think it's right to compare Muslims killing people in *obedience* to the Quran with Christians killing people in *disobedience* to the Bible?

---

W. St. Clair Tisdall brings up an interesting point regarding Muhammad's use of the sword. He notes that in Islam hypocrites are hated so much by Allah that he assigns them to the lowest pit of hell. Yet Muhammad was permitted to use the sword to *force* people to subscribe to a religion whether or not they truly believed in it. Hence, in a way, Muhammad's use of the sword yielded hypocrisy among innumerable people.[6] Does this sound like a religion of truth?

## ____ *Ask...* ____

*As a preface to these questions, it is generally not wise to overtly criticize Muhammad in your early discussions with a Muslim. It is often better to set forth a positive presentation of the Bible, Jesus, and the gospel. But once you develop a trusting relationship and discussions become more comfortable, the following questions might yield fruitful discussion.*

- Do you see any significance in the fact that the Quran says Jesus was sinless, whereas Muhammad had to ask for forgiveness for his sins? (See Suras 40:55; 48:2.)

- If the Quran says men can have no more than four wives (Sura 4:3), why did Muhammad have 11 wives after the death of his first wife, Khadija?

- Do you think it is right for a man who sets out to be a good moral example to raid caravans and keep one-fifth of the booty?

- Is it right for Muhammad to *force* people to believe the way he believes by use of the sword? Does not the Quran state, "Let there be no compulsion in religion" (Sura 2:256)?

---

## Islam's Rapid Growth Is Not a Gauge of Divine Blessing

While it is true that Islam has grown at a rapid pace, popularity does not necessarily equate to being "blessed by God." It is notable that Muhammad's movement started very slowly, and had just a handful of converts (a mere 40) during the first years of his ministry. The reality is that most Meccans rejected Muhammad's message. Muslims would make a stronger case if they could argue that Islam *immediately* became immensely popular as soon as it emerged. But that is not what happened. Even if it had happened, that still would not prove blessing by God, for many things throughout history have become popular that were not blessed by God. (Consider how popular unhealthy fast food is today. Consider how popular pornography is today.[7])

Besides, it was only after Muhammad sanctioned use of the sword that Islam began to grow rapidly. This hardly constitutes proof of divine blessing. Certainly a person would rather become a Muslim than be pierced through with a sword.[8] And when Muhammad started teaching that those who die fighting for Allah's cause will immediately go to paradise, this was all the more reason for people to join up with Islam. Islam's rapid growth thus has viable explanations other than "divine blessing."

It is worth noting that Christianity grew explosively in the first few centuries after Christ *without* use of the sword. In fact, the sword was used *against* the Christians by Roman soldiers. But Christianity still grew! That seems much more of a miracle than Islam's growth.

## _____ *Ask...* _____

- Muhammad's movement started very slowly, and had just 40 converts during the first years of his ministry. Where was the "divine blessing" then?

- If numerical growth is a gauge of divine blessing, couldn't other religions like Hinduism and Christianity also make the claim of divine blessing?

- It is a historical fact that Islam grew as a result of the sword. Christianity grew *without* use of the sword. In fact, Christianity grew despite the fact that the Romans wielded the sword against Christians. How do you explain that? *(The Muslim may rebut by mentioning the Crusades, so be ready.)*

- Have you considered the possibility that numerical growth may not necessarily be an indicator of divine blessing? After all, there are many things that are popular today that are not blessed by God. Can you think of any examples of this?

---

## Muhammad Did Not Truly Perform Miracles

Contrary to the claim of some Muslims, Muhammad was not a true miracle-worker. In fact, nowhere in the Quran does it record Muhammad's performing *any* supernatural feats of nature. He explicitly disavowed such ability. When asked why he did not perform miracles like the other prophets did, he responded that the Quran was his miracle (Sura 29:48-50).

Aside from (and in contradiction to) the Quran, however, there are literally hundreds of miracle stories of Muhammad in the Hadith (tradition). But there is good reason for doubting the veracity of these miracle claims[9]:

- Foundationally, the primary authoritative source for Muslims—the Quran—has no record of such miracles, but rather portrays Muhammad refusing to do miracles (Suras 3:181-84; 4:153; 6:8-9). Why should we consider the miracle legends contained in Muslim traditions (the Hadith) authentic, when the Quran portrays Muhammad as refusing to perform such miracles? If the Quran has a higher authority for the Muslim than Muslim traditions, then why do Muslims give credence to the traditions over the Quran in this matter?

- Most of the individuals who collected miracle stories about Muhammad lived between 100 and 200 years after Muhammad's time—meaning they were not eyewitnesses to Muhammad's life. Two hundred years is plenty of time for miracle legends to develop.

- One must wonder whether some of these miracle stories were invented specifically to answer Christian apologists who tried to show Jesus' superiority because of *His* miracles.

- Many of these miracle stories seem quite similar to the legendary stories of Jesus contained in the New Testament Apocrypha, written long after the time of Jesus.[10] Such accounts are obviously inauthentic when compared to the historically verifiable documents of the New Testament. Because the Muslim traditions bear such a strong similarity to the nature of the apocryphal books, they should be doubted every bit as much as the apocryphal books.

## _Ask..._

*Use your judgment to discern whether it is an appropriate time to ask these questions about Muhammad.*

- Why should we consider the miracle legends contained in Muslim traditions (the Hadith) authentic, when the Quran portrays Muhammad as refusing to perform such miracles (Suras 3:181-84; 6:8-9; 29:48-50)?

- Since these miracle traditions were composed between 100 and 200 years after Muhammad, is it possible that some of them were just made up?

- By contrast, Muslims *do* acknowledge that Jesus did miracles, right?

### Was Muhammad Illiterate?

There is reason to doubt the claim that Muhammad was an illiterate prophet. Christian scholars Bruce A. McDowell and

Anees Zaka point out that, according to certain Hadith sources, Muhammad is portrayed asking for paper and ink to write his will. And when he made a treaty with the Meccans, they refused to concede that he was an apostle of Allah, so he struck out that phrase on the treaty and wrote, "Muhammad, son of Abdullah."[11]

Further, as a successful businessman (merchant), one wonders how he could have done as well as he did without being literate. Scholars W. Montgomery Watt and Richard Bell comment that, while there is "no convincing proof that Muhammad was able to write, it is not improbable that he could. He may well have learned the art in Mecca itself. Since he conducted business for Khadija in his youth, and probably also on his own behalf, he must surely have been able to keep accounts."[12]

## ____ Ask... ____

- Do you think it is possible for Muhammad to have been the successful merchant he was without being able to write?

- If Muhammad could not write, how could he have signed a treaty with the Meccans, as history reveals he did?

---

## There Are No References to Muhammad in the Old Testament

### DEUTERONOMY 18:15,18 *Refers to Jesus, Not Muhammad*

#### The "prophet" had to be a Jew.

Muslims believe Muhammad was a perfect fulfillment of the prediction in Deuteronomy 18:15,18 of "a prophet like me from among your own brothers," of whom God said, "I will put my words in his mouth, and he will tell them everything I command him." Such a view, however, violates the biblical data.

First, the term "brothers" in this passage refers to Israelites, not to Arabs, who historically have been enemies of Israel.[13] Elsewhere in Deuteronomy the term "brothers" refers to fellow Israelites, not to foreign enemies. For example, God instructed the Israelites to choose a king "from among your own brothers," not from among foreign enemies (Deuteronomy 17:15). Well-known Old Testament expositors Keil and Delitzsch say that this phrase means "from [your] own people, not a foreigner or non-Israelite."[14] The reality is that there has never been an instance in the history of Israel in which a non-Jewish king was chosen to rule over the nation. We are also told in Deuteronomy 18:1-2 that the Levite priests "shall have no inheritance *among their brothers;* the Lord is their inheritance" (emphasis added). Clearly, the "brothers" in this verse are Jewish brothers (among other Jewish tribes, aside from the Levites). Similarly, the prophet mentioned in Deuteronomy 18 who is "from among your own brothers" must be Jewish.

There is more proof for this position in the book of Genesis. We know that the Jews are descended from Abraham through Isaac, and the Arabs claim descent from Abraham through Ishmael. In Genesis 17:18 Abraham said to God, "If only Ishmael might live under your blessing!" God emphatically answered that, while He would bless Ishmael, "My covenant I will establish *with Isaac,* whom Sarah will bear to you by this time next year" (verse 21, emphasis added). Later in the book of Genesis God repeated this: "It is *through Isaac* that your offspring will be reckoned" (21:12, emphasis added). Clearly, the fulfillment of God's future plans for Israel (including the future *prophet* of Israel) would take place through Isaac's line, not through Ishmael's line. This means the prophet mentioned in Deuteronomy 18 cannot be a non-Jew.[15]

### Jesus was the "prophet."

Still further, an examination of the Bible makes clear that Deuteronomy 18:15-18 is referring to Jesus. As Norman Geisler and I point out in our book *When Cultists Ask,*

Jesus perfectly fulfilled this verse, since (1) He was from among His Jewish brethren (cf. Gal. 4:4). (2) He fulfilled Deuteronomy 18:18 perfectly: "He shall speak to them all that I [God] command Him." Jesus said, "I do nothing of Myself; but as My Father taught Me, I speak these things" (John 8:28). And, "I have not spoken on My own authority; but the Father who sent Me gave Me a command, what I should say and what I should speak" (John 12:49). (3) He called Himself a "prophet" (Luke 13:33), and the people considered Him a prophet (Matt. 21:11; Luke 7:16; 24:19; John 4:19; 6:14; 7:40; 9:17). As the Son of God, Jesus was *prophet* (speaking to men for God), *priest* (Heb. 7–10, speaking to God for men), and *king* (reigning over men for God, Rev. 19–20).[16]

Moreover, scholar Gerhard Nehls observes that as babies both Moses and Jesus had death plots initiated against them (Exodus 1:15-16,22; Matthew 2:13ff.); both of them were rescued as a result of divine intervention (Exodus 2:2-10; Matthew 2:13ff.); both of them were authenticated by signs and wonders (Exodus 7:10,19,20; 8–12; Matthew 8:14ff.; Luke 7:11ff.; Matthew 14:13-14); Moses liberated the Israelites from bondage in Egypt, while Christ liberated believers from the bondage of sin (Exodus; Isaiah 53; John 8:32-36; Romans 6:18-22; 8:2; Galatians 5:1); Moses spoke to God "face to face," as did Christ on the Mount of Transfiguration (Exodus 33:11; Matthew 17:3); and Moses was the mediator of the Old Covenant, whereas Christ was the mediator of the New Covenant (Exodus 19–20; Hebrews 12:24).[17] Hence, Christ truly was a prophet "like" Moses.

Additionally, in the New Testament the apostle Peter indicates that Jesus is the fulfillment of the prophet prophesied in Deuteronomy 18. In Acts 3:19-23 Peter speaks to the men of Israel:

> Repent, then, and turn to God, so that your sins may be wiped out, that times of refreshing may come from the Lord, and that he may send the Christ, who has been appointed for you—even Jesus. He must remain in heaven until the time comes for God to restore everything, as he promised long ago through his holy prophets. For Moses said, "The Lord your God will raise up for you a prophet like me from among your own people; you must listen to everything he tells you. Anyone who does not listen to him will be completely cut off from among his people."

Peter here indicates that God foretold the coming of Jesus through all the prophets—including Moses in Deuteronomy 18. In keeping with this, Jesus elsewhere said to some Jewish critics, "If you believed Moses, you would believe me, for he wrote about me" (John 5:46). A fundamental principle of interpreting the Bible is that *Scripture interprets Scripture*. As we consult all the Scriptures that pertain to the fulfillment of Deuteronomy 18:15-18, it is clear that Jesus was the fulfillment of the prophecy.

## _____ *Ask...* _____

- Since the word "brothers," when occurring in contexts relating to Israel, always refers to *Jewish* brothers in the book of Deuteronomy, is it not clear that the prophet who would come "from among your own brothers" in Deuteronomy 18:15 would be Jewish?

- Did you know that the Quran in Sura 29:27 says the prophetic line came through Isaac? Is it not clear, then, that the prophet of Deuteronomy 18 would be Jewish?

- Have you considered how Jesus was a perfect fulfillment of the prophet mentioned in Deuteronomy 18:15-18? He was from among Jewish brethren (Galatians 4:4); He

spoke all that God commanded (John 8:28); and He is
called a prophet in the New Testament (Luke 13:33).

• Did you know the apostle Peter confirmed that Jesus was
the fulfillment of the prophet of Deuteronomy 18:15-18
(in Acts 3:19-23)?

## DEUTERONOMY 33:2 *Does Not Refer to Muhammad*

Muslims believe that Deuteronomy 33:2 predicts three separate visitations of God—one on "Sinai" to Moses, another in
"Seir" to Jesus, and a third in "Paran" to Muhammad, who came
to Mecca with an army of ten thousand. However, such a view is
geographically impossible. Paran refers to the wilderness region
in the central part of the Sinai Peninsula,[18] while Seir refers to the
mountain land of the Edomites where Esau and his descendants
lived (Genesis 14:6; Numbers 10:12; 12:16–13:3).[19] Seir is
nowhere near Palestine, where Jesus ministered; Paran is nowhere
near Mecca, where Muhammad ministered. Further, this verse is
speaking of the "Lord" coming, not Muhammad. And He is portrayed as coming with ten thousand *holy ones* (myriads of angels),
not ten thousand *soldiers* who kill people, as Muhammad did.[20]

## DEUTERONOMY 34:10 *Does Not Refer to Muhammad*

Muslims assert that Deuteronomy 34:10 proves the predicted
prophet could not have been an Israelite, but was instead
Muhammad, for "there arose not a prophet since in Israel like
unto Moses…" (KJV). The primary error of this view is that Muslims are reading far too long a time frame into this verse. The
word "since" is referring to the time beginning with Moses' death
and ending at the time Deuteronomy's last chapter (chapter 34)
was written (apparently by Joshua). Seen in this light, the statement in Deuteronomy 34:10 cannot be taken to exclude Jesus,
who would be born many centuries later. Further, Muhammad
was certainly *not* like the prophet Moses, who did "miraculous

signs and wonders" and interacted with God "face to face" (see Deuteronomy 34:10-11). Jesus *was* like Moses in these ways.[21]

## PSALM 45:3-5 *Does Not Refer to Muhammad*

While Muslims say that Psalm 45:3-5 refers to Muhammad with its mention of one coming with a "sword," the very next verse in the psalm indicates the person spoken of is God (verse 6). Moreover, Hebrews 1:8-9 applies Psalm 45:6-7 (and, by extension, the preceding verses in Psalm 45) specifically to Jesus Christ. This psalm has long been recognized as a messianic psalm, a psalm referring to a promised descendant of David who would be a conquering king, subduing the nations and sitting on David's throne to rule forever (see 1 Corinthians 15:25,28).[22] Jesus is clearly the fulfillment of the passage. Of course, Jesus Himself claimed to be the divine Messiah (John 4:26; 8:58; 10:30), and Scripture indicates that at His second coming He will be accompanied by the armies of heaven, and "from His mouth comes a sharp sword, so that with it He may strike down the nations" (see Revelation 19:11-16 NASB).[23]

## ISAIAH 21:7 *Does Not Refer to Muhammad*

While Muslims take the rider on the "donkeys" in Isaiah 21:7 to be Jesus and the rider on "camels" to be Muhammad (whom they believe supersedes Jesus), such an interpretation has no basis in the text of Scripture. Indeed, this verse is speaking of Babylon's fall (see verse 9), and how the news of this fall is spread by people riding on horses, donkeys, and camels. There is absolutely nothing here about the prophet Muhammad.[24]

## HABAKKUK 3:3 *Does Not Refer to Muhammad*

In Habakkuk 3:3 we read, "God came from Teman, the Holy One from Mount Paran. His glory covered the heavens and his praise filled the earth." Muslims say this verse refers to Muhammad coming from Paran.

Contrary to this view, Paran is nowhere near Mecca where Muhammad ministered. As noted earlier, Paran refers to the wilderness region in the central part of the Sinai Peninsula.[25] Further, the subject of the verse is God, not Muhammad. In this verse "God" and "the Holy One" are parallel references to one being— God. Moreover, the word "praise" does not refer to Muhammad (whose name means "the praised one"), for God Himself is clearly the object of the praise of the people of the earth and it is His glory that covers the heavens (see Psalm 48:10).[26] Muhammad is nowhere in sight in this verse.

## JOHN 14:16 *Does Not Refer to Muhammad*

In John 14:16 we read Jesus' words, "I will ask the Father, and he will give you another Counselor to be with you forever." Muslims see in this reference to the promised "Counselor" (Greek, *paraclete*) a prediction of Muhammad, for the Quran (Sura 61:6) refers to Muhammad as "Ahmad" *(periclytos),* which they take to be the correct rendering of *paraclete.*

As Norman Geisler notes, such a view is impossible to fit with the context.[27] He explains that over 5300 New Testament manuscripts have *paraclete,* not *periclytos* (they are two different words). Further, Jesus identified the "Counselor" or "Comforter" as the Holy Spirit (John 14:26). This Comforter was given *to Christ's apostles* (John 14:16), and would testify *about Christ*— not Muhammad (John 15:26). He would abide with God's followers "forever" (Muhammad has been dead 1300 years).

Jesus affirmed that the apostles "know" the Comforter (the Holy Spirit—John 14:17), but they did not know Muhammad. The Comforter would be sent in Jesus' name (John 14:26), but Muhammad did not come in Jesus' name. Jesus told His apostles that the Comforter would be "in you" (verse 17), but Muhammad was not "in" Jesus' apostles. The Comforter would "glorify" Jesus (John 16:14), but Muhammad claimed to supersede Jesus. Further, the fulfillment of Jesus' words took place ten days later on the day of Pentecost (Acts 1:4-5), not 600 years later in a city hundreds of miles from Jerusalem.

## ___ *Ask...* ___

- Did you know there are over 5300 New Testament manuscripts that have the Greek word *paraclete*, not *periclytos*?

- Were you aware that Jesus personally identified the Counselor as the Holy Spirit, not as Muhammad (John 14:26)?

- While John 14:16 indicates the Counselor would abide with God's followers "forever," hasn't Muhammad been dead for 1300 years?

- Since John 16:14 says the Counselor would "glorify" Jesus, isn't it a stretch to say the verse is referring to Muhammad, since Muhammad did not glorify Jesus but rather claimed to supersede Him?

- Did you know that the Bible teaches that the fulfillment of Jesus' words about the Counselor took place ten days later on the day of Pentecost (Acts 1:4-5), not 600 years later in a city hundreds of miles from Jerusalem?

---

## Muhammad's Confusion as to the Source of His Revelations

When the prophets in biblical times received revelations from God, they were quite sure as to the source—God. Over 100 times in the Old Testament alone, we find the prophets of God beginning their utterances "Thus saith the Lord," which is more literally "Thus saith Yahweh." They knew they were communicating Yahweh's words. God even said to Isaiah, "I have put my words in your mouth" (Isaiah 51:16), and "My Spirit, who is on you, and my words that I have put in your mouth will not depart from your mouth" (Isaiah 59:21). Jeremiah wrote, "The LORD reached out his hand and touched my mouth and said to me, 'Now, I have put my words in your mouth'" (Jeremiah 1:9).

By contrast, Muhammad was initially quite *unsure* as to the source of his revelation. He thought he might be possessed by a demonic spirit. It was his wife Khadija who convinced him Allah was speaking through him and who encouraged him to be obedient to the revelations. This does not sound like a true prophet of God!

One must wonder, what authority or experience or qualification did Khadija have to definitively affirm that the source of Muhammad's messages was God and not an evil spirit?[28] She made no claims to be a prophetess, so how did she know?

## _____ *Ask...* _____

*If the timing is appropriate, ask this question.*

• What authority or experience or qualification did Khadija have to definitively affirm that the source of Muhammad's messages was God and not an evil spirit?

## There Is Good Reason to Suspect Demonic Activity in Muhammad

Is it possible Muhammad was correct in his initial assessment that a demon was speaking through him? My examination of the content of Muhammad's revelation, as well as the manner in which he received these revelations, leads me to conclude that a demon indeed was speaking through him. We know Satan is a great deceiver and that he likes to mimic angels of light (2 Corinthians 11:14). In this case, he apparently mimicked Gabriel. This is one reason the Bible exhorts Christians, "Dear friends, do not believe every spirit, but test the spirits to see whether they are from God, because many false prophets have gone out into the world" (1 John 4:1).

Because Muhammad delivered revelations that completely contradict the biblical record, we can only conclude that it was not the Spirit of God speaking through him, but rather an unclean spirit. This assessment seems correct especially in view of the manner in which the revelations were received. Indeed, when Muhammad received revelations, he would often fall to the ground and foam at the mouth, and perspiration would pour down his face.[29]

My apologetics colleagues John Ankerberg and John Weldon write,

> Muhammad's inspiration and religious experiences are remarkably similar to those found in some forms of spiritism. Shamanism, for example, is notorious for fostering periods of mental disruption as well as spirit-possession. Significantly, Muhammad experienced Shaman-like encounters and phenomena. Further, many authorities have noted that spirit possession frequently leads to the kinds of experiences that Muhammad had.[30]

Though I take no pleasure in saying that a demonic spirit spoke through Muhammad, this is precisely what the evidence seems to indicate. If I am correct in this assessment, then over a billion people have been deceived by revelations given to Muhammad by a demonic spirit.

## A Closing Admonition

There is a time and a place for everything (Ecclesiastes 3:1). I bring this up only because—as alluded to earlier in the chapter—you need to be sensitive in your timing regarding *what* you share with your Muslim acquaintance and *how* you share it. If you come right out in your first discussion and say, "Muhammad was a demon-possessed man who was a false prophet and a bad moral example to humanity," you would be technically correct, but your chances of fruitful evangelism just went out the window. It could be that down the road, once you have made some progress in talking about a broad range of issues with your Muslim friend, that a frank discussion about Muhammad could occur—but even then you must be humble and sensitive in how you share information.

One good approach to use, if the issue of Muhammad comes up early on (in your first few discussions), is to say that since Muhammad is not spoken of (or prophesied to come) in either the Old Testament or the New Testament, Christians do not recognize Muhammad as a prophet. It could be that if you say this, the Muslim might bring up one of the Bible verses discussed above that allegedly speak of Muhammad. In that case, the door is now open for you to talk about what the Bible really teaches about the verses the Muslim mentions, as well as other verses. But again, be *humble, sensitive,* and *tactful*.

# 4

# *The Quran—The Scriptures of Islam*

The respect in which the Quran is held and its influence in Islamic lands cannot be overstated. Indeed, the Quran is the most revered and venerated book in any Muslim home. The first thing Muslims hear upon birth and the last thing they hear just before the moment of death is a reading from the Quran. Verses from the Quran are often inscribed on the walls of Muslim homes. The Quran is also a textbook on Islam for Muslim children.

Muslims recite the Quran daily. Some Muslims become *professional* reciters. Such recitation is considered an art form, and high acclaim is given to individuals who do it well, adding inflections so that each verse rings out as a "well-shaped musical line."[1]

The Quran is memorized by many Muslims, including children. Such memorization is considered a great act of piety, and those who do it are shown great respect. Jamal J. Elias tells us that "one who knows it in its entirety is called *hafiz* (literally 'guardian'), an honorific title which hearkens back to a time when the Quran was transmitted orally and committing it to memory was to participate in guarding the text from loss or corruption."[2] Elias also tells us that pious Muslims seek to read a thirtieth of the Quran each night. That way they can finish the Quran every month.[3]

One pious exercise that is believed to bring merit before Allah is to write out a copy of the Quran by hand. Many great Islamic men of the past, including Islamic leaders, have engaged in this exercise.[4]

Muslims typically view the Quran as a miraculous wonder. One Muslim comments,

> The Quran is the greatest wonder among the wonders of the world. It repeatedly challenged the people of the world to bring a chapter like it, but they failed and the challenge remains unanswered up to this day....This book is second to none in the world according to the unanimous decision of the learned men in points of diction, style, rhetoric, thoughts and soundness of laws and regulations to shape the destinies of mankind.[5]

In bookstores in Islamic lands, the general practice is to not attach a price tag to copies of the Quran. After all, the Quran is priceless. Instead, the proper etiquette is for a customer to ask the storekeeper what a suitable "gift" would be for the priceless book.[6]

Muslims treat their copies of the Quran with great respect. The book is never to be laid on the ground and is not to come into contact with any unclean substance. Nothing is ever to be placed on top of it. It is often wrapped in a beautiful cover,[7] and is typically read from an ornate stand specially made for holding it.[8] Scholar John Gilchrist notes that

> it is also customary to have a small ledge as close to the roof as possible upon which the Quran is

to be placed when it is not being read as it should obtain the highest place in the home. Muslims will also not leave a Quran on a chair, seat or bed as this is believed to be common property where people have sat or lain and unsuitable for such a book.[9]

When Muslims speak of the Quran, they often attach titles to it that signify great respect, such as *Quranal-Karim* (the Noble Quran), or *Quranal-Azim* (the Magnificent Quran), or *Quranal-Majid* (the Glorious Quran).[10] The Quran is often treated as an item almost worthy of worship. Dr. J. Christy Wilson, a professor at Princeton University, wrote that "next to the Bible, [the Quran] is the most esteemed and powerful book in the world."[11]

## The Finality of the Quran

Muslims believe that Allah's revelation is eternal, and hence the substance of all the holy books that derive from him are the same. Why, then, are there differences between, for example, the Quran and the Christian Bible? The answer most often given is that the Bible was tampered with through the years so that what passes as the Bible today is not the same as the Bible originally given to man. Other Muslims point out that there is a progressive nature to Allah's revelation to humankind, for man was not always ready for the fullness of Allah's message. Hence, man was only given as much as he could digest at a given time. These progressively more comprehensive revelations from Allah culminated in the Quran, which is Allah's final and complete revelation to humankind. Muslim writer Badru Kateregga thus asserts,

> The Quran, as the final revelation, is the perfection and culmination of all the truth contained in the earlier Scriptures (revelations). Though sent in Arabic, it is the Book for all times and for all mankind. The purpose of the Quran is to guard

the previous revelations by restoring the eternal truth of Allah. The Quran is the torchlight by which humanity can be rightly guided onto the straight path.[12]

## The Arrangement of the Quran

The Quran is composed of 114 suras (chapters), arranged in order according to length, with the longer chapters first and the shorter ones last. Because the material is arranged in this order, non-Muslim readers are often confused because they are more used to topical or chronological arrangement.[13] The Quran contains a total of 6247 verses and is about four-fifths the length of the New Testament.

## The Quran Is an Exact Copy of the Original in Heaven

Muslims believe the Quran is an exact and faithful reproduction of the original in heaven. This original in heaven is viewed as a well-guarded engraved tablet that has existed for all eternity in the presence of Allah.[14] The angel Gabriel took more than 20 years to bring the Quran to Muhammad, communicating only isolated sections at any single time, portion by portion, while Muhammad was in a prophetic trance. The Quran is thus viewed not as the word of Muhammad but as the very word of Allah.

Because the Quran was originally brought from heaven to earth via Gabriel in Arabic form, the Arabic language is considered an essential component of the Quran. Many Muslims believe the Quran cannot be divorced from the Arabic language in which it was communicated. Hence, unlike the Christian practice of translating the Bible into as many languages as possible, Muslims have always been reluctant to publish the Quran in other languages for non-Arabic readers. Even if the words are skillfully rendered in another language, Allah's words to Muhammad were *in Arabic*, and many believe it should remain so. For instance, a well-known translation of the Quran into English is that made by Islam convert Marmaduke Pickthall, and he appropriately titled his translation *The Meaning of the Glorious Quran* instead of just *The Quran*.[15] His title reflects the Muslim belief that the Arabic language is an essential part of the Quran. All we can do is communicate the *meaning* of the Quran in other languages.

## The Compiling of the Quran

Following the death of Muhammad in A.D. 632, there was no complete manuscript of the Quran. The need to collect and compile his fragmented revelations became a pressing concern. When Muhammad uttered his revelations, his followers generally recorded them on any material that was available—including bits of parchment, leaves, flat stones, and pieces of bone (such as the shoulder blades of camels). Of course, many of his followers also memorized his sayings. All these fragmented recordings of Muhammad's revelations had to be collected, and this process took time.[16]

About a year after Muhammad's death, some of Muhammad's companions, because of the prompting of Umar (who would later become the second caliph), ordered the collection of the Quran for fear that it might fade away. Zaid, a trusted secretary of Muhammad, was appointed to the task. Zaid said, "During the lifetime of the prophet the Quran had all been written down, but it was not yet united in one place nor arranged in successive order."[17] So Zaid engaged in collecting bits and pieces of revelation in order to compile this initial version.

Some time later, during the reign of the third caliph, Uthman, it was reported to him that several Muslim communities in Syria, Armenia, and Iraq were reciting the Quran in a way different from that in which those in Arabia were reciting it. This was unacceptable to Uthman. It would do damage to Islam if there were different versions of the Quran in wide distribution. Uthman thus called upon Zaid to oversee the production of a definitive and final *authorized* version of the Quran that would become the standard for all Muslims everywhere.[18] Once Zaid's task was completed, Uthman had copies of the authorized version made, and these were distributed to Islamic learning centers in Mecca, Medina, Basra, Damascus, and other cities. All other copies of the Quran were burned so there could be no challenge to the authorized text.[19]

## The Divine Nature of the Quran

*The unity of copies of the Quran proves its divine nature.* The fact that there were various versions of the Quran in distribution in the years following Muhammad's death is not something generally acknowledged by most Muslims. Today Muslims often argue for the divine nature of the Quran by virtue of the "absolute unity" of the copies of the Quran. One Muslim claims that "the Quran is one, and no copy differing in even a diacritical point is met with in one among the four hundred millions of Muslims....A manuscript with the slightest variation in the text is unknown."[20]

Muslims claim the unity of the copies of the Quran is greater than that of any other holy book in existence. Indeed, we are told that "the Holy Quran is the only divinely revealed Scripture in the history of mankind which has been preserved to the present time in its exact original form."[21] It is thus asked, how can such unity be accounted for unless God is behind the Quran?

*The diction and style of the Quran show it to be divine.* Muslims often argue for the divine nature of the Quran by saying that both the style and diction are such that it cannot be man-made. The Quran is said to be the most excellent Arabic poetry and prose ever written or recited in human history.[22] The Quran's beauty is especially a miracle, Muslims claim, in view of the fact that Muhammad was an "unlettered prophet" (that is, he was illiterate).

*The fact of changed lives proves the Quran is divine.* Muslims often claim that, because more than a billion people's lives have been changed by the Quran, this is sure proof the Quran is divine and not man-made. What human book, it is asked, could bring about such a massive change in the lives of so many people around the world? To Muslims, the incredible growth of Islam is an ironclad proof of the Quran's divine source.

***The agreement of modern science with the Quran proves its divine nature.*** Muslims often argue that the agreement of modern science with the Quran proves it is a divine book. Indeed, a book produced in the seventh century could not agree with modern science unless God were behind it, for the Quran states many things that were scientifically unknown in the seventh century. (Later in this book, I will show how Muslims argue against the veracity of the Christian Bible because of alleged scientific errors contained within its pages.)

***Prophecy proves the divine nature of the Quran.*** Some Muslims offer the predictive prophecies in the Quran as a proof that Muhammad could perform miracles, and that hence the Quran must indeed be a divine book. After all, how could Muhammad prophesy the future without God being involved? One example is that Muhammad prophesied that the Muslims would be militarily victorious at home and abroad. This literally came to pass. Hence, the Quran is proven to be divine.

## The Quran and Abrogation

Muslims say that a prerogative of the Quran is *abrogation,* which involves the annulling of a former law by a new law. Sura 16:101 says, "When We substitute one revelation for another, and God knows best what He reveals (in stages), they say, 'Thou art but a forger': but most of them understand not."

What this means is that Allah is not bound to his revelations. If he wants, he is free to bring new revelation that completely contradicts former revelation. If circumstances call for it, Allah is free to rescind earlier revelations and bring about something entirely new and different.

An example of such a change is that, originally, Muhammad ordered his followers to pray toward Jerusalem (Sura 2:150). However, when the Jews rejected him and called him an impostor, he received new revelation to the effect that the correct direction of prayer should be toward Mecca (Sura 2:125). This change is in keeping with what we read in Sura 2:106: "If we abrogate a verse or consign it to oblivion, we offer something better than it or something of equal value."

Islamic scholars do not agree among themselves as to the precise number of verses that have become abrogated by other revelations. But there are at least 20 instances in which a newer revelation has been said to supersede, contradict, or abrogate a previous revelation.[23] All this has given rise to a Quranic science known as *Nasikh wa Mansukh,* that is, "the Abrogators and the Abrogated."[24]

## Muhammad's *Sunnah* ("Path") and the *Hadith* ("Tradition")

As Islam expanded, many situations arose among Muslims for which the Quran contained no explicit instructions. For the answers, Muslims eventually began to appeal to traditions relating to the life of Muhammad. These Muslims believed that God directed Muhammad in all he said and did, so they came to depend on traditions regarding the way he lived to guide them in every area of life—personal, social, political, and religious.

Muhammad was widely regarded as the ideal human being and was therefore a model worthy of imitation. During his life, Muhammad had settled many questions posed to him not by divine revelation from Allah, but by decisions he made on a case-by-case basis. For this reason his words and actions were recognized, even during his own lifetime, as being worthy of imitation. It is also for this reason that his teachings and deeds were fixed in writing and became a standard of behavior alongside the Quran.[25]

Muhammad's teachings and deeds are called the *Sunnah* ("path") of the prophet, and they are found in numerous collections of the *Hadith* ("traditions"), which were compiled over many years. Scholar Gerhard Nehls tells us that "Sunnah and Hadiths are technically synonymous terms, but sunnah 'implies the *doings* and *practices* of Muhammad'....It is thus a concrete implementation, a tangible form and the actual embodiment of the Will of Allah."[26]

The Sunnah, found in collections of the Hadith, represents Muhammad's way of acting or thinking in any given situation. According to J. Christy Wilson, the Hadith contains "records of what Muhammad did, what he allowed, and what he enjoined. As such they form a model for conduct and a basis for law."[27] Whenever one does not find the answers he is looking for in the Quran, one should then consult the Hadith. Muslims believe the Hadith ranks second only to the Quran, and it is said to be complementary to the Quran. The Hadith helps to explain and clarify the meaning of the Quran and to present it in a more practical form.[28]

Following Muhammad by consulting the traditions brings a unity to Muslims all over the world—even Muslims of different nationalities. One Muslim scholar explains it this way:

> For nearly 1400 years Muslims have tried to awaken in the morning as the Prophet awakened, to eat as he ate, to wash as he washed himself, even to cut their nails as he did. There has been no greater force for the unification of the Muslim peoples than the presence of this common model for the minutest acts of daily life. A Chinese Muslim, although racially a Chinese, has a countenance, behavior, manner of walking and acting that resembles in certain ways those of a Muslim

on the coast of the Atlantic. That is because both
have for centuries copied the same model. Something of the soul of the Prophet is to be seen in
both places. It is this essential unifying factor, a
common Sunnah or way of living as a model,
that makes a bazaar in Morocco have a "feeling"
or ambiance of a bazaar in Persia, although the
people in the two places speak a different language and dress differently.[29]

This similarity in behavior is brought about in an immediate
and tangible way through the "presence" of Muhammad in his
community by virtue of his Hadith and Sunnah. The prophet virtually *lives on in his tradition.*

To sum up, the holy and venerated book for Muslims is the
*Quran,* while the traditions upon which Muslims base their lives
is the *Hadith.* In the next chapter, I will seek to provide a Christian response to the claims Muslims make about the Quran and
the Hadith.

# 5

# *A Christian Critique of the Quran*

Though Muslims often declare that the Quran is divine because "no error, alteration, or variation" has touched its copies since its inception, such a view does not accurately reflect the facts. It *is* true to say that the Quran of today is a nearly perfect copy of its seventh-century counterpart (the seventh-century authorized version produced under Uthman's supervision). But Christians challenge the idea that these copies reflect the exact words *as handed down by Muhammad*. As we noted in chapter 4, historical sources prove there were several differing texts circulating in Syria, Armenia, and Iraq prior to the final revision produced by Uthman. Muhammad's long-time secretary Zaid was called in by Uthman to oversee the final and definitive authorized version of the Quran. All other copies of the Quran were then burned so there could be no challenge to the authorized text.

## _____ *Ask...* _____

- Why would Caliph Uthman produce an authorized version of the Quran if the Quran had been perfectly preserved from the beginning?

Alfred Guillaume, perhaps the most famous scholar on Islam from the non-Islamic world, points out that not all Muslims accepted Uthman's recension (critical revision), nor are all versions of the Quran identical:

> Only the men of Kufa refused the new edition, and their version was certainly extant as late as A.D. 1000. Uthman's edition to this day remains the authoritative word of God to Muslims. Nevertheless, even now variant readings, involving not only different reading of the vowels but also occasionally a different consonantal text, are recognized as of equal authority one with another.[1]

A simple comparison of different transmitted versions of the Quran proves that there are variants between them—variants involving letter differences, differences in diacritical marks, and vowel differences. For illustration purposes, let us consider some transliterated words from the *Hafs* transmission and the *Warsh* transmission of the Quran. (The Hafs transmission is used in most parts of the Islamic world, while the Warsh transmission is used in west and northwest Africa.) In Sura 2:132 the Hafs transmission has the word *wawassa,* whereas the Warsh transmission has *wa'awsa.* In Sura 5:54 the Hafs transmission has the word *yartadda,* whereas the Warsh transmission has *yartadid.* In Sura 2:140 the Hafs transmission has the word *taquluna,* whereas the Warsh transmission has *yaquluna.* In Sura 20:63 the Hafs transmission has the word *hazayni,* whereas the Warsh transmission has *Inna hazani.* This sampling of variants demonstrates that the Muslim claim of perfect unity in the copies of the Quran is incorrect.[2]

## _____ *Ask...* _____

- Were you aware that even today, there are variants between different transmitted versions of the Quran—such as the Hafs transmission and the Warsh transmission?

- Since there are copies of the Quran that have variant readings, how can it be argued that there has always been "perfect unity" in the copies of the Quran?

---

Norman Geisler and Abdul Saleeb, in their excellent book *Answering Islam,* point out that even if today's Quran *were* a perfect copy of Muhammad's original, it still would not prove the original was inspired by God:

> All it would demonstrate is that today's Quran is a carbon copy of whatever Muhammad said; it would say or prove nothing about the truth of what he said. The Muslim claim that they have the true religion, because they have the only perfectly copied Holy Book, is as logically fallacious as someone claiming it is better to have a perfect printing of a counterfeit thousand dollar bill than a slightly imperfect printing of a genuine one![3]

There is one further point that bears mentioning here. Since Muslims believe that God has been giving revelations to humankind throughout history—including through the psalms of David and the gospel of Jesus Christ—one wonders why it is claimed that the Quran was preserved by Allah in infallible copies, whereas Allah was apparently singularly incapable of accomplishing the same feat with all his previous revelations. Missionary John Gilchrist says, "We find such a paradox impossible to believe—for the Eternal Ruler of the universe will surely act consistently at all times."[4]

## _____ *Ask...* _____

- While it is claimed that Allah preserved the Quran in infallible copies, are we to conclude that Allah was incapable of accomplishing the same feat regarding all his previous revelations, like the psalms of David and the gospel of Jesus Christ? Do you see an inconsistency with such a viewpoint? *(Of course, in reality the psalms and the gospel of Jesus Christ were not revelations of Allah but of Yahweh. The above question is only intended to communicate that the Muslim view is inconsistent.)*

---

## The Quran's Beauty and Eloquence Do Not Prove It Is Divine

Though Muslims often argue that the Quran's beauty and eloquence prove that the author is God (considering that Muhammad was an "unlettered prophet"), I must stress that beauty and eloquence are not tests for divine inspiration. If that were true, then many other works of art throughout human history would have to be deemed "divinely inspired." For example, the musical compositions of Mozart, Beethoven, and Bach, and the writings of Shakespeare and other literary giants, would have to be considered divinely inspired.

## *Ask...*

- If beauty and eloquence are tests for divine inspiration, must we not conclude that all the writings of Shakespeare are divinely inspired?

---

One must wonder whether Muslims would accept a challenge to produce a work comparable to any of Shakespeare's writings, or else be willing to accept that his writings are "divinely inspired."[5] That may seem a silly challenge, but it is akin to the Muslim challenge to the world to produce a single chapter comparable to a chapter in the Quran.

## _Ask..._

- Hypothetically speaking, what would you think of a challenge issued to the world to produce a work comparable to any of Shakespeare's writings, or else be willing to accept that his writings are "divinely inspired"?

  *(After asking the question, emphasize that the point you are making is that beauty and eloquence are not tests for divine inspiration.)*

---

One fact that seems to argue *against* the eloquence and beauty of the Quran is that it contains many grammatical errors. Christian apologist Ravi Zacharias has written,

> Let us consider just one troublesome aspect, the grammatical flaws that have been demonstrated. Ali Dashti, an Iranian author and a committed Muslim, commented that the errors in the Quran were so many that the grammatical rules had to be altered in order to fit the claim that the Quran was flawless. He gives numerous examples of these in his book, *Twenty-three Years: The Life of the Prophet Mohammed.* (The only precaution he took before publishing this book was to direct that it be published posthumously.)[6]

Arranging for the book to be published posthumously was a wise move, for Dashti surely would have been marked for death if he had published the book while he was alive. In his book, Dashti writes:

> The Quran contains sentences which are incomplete and not fully intelligible without the aid of commentaries; foreign words, unfamiliar Arabic

words, and words used with other than the
normal meaning; adjectives and verbs inflected
without observance of the concord of gender and
number; illogical and ungrammatically applied
pronouns which sometimes have no referent; and
predicates which in rhymed passages are often
remote from the subjects. These and other such
aberrations in the language have given scope to
critics who deny the Quran's eloquence....To
sum up, more than 100 Quranic aberrations from
the normal rules and structure of Arabic have
been noted.[7]

## Fulfilled Prophecy Does Not Prove the Quran Is Divine

The fact that the Quran prophesied that Muslims would be victorious at home and abroad (for example, Sura 30:1-5) hardly shows the book is divine. Unlike the Christian Bible, which makes very precise predictions many hundreds of years in advance—for example, precisely predicting that Jesus would be born in Bethlehem (Micah 5:2), that He would be born of a virgin (Isaiah 7:14), that he would be "pierced" for man's sins (Zechariah 12:10), and the like—the prediction that Muslims would be militarily victorious (especially considering Muhammad's overwhelming military force) is unimpressive.

A number of Christian apologists have noted that the prediction of Islamic military victory at home and abroad makes more sense when understood as a pre-battle victory speech from Muhammad to boost the morale of his followers, not as a supernatural prediction. It would be much like the leader of an army saying to his troops, "Fight bravely, for we will be victorious!"

Scholar Gerhard Nehls points out that

> with regard to the victories, it is impossible to prove these to be valid predictions, since the time between prediction and fulfillment was almost nil. We also realize that Mohammed obviously *expected* victory, otherwise he would not have been fighting. Besides that, he also needed to encourage his warriors. In every war that has been fought, both parties have expected and predicted victory. One of the two parties has *always* been right; therefore we cannot regard these predictions as prophecies.[8]

## ____ *Ask...* ____

- Have you considered the possibility that Muhammad's prediction of Islamic military victory at home and abroad makes more sense when taken as a pre-battle victory speech to boost the morale of his followers, not as a supernatural prediction? Couldn't we take his words as akin to an army leader saying to his troops, "Fight valiantly, for we are going to win"?

- Do you know of any prophecies in the Quran akin to prophecies in the Bible—such as the prophecy hundreds of years in advance that Jesus would be born in Bethlehem (Micah 5:2)? Or the prophecy hundreds of years in advance that Jesus would be born of a virgin (Isaiah 7:14)?

To say Muhammad was a prophet simply because he accurately predicted military victory (by his overwhelming military force) is kind of like a modern soothsayer saying there is going to be an earthquake in California—or a Florida weather forecaster, aware of an approaching hurricane off the coast, predicting high winds and rain. The odds are heavily stacked in favor of the prediction.

## The Quran's Affinity with Modern Science Does Not Prove It Is Divine

The claim that the Quran's remarkable affinity with modern science proves its divinity is an unconvincing argument. Foundationally, conformity to modern science is not a proof of divine inspiration. As modern scientists themselves admit, scientific models are constantly changing, so they are not an absolute gauge of what is true or false. What was accepted as scientifically true yesterday may not necessarily be accepted as scientifically true tomorrow. Any who doubt that scientific models constantly change should read Thomas Kuhn's book *The Structure of Scientific Revolutions*.

Further, there are some highly questionable scientific statements in the Quran—such as the statement that human beings are formed from a clot of blood (Sura 23:14). Certainly no reputable scientist would go along with that statement. Further, in Sura 18:86 in the Quran we are told that the sun sets in a spring of murky water. No scientist (or even nonscientist) would entertain such an idea.

## _____ *Ask...* _____

- Since scientific models are constantly changing, how can science be considered an ultimate gauge as to what is true or false?

- What about the Quran's claim that human beings are formed from a clot of blood (Sura 23:14)? Do you know of any scientists who accept that claim?

- What about the Quran's claim that the sun sets in a spring of murky water (Sura 18:86)? Do you know of any scientists who accept that claim?

It is noteworthy that many of the world's greatest scientists have been Christians working from within a Christian worldview—including men such as Nicolaus Copernicus, Johannes Kepler, and Sir Isaac Newton. These brilliant men found to be true what many others have discovered: *The Bible is a book that can be trusted.* (See chapters 12 and 13—"A Defense of the Bible, Part One and Part Two.")

## The Doctrine of Abrogation Is Problematic

The doctrine of abrogation is extremely problematic for the view that the Quran is a divine book. This is especially so since the Quran on earth is viewed as a perfect copy of the eternal Quran engraved on a tablet in heaven, which is in the presence of Allah. The problem, simply put, is this: If the Quran is eternal, authored by almighty God, why the need for changes in the revelation given to Muhammad? Does God change His mind? If God is all-knowing, then wouldn't the initial revelation given to Muhammad be final—and absolutely beyond the need for change? As Gerhard Nehls observes, "We should like to find out how a divine revelation can be improved. We would have expected it to have been perfect and true right from the start."[9]

## _____ *Ask...* _____

- If the Quran is truly eternal, authored by Allah, why the need for changes in the revelation given to Muhammad?

- If Allah is all-knowing, then wouldn't the initial revelation given to Muhammad be final—and absolutely beyond the need for change?

My former colleague at the Christian Research Institute, Dr. Walter Martin, suggested that six overwhelming theological problems emerge if the doctrine of abrogation is legitimate. I summarize them here:

1. We cannot trust the Quran, not only because it has divinely inspired contradictions, but because we have no assurance that God will not abrogate part of it again and annul the present revelation.

2. Muslims may argue that future abrogation will not occur because Muhammad was the last prophet, but what if God abrogates that and brings *still another* prophet?

3. How can we trust God with our eternal souls, knowing it is possible that God could abrogate his mercy on us?

4. Abrogation involves not just adding new revelation, but contradicting and annulling former revelation. This necessarily means that God has either changed his mind on a matter, or that he was unaware of how future contingent events would turn out, and thus was forced to make a change.

5. Abrogation calls into question God's attributes, such as his foreknowledge (that is, he did not have sufficient knowledge to avoid abrogation).

6. Since God is inconsistent, what basis is there for morality and ethics? There is no absolute right and wrong that serve as a foundation for our ethics.[10]

## _Ask..._

- How can we have assurance that God will not abrogate something again and annul the present revelation in the Quran?

- Though it is presently said that Muhammad is the last prophet, how do we know that Allah won't abrogate that and bring still another prophet?

- How can we trust God with our eternal souls, knowing that he may decide to abrogate his mercy toward us?

Many Christians have wondered why Muslims persist in arguing against the veracity of the Bible because of its alleged contradictions while at the same time holding to the doctrine of abrogation in the Quran. This does not seem to make much sense. Christians have also noted that whereas one verse in the Quran *affirms* the doctrine of abrogation (Sura 2:106), another verse says, "No change can there be in the words of God" (Sura 10:64). It is not clear how Muslims reconcile these verses.

## _____ *Ask...* _____

- Why do Muslims argue against the veracity of the Bible because of its alleged contradictions while at the same time holding to the doctrine of abrogation in the Quran?

- How do you explain the fact that one verse in the Quran affirms the doctrine of abrogation (Sura 2:106), whereas another verse says, "No change can there be in the words of God" (Sura 10:64)?

### The Quran Does Not Seem to Be Eternal

The Quran does not seem to be an eternal book, as Muslims claim. Indeed, if the Quran is eternal, then why does it allocate so many words to dealing with temporal issues that existed among Muhammad's own family and fellow Muslims? Professor Gleason Archer notes there are suras pronouncing a curse against Muhammad's uncle (Sura 111), an admonition to Muhammad's wives to remain subject to him (Sura 33), and words against the elephant brigade of Abraha, the Christian ruler of Abyssinia, who had come against the Muslims in Mecca (Sura 105). Archer thus concludes,

> The atmosphere of the Quran is saturated with the atmosphere and historical setting of Muhammad's

own time. This seems to be hardly compatible with a holy revelation of God composed before the beginning of time and co-eternal with God himself....The fact that it is so focused on the lifetime of Muhammad himself strongly suggests that it was actually Muhammad who composed the book himself, rather than it being dictated to him by some angelic spokesman of Allah.[11]

## _Ask..._

- If the Quran is eternal, then why does it allocate so many words to dealing with temporal issues that existed among Muhammad's own family?

- If the Quran is eternal, why do we find suras pronouncing a curse against Muhammad's uncle (Sura 111) and an admonition to Muhammad's wives to remain subject to him (Sura 33)?

- Do these sound like revelations composed before the beginning of time?

## Changed Lives Are Not a Proof That the Quran Is Divine

Though Muslims claim the Quran is divine because it has changed so many lives, the reality is that changed lives are not a proof of divine inspiration. Indeed, Mormons declare that their lives have been changed by the _Book of Mormon_. Members of the Unification Church say their lives have been changed by Reverend Moon's _Divine Principle_. Hindus say their lives have been changed by the Vedas. Satanists claim the _Satanic Bible_ has changed their lives. Karl Marx's _Das Kapital_ is said to have changed many lives. New Agers declare that the writings of Shirley MacLaine have changed their lives. Yet not one of these books is divinely inspired.

The reality is, any set of ideas that is put into practice in a person's life can have a life-changing effect on that person. But that does not mean those ideas are inspired by God. Hence, for Muslims to argue for the divinity of the Quran because it has changed many lives is not valid.

## _____ *Ask...* _____

- Did you know that millions of Mormons claim their lives have been changed by the *Book of Mormon?*

- Did you know that millions of Hindus say their lives have been changed by the Vedas?

- Yet you would not say such books are divinely inspired, would you?

- Doesn't it make sense to say that *any* set of ideas that is put into practice in a person's life can have a life-changing effect on that person, and yet not necessarily be divine?

---

### Circular Reasoning Among Muslims

Christian logicians have noted that Muslims sometimes propose circular arguments in setting forth their case for Muhammad, the Quran, and Allah. A circular argument involves assuming in one's basic premise what one intends to state in one's conclusion. If one engages in such circular reasoning, one has really proved nothing.

Dr. Robert Morey notes that

- proving Allah by the Quran and then proving the Quran by Allah is circular reasoning.

- proving Muhammad by the Quran and then proving the Quran by Muhammad is circular reasoning.

- proving Islam by the Quran and then proving the Quran by Islam is circular reasoning.[12]

If you detect such circular reasoning from your Muslim acquaintance, lovingly point out the problem to him or her.

## The Quran Is Not God's Word

The numerous contradictions between the Quran and the Bible are such that if one of the books came from God, there is no way the other could have come from God. Though Muslims try to argue that differences between the Quran and the Bible relate to corruptions in the biblical text, I have presented evidence in this chapter showing that the real problem is with the Quran.

Following are some of the notable contradictions between the Quran and the Bible, which lend support to the Christian view that the Quran is not from God.

- Genesis 8:4 says Noah's ark rested on the mountains of Ararat, while the Quran says Noah's ark rested on Mount Judi (Sura 11:44).

- Genesis 11:27 says Terah was Abraham's father, whereas the Quran says Azar was his father (Sura 6:74).

- Exodus 2:5 says the daughter of Pharaoh found the baby Moses in an ark and adopted him as her son, while the Quran says Pharaoh's wife adopted Moses (Sura 28:8-9).

- Matthew 27:35 says Jesus was crucified, while the Quran says He was not crucified nor even killed (Sura 4:157).

- Luke 1:20 indicates Zechariah's punishment for doubt was that he would not be able to speak until his son was born, while the Quran says he would not be able to speak for three nights (Sura 3:41).

- Luke 2:6-7 says Mary gave birth to Jesus in a stable, whereas the Quran says she gave birth under a palm tree (Sura 19:23).

- Hebrews 1:1-3 indicates Jesus is the brightness of God's glory and the express image of His person, while the Quran says Jesus was no more than a messenger (Sura 5:75).

- John 3:16 says God loves all people, while the Quran says Allah loves only those who follow him (Sura 3:32,57).

- Romans 5:8 indicates that God loves even sinners, while the Quran indicates that Allah does not love transgressors (Sura 2:190).

- Ephesians 5:25-28 says husbands are to love their wives as Christ loved the church, whereas the Quran says husbands can beat their wives if there is reason for it (Sura 4:34).

## Muslim Tradition Is Unreliable

Scholars believe that many traditions presently contained in the Hadith were deliberately invented between 100 and 200 years after the time of Muhammad by various Muslims in order to support the customs or beliefs of rival parties as divisions arose in Islam. Hence, not all that is in the Hadith is actually based on the life and teachings of Muhammad. Even some Muslim scholars admit that not all traditions about Muhammad are legitimate. In fact, Muslim scholars have developed methods of sifting through the sayings contained in the Hadith to evaluate them, weed out questionable or spurious ones, and preserve authentic ones in systematically arranged collections.[13] Even with these methods, however, there is no foolproof way of knowing for sure what is authentic and what is not.

An example of inauthentic traditions relates to some of the miracle stories about Muhammad in the Hadith. I noted previously that the Quran has no record of such miracles, but rather portrays Muhammad *refusing* to do miracles (Suras 3:181-84; 4:153). Since the Quran is a higher authority than the Hadith, it would seem that the miracle stories of Muhammad in the Hadith are not genuine.

## _____ *Ask...* _____

- Since the Quran portrays Muhammad as refusing to do miracles (Suras 3:181-84; 4:153), why should we believe the miracle stories in the Hadith?

- One scholar has noted that "tradition is like a garden in which the new plants have overwhelmed the original ones; it is very hard to tell which ones were there at the beginning."[14] How do you know objectively which traditions of Muhammad are true and which are not true?

### A Closing Admonition

I close with a caution similar to the one I suggested earlier in the book: *Be careful in your timing when bringing up problems with the Quran.* Especially if you have just begun conversations with a Muslim acquaintance, do not start off by insulting the Quran. Muslims greatly revere this book. An insult can quickly and permanently close the door to further discussion and can easily cause the Muslim to become even more "Muslim" than before. For this reason, I recommend that you start off by setting forth a positive defense of the Bible, Jesus, and the gospel. After a while, once you have developed a trusting and comfortable relationship, *then* bring up some of the issues in this chapter. But do so tactfully.

# 6

## *Allah—The God of Islam*

Muslims believe there is only one true God, whose name is Allah. The term "Allah" is probably derived from *al illah,* which means "the god."[1] Allah is said to have seven primary characteristics: Foundationally, he has absolute unity—that is, he is "one," and there is no such thing as a Trinity (more on this below). He is also all-seeing, all-hearing, all-speaking, all-knowing, all-willing, and all-powerful.

As a preface, people in pre-Islamic Meccan culture believed in many different gods, a view known as polytheism. For the most part, local and tribal gods received the most attention, and the people of that time often carved images of these gods and made blood sacrifices to them. They also believed in angels and fairies, who were considered kind spirits.[2]

Among this pantheon was the chief God, who went by the name of Allah. Before Muhammad even arrived on the scene, Allah was already known as the supreme deity or "high God" to the Bedouin peoples of northern Arabia.[3] This "high God" was considered to be the creator and sustainer of the universe, the

95

one who brought help in time of need.[4] As Muhammad grew from boyhood to manhood, he increasingly became convinced that Allah was the only true God, and all others were mere idols. In what follows, I will set forth Muhammad's teachings on Allah.

## Allah Has Many Names

The Quran reveals that Allah has many names. In Sura 59:22-24 we read,

> God is He, than Whom there is no other god; Who knows (all things) both secret and open; He, Most Gracious, Most Merciful. God is He, than Whom there is no other god; the Sovereign, the Holy One, the Source of Peace (and Perfection), the Guardian of Faith, the Preserver of Safety, the Exalted in Might, the Irresistible, the Supreme: Glory to God! (High is He) above the partners they attribute to Him. He is God, the Creator, the Evolver, the Bestower of Forms (or Colors). To Him belong the Most Beautiful Names: whatever is in the heavens and on earth, doth declare His Praises and Glory: and He is the Exalted in Might, the Wise.

Though Allah has many names, Muslims most often refer to him, with great awe and respect, as simply "Allah." As one listens to the speech of Muslims, Allah's name is often sprinkled in. If a Muslim promises to do something, he may well add the qualification "If Allah wills." If he sneezes, he might be heard saying "Praise Allah!" If he witnesses a beautiful sight, he might be heard saying "Glory to Allah!" No matter what he might encounter in day-to-day life, he might be heard saying "Thanks be to Allah!"[5] Just as Muslims revere the name of Muhammad as a prophet, so they revere Allah as the only true God.

## Allah Is Singularly "One"

Muslims view Allah as being absolutely *one*. He was not begotten by anyone, nor did he beget anyone. He is *singularly* one. Because Allah is "one," he has no partners or associates.

Allah is viewed as being different from anything that man can conceive of. For this reason, Muslims often describe Allah using negative terms—such as, Allah is not a spirit. (They say angels are created beings and are spirits, and so to say that God is a spirit would imply he is a created being.[6]) Muslims also say that Allah cannot be seen by anyone, and that he does not have parts or members. But they also sometimes speak in positive terms, noting that Allah is full of compassion and mercy.

Some Muslims prefer to use the term "unicity" to emphasize Allah's oneness and utter uniqueness.[7] Allah is said to be entirely separate from the creation, and is not manifested in any way. While Allah's *will* is manifested (in the pages of the Quran), Allah *himself* is not manifested. Allah is utterly transcendent. He is so separate and divorced from the creation, and so unified to himself, that he cannot be associated with creation. Any talk of God revealing *himself* would compromise his transcendence. In the Muslim mindset, it is simply not permissible to speak in terms of God compromising or reducing his transcendence in any way.

Muslims thus understand God as being beyond virtually every quality and state that belongs to creatures. Allah is inaccessible. We cannot know him in his true nature, for he is beyond us. He is wholly other and totally different. This ultimately means that the Allah of the Quran is an unknowable entity. Yet, at the same time, the Quran teaches in one place that Allah is closer to man than his jugular vein (Sura 50:16). Nonetheless, Allah does not personally manifest himself to those he is "close" to.

Despite the absolute transcendence of Allah, we can at least know something of him via his attributes that are revealed in the Quran. As Islam scholar Jamal J. Elias points out, "Human beings can know God through his attributes (such as mercy, justice, compassion, wrath, and so on), but the ultimate essence of God remains unknowable."[8] There is no personal fellowship with the Allah of the Quran. The main emphasis in Islam is not personal fellowship with God, but rather service, obedience, and allegiance to him. There is no concept of God as father at all.

## Allah Is Not a Trinity

The emphasis on the absolute oneness of Allah is the primary reason Muslims reject the Christian doctrines of the Trinity and of Jesus being the "Son of God." They take this latter phrase quite literally and believe it implies that Allah had a sexual partner in order to beget Christ. It is for this reason that Muslims also reject the idea that God (Allah) is a "Father." In the Muslim mindset, the term "father" cannot be divorced from the physical realm. Hence, to call Allah a "Father" or "heavenly Father" is viewed as blasphemous because it amounts to saying that Allah had sexual relations to produce his "Son" Jesus Christ.

When Muslims bring up the subject of the Trinity, they typically describe it in terms of tritheism—belief in three gods—instead of correctly describing it as belief in one God eternally manifest in three persons.[9] Muslims thus accuse Christians of worshiping three gods. The Quran states, "So believe in God and His apostles. Say not 'Trinity': desist: it will be better for you: for God is one God: Glory be to Him: (far exalted is He) above having a son" (Sura 4:171). Muslims will also typically say that the doctrine of the Trinity is contradictory, for how can something be both three and one at the same time? It does not make sense, they say.

A particularly strange idea that often surfaces in discussions of the Trinity with Muslims is that Christians allegedly believe the Trinity is made up of God, Mary, and Jesus. This idea seems to be based on Sura 5:116 in the Quran: "And behold! Allah will say: 'O Jesus the son of Mary! Didst thou say unto men, worship me and my mother as gods in derogation of Allah?'" This may well be the way Muhammad understood the Christian belief in the Trinity. (Muhammad actually misunderstood a number of

Christian doctrines. Scholars are convinced that Muhammad never knew the correct doctrines of historic, orthodox Christianity, and hence was unable to reject it. What he rejected were *distortions* of Christianity.) In any event, based on Sura 5:116, it is easy to see how a Muslim might conclude that Christians worship three gods. But, of course, this is not the correct view of the Trinity (more on this later).

Scholars Bruce McDowell and Anees Zaka have suggested there may be several possible historical sources for the God–Jesus–Mary concept of the Trinity.[10] They note that since the Syriac word for "spirit" is feminine, some Syriac Christians may have concluded that the Holy Spirit is a "she." There is also an apocryphal gospel—*The Gospel According to the Hebrews*—that makes reference to "my mother, the Holy Spirit." We also know that the Abyssinian Christians highly venerated the Virgin Mary. Still further, there was a Christian sect—the Choloridians—which held a view similar to that described in the Quran. Since all of these had proximity to Muhammad, any or all of these factors may have played a role in Muhammad's inclusion of Sura 5:116 in the Quran, and the subsequent view that the Trinity is composed of God, Jesus, and Mary.

## Allah Brings About Good *and* Evil

One of the more controversial aspects of the Muslim view of Allah relates to his absolute sovereignty. The Quran tells us, "God hath power over all things" (Sura 3:165). In the Muslim view, God brings about both good and evil. God can guide men in righteousness, or he can lead them to evil. In some 20 passages of the Quran, Allah is said to lead men astray. Abdiyah Akbar Abdul-Haqq observes: "Even if a person desires to choose God's guidance, he cannot do so without the prior choice of God in favor of his free choice."[11]

Everything that happens in the universe, whether good or bad, is said to be foreordained by the unchangeable decrees of Allah. Muslims believe that all our thoughts, words, and deeds (good or evil) were foreseen, foreordained, determined, and decreed from all eternity. Allah is thus variously described as the bringer-down, the Compeller, the Tyrant, or the Haughty.[12] One Muslim theologian, al-Ghazali, put it this way:

> He willeth also the unbelief of the unbeliever and the irreligion of the wicked and, without that will, there would neither be unbelief nor irreligion. All we do we do by His will: what He willeth not does not come to pass. If one should ask why God does not will that men should believe, we answer, "We have no right to inquire about what God wills or does. He is perfectly free to will and to do what He pleases." In creating unbelievers, in willing that they should remain in that state; in making serpents, scorpions and pigs: in willing, in short, all that is evil, God has wise ends in view which it is not necessary that we should know.[13]

Another Muslim theologian, Risaleh-i-Barkhawi, goes so far as to say,

> Not only can he (God) do anything, he actually is the only one who does anything. When a man writes, it is Allah who has created in his mind the will to write. Allah at the same time gives power to write, then brings about the motion of the hand and the pen and the appearance upon paper. All other things are passive, Allah alone is active.[14]

There is thus a very strong strain of fatalism in Islam. A frequent statement one hears among devout Muslims is *"im shallah"*—if God wills it.[15] This strong sense of fatalism can lead to irresponsible actions. McDowell and Zaka speak of children in apartment buildings in Teheran, Iran, who would fall over low balcony railings to their deaths, and because of the belief that this must have been the will of Allah, nothing was done to heighten the railings to prevent such tragedies in the future.[16] Fatalism thus leads to a diminished sense of moral responsibility. John Gilchrist summarizes the Muslim mindset this way: "If no one can resist [Allah's sovereign will], why strive for one's own advancement at all? Simply take what comes, for it will surely come just as he purposes."[17] This attitude pervades the mentality of many Muslims.

Some Muslims try to explain this contradiction in Allah (his causing both good and evil) as relating not to his *nature* but rather to his *will*. However, such an explanation seems less than satisfactory in view of the fact that actions that stem from the *will* are rooted in a person's *nature*. Or as apologists Norman Geisler and Abdul Saleeb put it, "Salt water does not flow from a fresh stream."[18]

One cannot help but notice that the Allah of the Quran seems to act in a quite arbitrary fashion. He can choose good, but he can just as easily choose evil. He can choose mercy, but he might just as easily choose severity. He could choose love, but he could just as easily choose hate. This is nowhere more clearly evident than in Sura 11:118-19: "If the Lord pleased, He had made all men of one religion,…but unto this has He created them; for the word of the Lord shall be fulfilled: verily I will fill hell altogether with genii and men." In other words, Allah misleads for the very purpose of populating hell.

Despite the heavy emphasis on God's absolute sovereignty, the Quran also teaches that human beings will be held morally accountable for the evil they engage in. Allah will judge them on the future Day of Judgment. It is never adequately explained *how* humans can be held accountable for that which Allah arbitrarily and sovereignly decreed from all eternity, but Muslims nevertheless believe it.

In view of the clear teaching of the Quran that Allah engages in both good and evil, it is not surprising to learn that there is no suggestion in the Quran that Allah is holy. The Quran seems to emphasize Allah's power rather than his purity, his omnipotence rather than his holiness. This, of course, is completely different from the God of the Bible, for the pivotal attribute of Yahweh is said to be holiness (see Exodus 3:5; 1 Peter 1:16).

## Allah Loves, but Only to an Extent

One attribute of the God of the Bible that is heavily emphasized, but that seems to be largely lacking in regard to Allah, is love. A Muslim can not truthfully say that "God is love" like the Christian can (see 1 John 4:16). The Quranic view is that Allah loves those who love him and serve him, but he does not love those who are unbelievers. Allah is merciful to those who do good, but he withholds mercy from those who do bad. In the Quran we read, "Allah loveth the beneficent" (Sura 2:135). We also read, "If ye do love God, Follow me: God will love you and forgive you your sins" (Sura 3:31). Notice that the motivation for loving Allah is *in order to attain* God's love and forgiveness, not to reciprocate heartfelt love already being received from Allah. The idea is, "Love me in order to be loved back!"

Muslims *do* point to two key verses in the Quran that at least *speak* of Allah's love. Both verses say that Allah is "all-loving" (Suras 11:90; 85:14). However, these two brief general affirmations come nowhere close to the heavy emphasis of God's personal love for sinful man in the Christian Bible. One will simply not find in the Quran the Christian emphasis of a filial love that a Father has for his own dear children. One will not find in the Quran a God who will sacrificially give of Himself to bring about the highest good of His children (like the death of Jesus on the cross).

Muslim theologian al-Ghazali goes so far as to say that it is inconceivable that Allah should love mankind because "when there is love there must be in the lover a sense of incompleteness, a realization that the beloved is needed for complete realization of self." This is quite impossible with Allah, he says, since Allah is perfectly complete in himself.[19]

In view of the Quranic teaching that Allah loves only believers who do good, the Muslim's goal is not to appeal to Allah's love for salvation, but rather to do all he or she can to hold back Allah's judging hand by doing good works and submitting to Allah's laws. I will demonstrate later in the book that Muslims do not have any concept of assurance of salvation.

# 7

# *The Biblical View of God*

Contrary to the Muslim viewpoint, the Bible reveals that God is a highly personal being with whom intimate personal relationships can be established and enjoyed. A person is a conscious being—one who thinks, feels, and purposes, and carries these purposes into action. A person engages in active relationships with others. You can talk to a person and get a response from him. You can share feelings and ideas with him. You can argue with him, love him, and even hate him if you so choose. Surely by this definition God must be understood as a person. After all, God is a conscious being who thinks, feels, and purposes—and He carries these purposes into action. He engages in relationships with others. You can talk to God and get a response from Him.

As inscrutable as it may seem to the human mind, our personal God specially constructed man with a capacity to know and have a relationship with Him. Our purpose—indeed, our highest aim in life—must be to know God.

"What were we made for? To know God!" exults J.I. Packer in his modern classic, *Knowing God*. "What aim should we set ourselves in life? To know God."[1] We read in Scripture, "This is what the Lord says: 'Let not the wise man boast of his wisdom or the strong man boast of his strength or the rich man boast of his riches, but let him who boasts boast about this: that he understands and knows me'" (Jeremiah 9:23-24).

Knowing Jesus Christ—who Himself *is* God, and is the full revelation of God to man—takes on similar importance in the New Testament. The apostle Paul said, "I consider everything a loss compared to the surpassing greatness of knowing Christ Jesus my Lord, for whose sake I have lost all things" (Philippians 3:8).

The Old Testament backdrop to all this is that when God created Adam, He declared Adam's loneliness to be "not good" (Genesis 2:18). *God made man as a social being.* Man was not created to be alone. He was created to enter into and enjoy relationships with others. The most important relationship man was created to enter into is that with God Himself. There is a hunger in the heart of man that none but God can satisfy, a vacuum that only God can fill. We were created with a need for fellowship with God. And we are restless and insecure until this becomes our living experience.

All this is rooted in the fact that God created man in His image (Genesis 1:26). While many have debated down through the centuries what it means for man to be created in God's image, one thing is certain: Part of that "image" is that man is a personal, social, and relational being. We were specifically engineered with a capacity to interact with the Creator on a personal level.

As God has a social nature, so He has endowed man with a social nature. And because man has been endowed with a social nature, man in his deepest heart seeks companionship with his Creator. He yearns for this relationship so that the void in his heart can be filled.

It seems clear from the biblical record that the first man and woman entered into intimate fellowship with God. After all, we read that on one particular day Adam and Eve "heard the sound of the LORD God as he was walking in the garden in the cool of the day" (Genesis 3:8). I believe the clear implication of this statement is that God in the form of a *theophany* ("appearance of God") entered the garden on a regular basis. It seems natural to surmise that God often came into the garden for the sole purpose of fellowshiping with the first man and woman. How blessed it must have been!

There can be no doubt that people in biblical times knew God intimately in their personal experience. In fact, knowing God was the main business among believers of ancient times. We read that Enoch and Noah walked with God (Genesis 5:24; 6:9). God spoke *directly* (not through an angel) to Noah (Genesis 6:13), to Abraham (Genesis 12:1), to Isaac (Genesis 26:24), to Jacob (Genesis 28:13), to Moses (Exodus 3:4), to Joshua (Joshua 1:1), to Gideon (Judges 6:25), to Samuel (1 Samuel 3:4), to David (1 Samuel 23:9-12), to Elijah (1 Kings 17:2-4), and to Isaiah (Isaiah 6:8). Likewise, in the New Testament God spoke to Peter, James, and John (Mark 9:7), to Philip (Acts 8:29), to Paul (Acts 9:4-6), and to Ananias (Acts 9:10). How unlike this is to the utterly remote Allah of Islam.

Scripture often describes the personal relationship believers can have with God in terms of being in His family—a family that lasts forever and ever. John 1:12-13 tells us that "to all who received [Jesus], to those who believed in his name, he gave the right to become children of God—children born not of natural descent, nor of human decision or a husband's will, but born of God." Galatians 3:26 tells us, "You are all sons of God through faith in Christ Jesus." This, of course, does not mean the Father has a female partner who has children. Rather, by *adoption* we are brought into the forever family of God (Romans 8:14). God adopts into His family *any* who believe in His Son, Jesus Christ. This is noticeably different from human adoptions, for human adults generally seek to adopt only the healthiest and best-behaved children. But *all* are welcome in God's family.

It is significant that in New Testament times an adopted son enjoyed all the rights and privileges of a natural-born son. Hence, Christians need not be fearful about coming to God, but can boldly approach His throne and say, "Abba, Father" (Romans 8:15). "Abba" is an Aramaic term of affection and intimacy—similar to the English word "daddy." The word speaks of a tender relationship with God.

Jesus, revered among Muslims as a great prophet, often spoke of God as a loving Father (see, for example, Matthew 6:9,26,32). Elsewhere in the New Testament we are told that God is the "Father of compassion" of all believers (2 Corinthians 1:3). He is often portrayed in Scripture as compassionately responding to the personal requests of His people. A few good examples may be found in Exodus 3:7-8; Job 34:28; Psalm 81:10; 91:14-15; 2 Corinthians 1:3-4; and Philippians 4:6-7. As we engage in discussions with our Muslim acquaintances, we must do all we can to communicate this wonderful personal relationship that we can have with the true God.

## _Ask_...

- Can I tell you what the Bible says about adoption into God's eternal family?

## The Biblical God Is Spirit

Contrary to Islam, which says God is not a spirit (since that would imply he is part of the created realm, like angels), the Bible informs us that God is indeed Spirit (John 4:24; see also Isaiah 31:3). Because God is a spirit, He is invisible and cannot be seen. First Timothy 1:17 refers to God as "the King eternal, immortal, invisible, the only God." Colossians 1:15 speaks of "the invisible

God." John 1:18 tells us, "No one has ever seen God [the Father], but God the One and Only [Jesus Christ], who is at the Father's side, has made him known." When Jesus became a man, He became a *visible* revelation of the *invisible* God.

Islam is incorrect in asserting that the suggestion that God is Spirit implies He is a created being, like angels. Scripture indicates that while God is Spirit, He is also eternal. *God is an eternal spirit*. God, as an eternal being, has always existed. He never came into being at a point in time. He is beyond time altogether. God is the King eternal (1 Timothy 1:17), who alone is immortal (6:16). God is the "Alpha and Omega" (Revelation 1:8) and is the "first and...the last" (see Isaiah 44:6; 48:12). God exists "from eternity" (Isaiah 43:13), and "from everlasting to everlasting" (Psalm 90:2). He lives forever from eternal ages past (Psalm 41:13; Isaiah 57:15).

## The Biblical God Is Transcendent *and* Immanent

The theological phrase "transcendence of God" refers to God's otherness or separateness from the created universe and from humanity. The phrase "immanence of God" refers to God's active presence within the creation and in human history (though all the while remaining distinct from the creation). While Allah is portrayed as radically transcendent, having no interaction with his creatures, the God of the Bible is portrayed as both transcendent *and* immanent—high above His creation, but at the same time intimately involved among His creatures.

A plethora of verses in both the Old and New Testaments speak of God's transcendence. For example, in 1 Kings 8:27 Solomon says, "But will God really dwell on earth? The heavens, even the highest heaven, cannot contain you. How much less this temple I have built!" In Psalm 113:5-6 the question is asked, "Who is like the LORD our God, the One who sits enthroned on high, who stoops down to look on the heavens and the earth?"

Likewise, many verses in Scripture speak of God's immanence. In Exodus 29:45-46 God states, "I will dwell among the
Israelites and be their God. They will know that I am the LORD
their God, who brought them out of Egypt so that I might dwell
among them." In Deuteronomy 4:7 the question is asked, "What
other nation is so great as to have their gods near them the way
the LORD our God is near us whenever we pray to him?"

Some verses in the Bible teach both God's transcendence and
His immanence. For example, Deuteronomy 4:39 says, "Acknowledge and take to heart this day that the LORD is God in heaven
above and on the earth below. There is no other." Isaiah 57:15
affirms, "This is what the high and lofty One says—he who lives
forever, whose name is holy: 'I live in a high and holy place, but
also with him who is contrite and lowly in spirit, to revive the
spirit of the lowly and to revive the heart of the contrite.'" In
Jeremiah 23:23-24 we read, "'Am I only a God nearby,' declares
the Lord, 'and not a God far away? Can anyone hide in secret
places so that I cannot see him?' declares the Lord."

Clearly, God is above and beyond the creation yet is simulta-
neously active *in the midst of* the Creation. Help your Muslim
acquaintance see that the fact of God's transcendence does not
rule out the wonderful reality that He is also immanent.

## _____ *Ask...* _____

- Like you, I believe that God is transcendent. But I also
  believe He is right here with us. Can I share with you what
  the Bible says about this?

## The Biblical God Reveals *Himself*—Not
## Just His Laws

Muslims believe that while Allah's *will* is manifested (in the
pages of the Quran), Allah *himself* is not manifested. Contrary to

this viewpoint, the Bible is clear that God has always been the initiator in making *Himself*—not just His laws—known. He has always taken the first step to reveal Himself to humankind. He does this through *revelation*.

When you think about it, the existence of revelation makes good sense in view of the fact that God is our Father. Consider for a moment: No loving parent would ever deliberately keep out of his or her child's sight so that the child grew up without knowing of the parent's existence. Such an action would be the height of cruelty. Likewise, for God to create us and then not communicate with us would not be in character for a loving heavenly Father.

The word "communication" brings to mind someone coming to us to tell us about himself, telling us what he knows, opening up his mind to us, asking for our attention, and seeking a response.[2] This is what divine revelation is all about. God has come to us to tell us about Himself, to tell us what He knows, to open His mind to us, to ask for our attention, and to seek a response from us.

There are two primary ways God has revealed Himself—through *general* revelation and *special* revelation. General revelation refers to revelation that is available to *all persons* of *all times*. An example of this would be God's revelation of Himself in the world of nature (Psalm 19). Special revelation refers to God's *very specific* and *clear* revelation in such things as His mighty acts in human history, the person of Jesus Christ, and His message spoken through Old Testament prophets and New Testament apostles.

If there really is a personal God who created humankind, then one would naturally expect that He would reveal Himself among human beings in the outworking of human history. And indeed, God *has* manifested Himself historically (read the Exodus account for a good example). God is the *living* God, and He has communicated knowledge of Himself through the ebb and flow of historical experience. The Bible is first and foremost a record of the history of God's interactions among Abraham, Isaac, Jacob, the twelve tribes of Israel, the apostles Paul, Peter, John, and all the other people of God in biblical times.

Though God revealed Himself in mighty acts in human history, the only way for Him to be able to *fully* do and say all that He wanted was to actually leave His eternal residence and enter the arena of humanity. This He did in the person of Jesus Christ. Jesus was Immanuel—"God with us." Jesus was God's ultimate "special" revelation.

A little backdrop makes it clear why it was so necessary for Jesus to come as God's fullest revelation. As noted above, God is Spirit. And because He is Spirit, He is invisible. With our normal senses, we cannot perceive Him, other than through what we can detect in general revelation.

Not only that, man is spiritually blind and deaf. Since the fall of man in the Garden of Eden (Genesis 3), man has lacked true spiritual perception. So humankind was in need of special revelation from God in the worst sort of way.

Jesus—as eternal God—took on human flesh so He could be God's fullest revelation to man (John 1:18; Hebrews 1:2-3). Jesus was a revelation of God not just in His person (as God), but in His life and teachings as well. By observing the things Jesus did and the things Jesus said, we learn a great deal about God.

Here are just a few of the ways that Jesus revealed God:

- God's awesome *power* was revealed in Jesus (John 3:2).

- God's incredible *wisdom* was revealed in Jesus (1 Corinthians 1:24).

- God's boundless *love* was revealed and demonstrated by Jesus (1 John 3:16).

- God's unfathomable *grace* was revealed in Jesus (2 Thessalonians 1:12).

These verses serve as the backdrop as to why Jesus told a group of Pharisees, "When a man believes in me, he does not believe in me only, but in the one who sent me" (John 12:44). Jesus likewise told Philip that "anyone who has seen me has seen the Father" (John 14:9). Jesus was the ultimate revelation of God!

Please notice that Muhammad is completely unlike Jesus in this regard. Muhammad never dared to make the claim that he was the revelation *of* Allah. He simply communicated revelation *from* Allah (via the angel Gabriel). Jesus did not just bring revelation *from* God. He Himself was a revelation *of* God in bodily form (Hebrews 1:2-3).

## The Biblical God Is a Trinity

I believe that at some point or another, it will become necessary for the Christian witness to speak to the Muslim about the doctrine of the Trinity. I realize that some missionaries to Muslims are hesitant to bring the subject up at all, but the reality is that Muslims believe the Trinity is the chief weak point in the Christian system of doctrine, and they invariably seek to attack it. For this reason, the Christian witness must be ready with answers.

To begin, the Christian witness must be aware that Muslims may come right out and ask, "Do you believe in the Trinity?" This is where the Christian must be cautious. As Sobhi Malek points out, if the Christian simply says, "Yes, I believe in the Trinity," and does not clarify the meaning of the term, the Muslim will conclude that the Christian believes in three gods, which is anathema to the Muslim. Yet if the Christian says, "No, I do not believe in the Trinity," he will be denying one of the basic doctrines of Christianity.[3] Hence, should the Muslim ask this question, the Christian must give a *qualified* "Yes"—that is, the Christian must clearly define what is meant by the term "Trinity."

Muslims typically reject the doctrine of the Trinity for several reasons. Primarily, the doctrine implies that God has partners, an idea Muslims interpret to be a heinous sin. Also repulsive to them is the idea that God can have a Son, which implies that God had a female partner who begat Jesus (I'll critique this idea when I examine the Muslim view of Jesus later in the book).

Some Muslim apologists even point out that the word "Trinity" is not in the Bible. One point you can make to a Muslim who argues this way is to point out that the Muslim term for God's unity *(tawhid)* is not in the Quran either.[4] Yet Muslims still believe in the *concept* of God's unity because they believe the whole of the Quran teaches it. Likewise, though the *word* "Trinity" is not mentioned in the Bible, the *concept* is clearly derived from Scripture.

## ____ *Ask...* ____

- Did you know the Muslim term for God's unity *(tawhid)* is not in the Quran? And yet Muslims believe the concept of God's unity is taught in the Quran, right?

- In the same way, cannot Christians believe that while the word "Trinity" is not in the Bible, the concept of the Trinity *is* in the Bible?

---

The Christian doctrine of the Trinity is based on 1) evidence that there is only one true God; 2) evidence that there are three persons who are God; and 3) scriptural indications for three-in-oneness within the Godhead.

Before we examine these three lines of evidence, it is important to clarify what we do *not* mean by the word "Trinity." In attempting to understand God's triune nature, two errors must be avoided. First, we must not conclude that the Godhead is composed of three separate and distinct individuals, such as Peter, James, and Paul, each with their own unique characteristics or attributes. Such a concept would lead to tritheism—the belief that there are three Gods rather than three persons within the Godhead. (Most Muslims understand the Trinity in tritheistic terms.) Second, we must not conclude that the Godhead is one person only and that the triune aspect of His being is no more than three fields of interest, activities, or modes of manifestation—a view known as *modalism*. The fallacy of these ideas will become clearer as we examine the biblical evidence for the Trinity.

## _____ *Ask...* _____

- Would you define your understanding of the Trinity? *(The Muslim will likely give a distorted view.)*

- Would you mind if I clarified what Christians really believe about the Trinity?

### Evidence for One God

The fact that there is only one true God is the consistent testimony of Scripture from Genesis to Revelation—something you will want to heavily emphasize to your Muslim acquaintance, since he thinks the Trinity involves the worship of three gods. The fact that God is one is like a thread that runs through every page of the Bible. An early Hebrew confession of faith, the *shema,* is an example of this consistent emphasis: "Hear, O Israel: The LORD our God, the LORD is one" (Deuteronomy 6:4). This verse is probably better translated from the Hebrew, "Hear, O Israel! The LORD is our God, *the LORD alone.*" In a culture saturated with false gods and idols, the *shema* would have been particularly meaningful for the ancient Israelites. The importance of the *shema* is reflected in the Hebrew practice of requiring children to memorize it at a very early age.

In the song of Moses—the song that Moses recited to the whole assembly of Israel following the exodus from Egypt—we find God's own words worshipfully repeated: "See now that I myself am He! There is no god besides me" (Deuteronomy 32:39).

After God had made some astonishing promises to David (see the Davidic Covenant in 2 Samuel 7:12-16), David responded by offering praise to God: "How great you are, O Sovereign LORD! There is no one like you, and there is no God but you" (2 Samuel 7:22). Later, in the form of a psalm, David again praised God with the words, "You are great and do marvelous deeds; you alone are God" (Psalm 86:10).

God Himself positively affirmed through Isaiah the prophet, "I am the first and I am the last; apart from me there is no God" (Isaiah 44:6; see also 37:20; 43:10; 45:5,14,21-22). God later declared, "I am God, and there is no other; I am God, and there is none like me" (46:9). God often demonstrated that He alone is God by foretelling the future, something that false gods could never do (46:5-7).

The oneness of God is also often emphasized in the New Testament. In 1 Corinthians 8:4, for example, the apostle Paul asserted that "an idol is nothing at all in the world and that there is no God but one." James 2:19 likewise says, "You believe that there is one God. Good! Even the demons believe that—and shudder." These and a multitude of other verses (including John 5:44; 17:3; Romans 3:29-30; 16:27; Galatians 3:20; Ephesians 4:6; 1 Thessalonians 1:9; 1 Timothy 1:17; 2:5; 1 John 5:20-21; Jude 25) make it absolutely clear there is one and only one God.

Make every effort to help your Muslim acquaintance understand that Christians worship *one God alone*. In his book *Christian Reply to Muslim Objections,* W. St. Clair Tisdall suggests that we say to the Muslim,

> We do not ask you to abandon monotheism.
> Belief in the unity of God is the very foundation
> of Christianity in general, and of the doctrine of
> the Trinity in particular. Anyone who abandons it
> and believes in three gods is a polytheist and not
> a Christian. Both in the Old Testament and in the

New the unity of God was taught ages before Muhammad's time.[5]

## _Ask..._

- Did you know Christianity taught the unity of God long before Muhammad was born?

- Did you know the unity of God is one of the major planks of the doctrine of the Trinity? Can I explain? _(Define the doctrine of the Trinity according to the information in this chapter.)_

## Evidence for Three Persons Who Are Called God

Though Scripture is clear that there is only one God, in the unfolding of God's revelation to humankind it also becomes clear that there are _three distinct persons_ who are called God. Be sure to emphasize that the three persons are not God, Jesus, and Mary (as many Muslims believe, based on Sura 5:116), but rather the Father, the Son Jesus, and the Holy Spirit.

Each of these three persons is called God in Scripture. Peter refers to the saints "who have been chosen according to the foreknowledge of God _the Father_" (1 Peter 1:2, emphasis added). The Father said of Jesus, "Your throne, O God, will last for ever and ever" (Hebrews 1:8). In Acts 5:3-4, we are told that lying to the Holy Spirit is equivalent to lying to God.

Besides being recognized as "God," the Father, Jesus, and the Holy Spirit are, on different occasions, seen to possess the attributes of deity. For example:

- All three persons possess the attribute of _omnipresence_ (that is, all three are everywhere-present): the Father (Matthew 19:26), the Son (Matthew 28:18-20), and the Holy Spirit (Psalm 139:7).

- All three have the attribute of *omniscience* (all-knowingness): the Father (Romans 11:33), the Son (Matthew 9:4), and the Holy Spirit (1 Corinthians 2:10).

- All three have the attribute of *omnipotence* (all three are all-powerful): the Father (1 Peter 1:5), the Son (Matthew 28:18), and the Holy Spirit (Romans 15:19).

- *Holiness* is ascribed to each of the three persons: the Father (Revelation 15:4), the Son (Acts 3:14), and the Holy Spirit (John 16:7-14).

- *Eternalness* is ascribed to each of the three persons: the Father (Psalm 90:2), the Son (Micah 5:2; John 1:2; Revelation 1:8, 17), and the Holy Spirit (Hebrews 9:14).

In addition to having the attributes of deity, each of the three persons were involved in doing the *works* of deity. For example, all three were involved in the creation of the world: the Father (Genesis 2:7; Psalm 102:25), the Son (John 1:3; Colossians 1:16; Hebrews 1:2), and the Holy Spirit (Genesis 1:2; Job 33:4; Psalm 104:30).

## Scriptural Indications for Three-in-Oneness

There are a number of scriptural indications for three-in-oneness in the Godhead. Perhaps one of the best illustrations is Matthew 28:19. After Jesus had been resurrected from the dead, He referred to all three persons of the Trinity while instructing the disciples: "Go and make disciples of all nations, baptizing them in the name of the Father and of the Son and of the Holy Spirit." It is highly revealing that the word "name" is singular in the Greek, indicating that there is one God, but three distinct persons within the Godhead—the Father, the Son, and the Holy Spirit.[6] Theologian Robert Reymond draws our attention to the importance of this verse for the doctrine of the Trinity:

Jesus does not say, (1) "into the names [plural] of the Father and of the Son and of the Holy Spirit," or what is its virtual equivalent, (2) "into the name of the Father, and into the name of the Son, and into the name of the Holy Spirit," as if we had to deal with three separate Beings [akin to the Muslim charge of tritheism]. Nor does He say, (3) "into the name of the Father, Son, and Holy Spirit" (omitting the three recurring articles), as if "the Father, Son, and Holy Ghost" might be taken as merely three designations of a single person. What He does say is this: (4) "into the name [singular] of *the* Father, and of *the* Son, and of *the* Holy Spirit," first asserting the unity of the three by combining them all within the bounds of the single Name, and then throwing into emphasis the distinctness of each by introducing them in turn with the repeated article.[7]

Still further evidence for God's three-in-oneness is found in Paul's benediction in his second letter to the Corinthians: "May the grace of the Lord Jesus Christ, and the love of God [the Father], and the fellowship of the Holy Spirit be with you all" (2 Corinthians 13:14). This verse shows the intimacy that each of the three persons has with the believer.

As you try to share the correct view of the Trinity with your Muslim acquaintance, it could be that he might say the doctrine does not make sense. How can there be three in one? Help your friend see that the Trinity does not involve *three gods in one god,* nor does it involve *three persons in one person.* Those kinds of statements would be illogical. But the Trinity involves one God who is eternally manifest in three persons. It may not be easy to understand, but it should not surprise us that *finite minds* cannot fully comprehend the nature of an *infinite God.*

_____ *Ask...* _____

- Is it your view that *finite* minds can fully comprehend the nature of an *infinite* God? (*Likely they will say no.*)

- If the *infinite* God were a Trinity, would you expect that *finite* minds would be able to fully comprehend it?

- Can I share with you what the Bible reveals about this doctrine so you can make an informed decision?

_____

You might share with your Muslim acquaintance how the great theologian Augustine struggled with this. One day while puzzling over the doctrine of the Trinity, he was walking along the beach, when he observed a young boy with a bucket, running back and forth to pour water into a little hole. Augustine asked, "What are you doing?"

The boy replied, "I'm trying to put the ocean into this hole."

Augustine smiled, recognizing the utter futility of what the boy was attempting to do.

After pondering the boy's words for a few moments, however, Augustine came to a sudden realization. He realized he had been trying to put an infinite God into his finite mind. It could not be done.[8]

We can accept God's revelation to us that He is triune in nature and that He has infinite perfections. But with our finite minds we cannot fully understand everything about God. *Our God is an awesome God.*

World religions scholar Dean Halverson says "the difficulty of understanding and explaining the concept of the Trinity is, in fact, evidence for its divine origin. It is unlikely that such a concept would be invented by mere humans."[9] This is not unlike something C.S. Lewis once said: "If Christianity was something we were making up, of course we could make it easier. But it is not. We cannot compete, in [terms of] simplicity, with people who are inventing religions. How could we? We are dealing with Fact. Of course anyone can be simple if he has no facts to bother about."[10] The *fact* is, God is a Trinity.

## _____ *Ask...* _____

- Have you considered the possibility that the difficulty of fully understanding the concept of the Trinity is, in fact, an evidence for its divine origin?

- After all, it isn't likely that human beings would just invent such a doctrine out of the blue, is it?

### The Biblical God Is Love

While "Allah loveth not those that do wrong" (Sura 3:140), the Christian Bible tells us that "God demonstrates his own love for us in this: *While we were still sinners,* Christ died for us" (Romans 5:8, emphasis added). In fact, the Bible quite clearly indicates that God loves all sinners (see John 3:16; Romans 5:1-10).

## _____ *Ask...* _____

- Doesn't the Quran teach that Allah does not love those who do wrong (Sura 3:140)?

- Did you know the Bible teaches that God loves us *while we are still sinners* (Romans 5:8)? Did you know that God loves *you?*

God is not just characterized *by* love. He is the very personification *of* love (1 John 4:8). Love permeates His being. And God's love is not dependent upon the lovability of the object—human beings, that is. God loves us despite the fact that we are fallen in sin (John 3:16). God loves the sinner, though He hates the sin. Consider 1 John 4:7-11:

> Dear friends, let us love one another, for love comes from God. Everyone who loves has been born of God and knows God. Whoever does not love does not know God, because God is love. This is how God showed his love among us: He sent his one and only Son into the world that we might live through him. This is love: not that we loved God, but that he loved us and sent his Son as an atoning sacrifice for our sins. Dear friends, since God so loved us, we also ought to love one another.

If you ask a Muslim if there is anything comparable to this in the Quran, he will be forced to say no. The God of the Bible loves people regardless of the lovability of the people. He loves them so much that He sent Jesus to die for them on the cross. John Gilchrist, a longtime apologist who evangelizes among Muslims, writes regarding 1 John 4,

> Herein lies the proof of the depth of God's love towards us. He has done the greatest thing he could possibly do to reveal his love for us—he gave willingly his very own Son Jesus Christ to die on a cross for our sins to redeem us to himself. No greater proof of God's love can be given to mankind than this. It is no wonder that John does not appeal to anything further to make his point. He has given the very best possible proof of God's love towards men.[11]

## The Biblical God Is Holy

God's holiness means not just that He is entirely separate from all evil but also that He is absolutely righteous (Leviticus 19:2).

He is pure in every way. God is separate from all that is morally imperfect. The Scriptures lay great stress upon this attribute of God:

- "Who is like you—majestic in holiness?" (Exodus 15:11).
- "There is no one holy like the LORD" (1 Samuel 2:2).
- "The LORD our God is holy" (Psalm 99:9).
- "Holy and awesome is his name" (Psalm 111:9).
- "Holy, holy, holy is the LORD Almighty" (Isaiah 6:3).
- "You alone are holy" (Revelation 15:4).

When one reads the Quran, one finds that the primary attributes of Allah are transcendence and sovereignty. While the Bible does portray God as being transcendent and sovereign, the foundational attribute of God's holiness is a thread that runs through the entire Bible. God never does anything that violates His intrinsic holiness in any way.

## The Biblical God Is *Singularly* Good, Just, and Righteous

A key emphasis in the Bible relates to the absolute unity of God's moral character. By "unity," I mean that God does not have within His nature dualistic ideas of good and evil, mercy and meanness. God is *singularly* good, just, and righteous. The God of the Bible abhors evil, does not create moral evil, and does not lead men astray.

Christian apologists have noted that in Islamic teaching, God is not essentially good but is only *called* good because he *does* good. He is named for his actions. There is an obvious fatal flaw in this line of thinking. Indeed, if God is called good because he does good, then should we *call* God evil because he *does* evil? It seems difficult to avoid this conclusion.[12]

Further, if God does evil, then doesn't this reveal something about His nature? Doesn't an effect resemble its cause? As Thomas Aquinas pointed out, one cannot produce what one does not possess.[13] Seen in this light, it is hard to escape the conclusion that evil is a part of Allah's nature.

## _____ *Ask...* _____

- If God produces evil, how can we escape the conclusion that he has evil in his nature, since one cannot produce what one does not possess?

---

Contrary to Islam, both good and evil cannot stem from one and the same essence (God). The Bible is clear that "God is light; in Him is no darkness at all" (1 John 1:5; compare with Habakkuk 1:13; Matthew 5:48). First John 1:5 is particularly cogent in the Greek, which translates literally, "And darkness there is not in Him, not in any way." John could not have said it more forcefully.

Related to this is a warning from the prophet Isaiah: "Woe to those who call evil good and good evil" (Isaiah 5:20). Saying that good and evil stem from the same essence of God is the same as calling evil "good" and calling good "evil." The Scriptures clearly portray God as *singularly good:*

- "How great is your goodness, which you have stored up for those who fear you" (Psalm 31:19).
- "Taste and see that the LORD is good; blessed is the man who takes refuge in him" (Psalm 34:8).
- "Good and upright is the LORD" (Psalm 25:8).
- "The LORD is good and his love endures forever" (Psalm 100:5).

- "Give thanks to the LORD, for he is good; his love endures forever" (Psalm 106:1).

- "The LORD is good, a refuge in times of trouble. He cares for those who trust in him" (Nahum 1:7).

The Scriptures also portray God as *singularly righteous:*

- "LORD, God of Israel, you are righteous!" (Ezra 9:15).

- "The LORD is righteous, he loves justice" (Psalm 11:7).

- "The LORD loves righteousness and justice" (Psalm 33:5).

- "Righteousness and justice are the foundation of your throne" (Psalm 89:14).

- "You are always righteous, O LORD" (Jeremiah 12:1).

God is also *singularly just.* That God is *just* means He carries out His righteous standards justly and with equity. There is never any partiality or unfairness in God's dealings with people (Zephaniah 3:5; Romans 3:26). His justness is proclaimed emphatically in both the Old and New Testaments (see, for example, Genesis 18:25; Psalm 11:7; John 17:25; Hebrews 6:10).

## ____ *Ask...* _____

- Would you mind if I shared with you what the Bible says about God being *singularly* good, righteous, and just?

---

### The Biblical God Is Sovereign, but He Allows for Free Will

God is absolutely sovereign in the sense that He rules the universe, controls all things, and is Lord over all (see Ephesians 1).

There is nothing that can happen in this universe that is beyond the reach of His control. All forms of existence are within the scope of His absolute dominion. Psalm 50:1 makes reference to God as the Mighty One who "speaks and summons the earth from the rising of the sun to the place where it sets." Psalm 66:7 affirms that "He rules forever by his power." We are assured in Psalm 93:1 that "the Lord reigns" and "is armed with strength." Isaiah 40:15 tells us that by comparison, "Surely the nations are like a drop in a bucket; they are regarded as dust on the scales; he weighs the islands as though they were fine dust." Indeed, "Before him all the nations are as nothing" (Isaiah 40:17). God is said to be "the blessed and only Ruler, the King of kings and Lord of lords" (1 Timothy 6:15).

Though Scripture portrays God as being absolutely sovereign (Acts 15:17-18; Ephesians 1:11; Psalm 135:6), Scripture also portrays man as having a free will (Genesis 3:1-7). It is certainly inscrutable to our finite understanding how both divine sovereignty and human free will can be true, but both doctrines are taught in Scripture. In fact, both of these are often seen side-by-side in the span of a single Scripture verse.

For example, in Acts 2:23 we read this of Jesus: "This man was handed over to you by God's set purpose and foreknowledge; and you, with the help of wicked men, put him to death by nailing him to the cross." Here we see *divine sovereignty* ("by God's set purpose and foreknowledge") and *human free will* ("you, with the help of wicked men, put him to death").

We also see both doctrines in Acts 13:48: "When the Gentiles heard this, they were glad and honored the word of the Lord; and all who were appointed for eternal life believed." God's sovereignty is clear ("all who were appointed for eternal life") as is man's free will ("believed").

There are numerous indicators in Scripture that human beings have a free will. In Matthew 23:37 Jesus is speaking to Jews who rejected him: "O Jerusalem, Jerusalem, you who kill the prophets and stone those sent to you, how often I have longed to gather your children together, as a hen gathers her chicks under her wings, *but you were not willing"* (emphasis added). Christ (God) was willing to affectionately gather these Jews close to Him, but *they chose* not to draw near to Him. Likewise, we see man's free will illustrated in Genesis following Adam and Eve's sin. After they had committed their rebellious act by eating the forbidden fruit, God came into the Garden and asked, "What is this *you* have done?" (Genesis 3:13, emphasis added). Adam and Eve couldn't pass the buck to God and say, "You decreed me to do it," but rather they were found guilty of their own act of rebellion against the Lord.

The difficulty, as noted above, is trying to figure out how human freedom and divine sovereignty can both be true at the same time. These are not easy concepts. It has been suggested that divine sovereignty and human free will are like parallel railroad tracks that are often found side by side in Scripture, and the tracks never come together on this side of eternity. When we enter glory, we will no doubt come to a fuller understanding of these biblical doctrines. Now we see as in a mirror darkly; then we shall see clearly (1 Corinthians 13:12).

## The Biblical God Has an Objective Basis for Forgiving Sinners

Humankind's dilemma of falling short of God's glory (Romans 3:23) pointed to the need for a solution. Man's sin—his utter unrighteousness—was such that there was no way of his coming into a relationship with God on his own. Humankind was guilty before a holy God, and this guilt of sin put a barrier between man and God.

God solved this seemingly insurmountable problem by "declaring righteous" all those who believe in Jesus. Because of Christ's work on the cross—taking our place and bearing our sins—God acquits believers and pronounces a verdict of "not guilty." Romans 3:24 tells us that God's declaration of righteousness is given to believers "freely by his grace." The word "grace" literally means "unmerited favor." It is because of God's unmerited favor that believers can freely be "declared righteous" before God.

Here is the important thing I want to emphasize: God's declaration of righteousness has an *objective* basis. God did not just subjectively decide to overlook man's sin or wink at his unrighteousness. That would be unjust. That would be unrighteous. Instead, Jesus died on the cross for us. He died in our stead and paid for our sins. He ransomed us from death by His own death on the cross.

There has been a great exchange. As the great reformer Martin Luther said, "Lord Jesus, you are my righteousness, I am your sin. You have taken upon yourself what is mine and given me what is yours. You have become what You were not so that I might become what I was not."[14] This is completely just and completely righteous. And as a result, we who trust in Christ are saved and have peace with God (Romans 5:1).

The reason I bring this up is that there is no *atonement* in Islam (I'll discuss this in greater detail later in the book), and therefore there is no objective basis for Allah to decide to forgive someone. This ultimately means that Allah is being unrighteous and unjust. Only through the cross could God remain *just* and *the justifier* of the ungodly who trust in Jesus. To imagine that God can righteously forgive sinners without requiring any atonement "is to impute immorality to God and make him a protector of sin rather than its condemner."[15]

## Ask...

- Can I explain to you how Jesus' death on the cross provides an objective basis for God to forgive the sins of human beings?

## The Biblical God Is Not Allah

Though it is often argued that the Allah of Islam and the God of the Bible are one and the same God, my knowledge of the Bible compels me to reject this line of thinking. Certainly there are similarities between the God of Islam and that of the Bible: Both are "one," are transcendent, are creators of the universe, sovereign, omnipotent, have communicated through angels and prophets, and will eventually judge all humankind. But there are also differences between the two—differences that are so substantive as to make impossible a common identity:

- Whereas the God of the Quran is a radical unity, the God of the Bible is a Trinity (one God eternally manifest in three persons—see Matthew 28:19).

- Whereas the God of the Quran cannot have a "Son," the God of the Bible has an eternal Son named Jesus Christ (John 3:16).

- Whereas the God of the Quran is not "spirit," the God of the Bible is spirit (John 4:24).

- Whereas the God of the Quran is wholly transcendent, the God of the Bible is both transcendent and immanent (Deuteronomy 4:39; Isaiah 57:15; Jeremiah 23:23-24).

- Whereas the God of the Quran brings about both good and evil, the God of the Bible never engages in evil and is singularly righteous (1 John 1:5).

- Whereas the God of the Quran is not a "Father" (Sura 19:88-92; 112:3), the God of the Bible is (Matthew 6:9).

- Whereas the God of the Quran loves only those who love him and obey him, the God of the Bible loves all people, including all sinners (see Luke 15:11-24).

- Whereas Allah desires to afflict people for their sins (Sura 5:49), the God of the Bible is "not wanting anyone to perish, but everyone to come to repentance" (2 Peter 3:9).

- Whereas the God of the Quran reveals only his laws and not himself, the God of the Bible has revealed Himself from the beginning.

- Whereas the God of the Quran has no objective basis for forgiving people, the God of the Bible does have an objective basis—the death of Jesus Christ on the cross of Calvary.

# 8

# *Jesus—A Prophet of Islam*

Muslims believe Jesus was one of the foremost prophets of Allah. He was a sinless man who was a messenger of God, bringing truth for His particular age. He was not the Son of God, nor was He God in human flesh. He was certainly not a partner of God, for that would constitute blasphemy against Allah. Jesus is spoken of with great honor, but no more honor than is due any other prophet of Allah. He is said to be a lesser prophet than Muhammad.

Muslims recognize this is quite different from what Christians have heard about Jesus. But they believe they understand Jesus' message and mission more accurately than Christians do.[1] They base their view on what the Quran teaches. And since, in their view, the Quran supersedes the corrupted Gospels of the Christian Bible, the Quran's teachings about Jesus are to be accepted as final and authoritative. While the Muslim view of Jesus is much less than that of the Bible, they do not believe they degrade Him, or belittle Him, or make Him to be less than He is. Indeed, they believe the Quran depicts Jesus in a most respectful way.

131

## An Apostle of Allah

While innumerable verses in the Christian Bible deal with the person of Jesus Christ, only a sparse 74 verses out of 6236 in the Quran deal with Him—and of those, some 42 are indirect references.[2] It is quite obvious that Jesus is not a "major player" in the Quran.

One of the more central verses in the Quran that deals with Jesus is Sura 4:171: "Christ Jesus the son of Mary was (no more than) an apostle of God, and His Word, which He bestowed on Mary, and a spirit proceeding from Him." Muslims believe this verse is rich in commendations for Jesus. He is called a prophet of Allah, even though He is a much lesser prophet than Muhammad. Muslims say Jesus never claimed to be more than a prophet. Indeed, He is just one among many thousands (allegedly 124,000) of prophets of Allah, and hence, even though great, He is not unique.

Jesus is also called the Word of God in this verse. At first glance, it may appear to the Christian that Muslims are ascribing to Jesus the same title for God that we find in John 1:1. This, however, is not the case. Muslim scholar al-Ghazali says that the title "Word of God" refers only to the idea that Jesus was created in Mary's womb by a divine command, not to Jesus as eternal God who came as a full and final revelation of God the Father.[3] Far from being a title of deity, "Word of God" to Muslims indicates that Jesus was *not* God.

Jesus is also called a spirit from Allah in Sura 4:171. This is not a *divine* spirit, but simply refers to a soul created by Allah.

Elsewhere, in Sura 3:45, we are told that Jesus' name is "the Messiah" (see also Suras 4:157,171). But again, Muslims do not mean by "Messiah" what Christians do. In fact, Muslims seem to have no awareness of the true significance of this term, and certainly have no conception of the Messiah as a divine being.

## A Miracle Worker

Muslims highly revere Jesus for the miracles He performed (Suras 3:49; 5:110). They think it is wonderful that He healed sick people and raised dead people to life. Christian scholar William Miller notes that even to this day, if a person wishes to compliment a doctor in Iran, he may say something like, "Doctor, you perform miracles; you have the breath of Jesus!"[4]

The fact that Jesus performed miracles that greatly benefited people has endeared Him to many Muslims. Yet, Muslims do not see miracles as a proof that Jesus was a divine being or that He was the Son of God. After all, Muslim apologists point out that even in the Christian Bible, false Christs and false prophets have the ability to perform miracles (Matthew 24:24), and hence miracles do not prove divine identity. Muslims argue that it was Allah who enabled Jesus to do such things.

## Jesus Was Not the Son of God

Muslims make every effort to argue against the idea that Jesus was the Son of God. People who believe Jesus is the Son of God are viewed as being deluded (Sura 9:30). In Muslim thinking, the suggestion that Jesus was the Son of God implies that Allah had sexual relations with a female partner (Mary), which resulted in the birth of Jesus. They are obviously taking a grossly anthropomorphic view of "Son of God." The Quran is clear that Allah has no consort: "How can He have a son when He hath no consort?" (Sura 6:101). The Quran also states of Allah: "No son has He begotten, nor has He a partner in His dominion" (Sura 25:2). Further, we are told that "He begetteth not, nor is He begotten" (Sura 112:3). Since Muslims believe it is blasphemy to say Allah could have a partner, the very idea that Jesus is the Son of God is highly offensive to them.

Part of the confusion relates to the fact that the King James Version of the Bible uses the term "begotten" of Jesus Christ (see John 1:14,18; 3:16). One Muslim apologist says, "The Muslim takes exception to the word 'begotten,' because begetting is an animal act, belonging to the lower animal functions of sex. How can we attribute such a lowly capacity to God?"[5]

Further, Muslims say, if Jesus was the Son of God, then why did He so often claim to be merely the Son of Man? Jesus' own words argue against the idea that He was the Son of God.[6]

## Jesus Was Not God

Muslims are emphatic that Jesus was not God in human flesh. Christians who hold to such an idea are guilty of blasphemy (Suras 5:17,73). To say that Jesus was God would ultimately mean there is more than one God, which constitutes a denial of their basic confession that there is only one God whose name is Allah (for example, Suras 5:116-17). Christians who make such a claim are infidels, for such a view greatly dishonors Allah.

One Muslim apologist goes so far as to say there is not a single unequivocal statement in the Christian Bible where Jesus claimed to be God or where He instructed His followers to worship Him.[7] Jesus never claimed to be more than a prophet and denied being deity.

Muslims believe Jesus was completely human. While it is true that He did many incredible miracles, He did these miracles not by His own power, but by the power of Allah. As a servant of Allah, Jesus received the ability to do miracles to glorify Allah, not Himself.

## Bible Verses That "Disprove" Jesus' Deity

Muslim apologists often cite verses from the New Testament with the sole purpose of proving that Jesus is not God. It is beyond the scope of this chapter to cover every single verse they cite, but in what follows I deal with some of the more representative verses. (I deal with other such verses in my previous book *The Complete Book of Bible Answers,* published by Harvest House Publishers.)

- *John 10:30.* Here Jesus affirmed, "I and the Father are one." Muslims realize Christians often cite this verse in support of the deity of Jesus, so they are quick to argue that Jesus and the Father are merely *one in purpose.* Both the Father and Jesus are portrayed as having the same purpose of seeing to it that believers remain in the faith.[8]

- *John 14:28.* In this verse we find Jesus asserting, "I am going to the Father, for the Father is greater than I." Muslims believe Jesus is here saying that the Father is greater than Him *in nature,* and hence Jesus cannot be God.

- *Mark 10:18.* Here we find Jesus saying the following to a rich young ruler who had referred to Him as "good": "Why do you call me good?...No one is good—except God alone." Muslims believe Jesus is denying He is God.[9]

- *John 20:28.* Thomas, after beholding the resurrected Jesus, said to Him, "My Lord and my God!" Realizing that Christians often cite this verse in support of the deity of Jesus, Muslim apologists argue that Thomas was simply uttering an exclamation: "My God!" He was not saying Jesus was his God and Lord.[10]

- *Mark 13:32.* In this verse Jesus said of His future second coming, "No one knows about that day or hour, not even the angels in heaven, nor the Son, but only the Father." Muslim apologists say that if Jesus were divine, He ought to have been omniscient, like God is (Sura 59).[11]

- *Mark 14:50.* Here we read that following the arrest of Jesus, "everyone deserted him and fled." Muslims say that since *all* the disciples fled (notice the word "everyone"), this means that there were no eyewitnesses of the events that followed—including the alleged crucifixion. The disciples' knowledge of the so-called crucifixion was mere hearsay: "They had heard that their master was hanged on the Cross; they had heard that he had given up the Ghost; they had heard that he was dead and buried for three days."[12] In reality, Muslims say, the crucifixion never occurred. Nobody saw what happened.

- *Matthew 16:20.* In this verse we find Jesus warning His disciples not to tell anyone that He was the Christ. Obviously, Muslims say, Jesus was reacting against any suggestion that He was deity.[13]

## Jesus Was Not Crucified, but Was Taken into Heaven by Allah

The Quran states that Jesus did not die by crucifixion: "...They said (in boast), 'We killed Christ Jesus the son of Mary, the Apostle of God'; but they killed him not, nor crucified him, but so it was made to appear to them, and those who differ therein are full of doubts, with no (certain) knowledge, but only conjecture to follow, for of a surety they killed him not" (Sura 4:157).

The question is, how was it "made to appear to them" that Jesus was crucified? Muslims offer a variety of different explanations in trying to make sense of what really happened to Jesus. Some Muslims argue that the Roman guards seized and arrested the wrong Jesus—*Barabbas* (tradition says he was also named "Jesus")—and crucified him. We are told that when Jesus encountered the disciples on the road to Emmaus (Luke 24), He was actually seeking to escape from Jerusalem before anyone discovered the error of arresting the wrong man.[14]

Another popular theory is that Judas was crucified on the cross. According to this theory, after Judas betrayed Jesus, Allah transformed Judas so that he looked like Jesus, and then Judas was nailed to the cross to die. Jesus, unharmed, was then taken directly into heaven. Abdul-Haqq says, "The shape of Jesus was put on Judas who had pointed him out, and they crucified him instead, supposing that he was Jesus. After three hours God took Jesus to Himself and raised him up to heaven."[15] This raising to heaven was not the ascension that is spoken of in the Bible (Acts 1:9-11), but was rather an Elijah-like transference of Jesus into God's presence without the experience of death.

A variation of the Judas theory is that when the Roman soldiers came to arrest Jesus, it was dark, and in the commotion the soldiers mistakenly arrested Judas instead of Jesus. Judas was then crucified while Jesus remained unharmed and was raised up to heaven by Allah.

Here is yet another variation of this theory:

> It is related that a group of Jews reviled Isa [Jesus].... Then the Jews gathered to kill him. Whereupon Allah informed him that he would take him up to heaven. Then Isa said to his disciples, "Which one of you is willing to have my likeness cast upon him, and be killed and crucified and enter paradise?" One of them accepted, and Allah cast the likeness of Isa upon him, and he was killed and crucified. It is said also that he was one who acted the hypocrite toward Isa, and went out to lead the Jews to him. But Allah cast the likeness of Isa upon him, and he was taken and crucified and killed.[16]

Still another theory is that it was actually Jesus that was crucified on the cross, but He did not die. He merely "swooned" and passed out, and was then mistaken for dead.[17] He later recovered just fine.

Why all the different theories "proving" that Jesus never died by crucifixion? The primary reason is that, in Muslim thinking, it is impossible that Allah would desert a prophet (like Jesus) in the fulfillment of His mission, and allow Him to die a degrading death. For Jesus to die on a cross would be contrary to Allah's omnipotence. Allah would surely rescue a prophet in danger. "As an arbiter of the destinies of all living creatures, God would not allow his prophet-servant to be defeated or humiliated by his enemies."[18] Indeed, "If Messiah Isa [Jesus] had been allowed to die in this cruel and shameful way, then God himself must have failed—which was an impossible thought."[19] In fact, Muslims sometimes argue that they honor Jesus more than Christians do because death by crucifixion would be a dishonor. Allah is said to have honored Jesus by taking Him straight to heaven.

Muslims know that Christians sometimes object by saying, "How is it possible that Muhammad, who lived over 600 years after the event, knew what really happened to Jesus?" Muslims typically respond by saying that the words Muhammad uttered in this regard were not his own, but rather were put into his mouth by Allah, the "All-Knowing, All-Seeing God."[20] Because Allah does not make mistakes, neither does the prophet through whom he speaks.

It is interesting to observe that some Muslim apologists have made bold assertions to the effect that Jesus *never* said anything like "I was dead and now I'm alive." One such apologist declared, "Throughout the length and breadth of the 27 books of the New Testament, there is not a single statement made by Jesus Christ that 'I was dead, and I have come back from the dead.'"[21]

## Jesus Did Not Atone for Man's Sins

Muslims not only argue that Jesus did not die on the cross, they also argue He was not an atoning sacrifice for the sins of humanity. The Quran states, "No bearer of burdens can bear the burden of another" (Sura 39:7). This means Jesus cannot take upon Himself the sins of humanity and atone for them. Muslims ask, "How could the punishment of one man be made applicable to all men?"[22]

## Jesus Did Not Rise from the Dead

In Luke 24:39 Jesus told His disciples, "Look at my hands and my feet. It is I myself! Touch me and see; a ghost does not have flesh and bones, as you see I have." Muslim apologists believe this verse proves Jesus did not die and therefore was not resurrected from the dead. A Muslim paraphrase of the verse might be this: "What is wrong with you disciples? Can't you see I am the same person who walked and talked with you, broke bread with you, flesh and blood in all respects?"[23] Jesus was simply telling the disciples that they should touch Him and handle Him so they could see He had not died and been resurrected in a spiritualized body. He was still physically alive and in their midst.

In keeping with this, Muslims argue that there was no ascension of a resurrected Jesus. Muslim apologist Ahmed Deedat asserts that the authors of the four canonical Gospels did not record a single word about the ascension of Jesus.[24] The doctrine is therefore pure myth.

## The Second Coming of Jesus

Muslims believe that one day Jesus will come back to earth, slay all who do not accept Islam as the one true religion, reign for 40 years, and then die and be buried next to Muhammad in Medina. Following this He will be resurrected with all other men and women on the last day. Contrary to the teachings of the New Testament, there is nothing unique about the resurrection of Jesus from the dead, for Jesus will simply be resurrected like all other people.

# 9

# *The Biblical View of Jesus, Part One*

Muslims say it would be blasphemous to say that Jesus is the Son of God, for it suggests that God engaged in a sexual union with a female. If Muslims were right in saying that the term "Son of God" demanded that God have sexual relations with a female, this doctrine would cause Christians to shrink back in horror every bit as much as Muslims do. But the Bible contains no such idea. The Bible indicates that Jesus is *eternally* the Son of God.

## What Does "Son of God" Mean?

Among the ancients, the term "son of…" often carried the important metaphorical meaning "of the order of." The phrase is often used this way in the Old Testament. For example, "sons of the prophets" meant "of the order of prophets" (1 Kings 20:35). "Sons of the singers" meant "of the order of singers" (Nehemiah 12:28 NASB). Likewise, the phrase "Son of God" means "of the order of God," and represents a claim to undiminished deity. There is no sexual connotation in the phrase.

Ancient Semitics and Orientals used the phrase "Son of…" to indicate likeness or sameness of nature and equality of being.

Hence, when Jesus claimed to be the Son of God, His Jewish contemporaries fully understood He was making a claim to be God in an unqualified sense. Indeed, the Jews insisted, "We have a law, and according to that law he [Christ] must die, because he claimed to be the Son of God" (John 19:7; see also 5:18). Recognizing that Jesus was identifying Himself as God, the Jews wanted to kill Him for committing blasphemy.

It is one thing to say Jesus *became* the Son of God; it is another thing altogether to say He *always was* (eternally) the Son of God. Clear evidence for Christ's eternal Sonship is found in the fact that Christ is represented as *already being* the Son of God before His birth in Bethlehem. For instance, recall Jesus' discussion with Nicodemus in John 3. Jesus said, "God so loved the world that he gave his one and only Son, that whoever believes in him shall not perish but have eternal life. For God did not send his Son *into* the world to condemn the world, but to save the world through him" (John 3:16-17, emphasis added). That Christ—as the Son of God—was sent *into* the world implies that He was the Son of God before the incarnation.

Further evidence for Christ's eternal Sonship is found in the fact that Hebrews 1:2 says God created the universe through His "Son"—implying that Christ was the Son of God *before* the creation. Moreover, Christ as the Son is explicitly said to have existed "before all things" (Colossians 1:17; see especially verses 13-14). As well, Jesus, speaking as the Son of God (John 8:54-56), asserts His eternal preexistence before Abraham (verse 58).

Hence, the Muslim view constitutes a gross misunderstanding. You should go to great lengths to help your Muslim acquaintance understand what the Bible means by this title. World religions scholar Dean Halverson suggests pointing the Muslim to how different Arabic words for "son of" can help explain the correct meaning of "Son of God":

> In the Arabic language there are two words for expressing "Son of": *walad* and *ibn*. *Walad* definitely denotes becoming a son through the union

of a male with a female. We as Christians would agree that Jesus was not a *waladdu'llah*—"Son of God"—in that sense....Unlike *walad,* however, the word *ibn* can be used in a metaphorical sense. For example, Arabs themselves talk about a traveler as being an *ibnu'ssabil*—"Son of the road." They obviously do not mean by such a phrase that one has had sexual relations with the road. It is in this wider metaphorical sense that Jesus is understood as being the Son of God.[1]

In the above example, the traveler is thought of as taking on the nature of the road, so he becomes its son, so to speak. This is a metaphor, a figure of speech. In the same way, the term "Son of God" is not intended to indicate a sexual act on the part of the Father, but is simply a metaphorical way of describing the eternal relationship between the Father and Jesus.

## ___ *Ask...* ___

- When Arabs talk about a traveler as being a "son of the road," what do they mean by this term? Isn't "son of the road" a figurative expression?

- Did you know the term "Son of God" is likewise a figurative expression?

- Can I explain to you what the Bible means by this expression?

Your Muslim friend may reply that Christ is said to be "begotten" (Greek, *monogenes,* pronounced mah-noh-ge-NAYS) in the New Testament (John 1:14,18 KJV). Actually, the Greek word *monogenes* does not mean that Christ was procreated, but rather means "unique" or "one of a kind."[2] Jesus is the "Son of God" in the sense that He uniquely has the same nature as the

Father—a divine nature. As noted earlier, whenever Christ claimed to be the Son of God in the New Testament, His Jewish critics tried to stone Him because they correctly understood Him as claiming to be God (see John 5:18). Help your Muslim acquaintance understand the correct meaning of *monogenes*.

## Why Is Jesus Called the "Son of Man"?

If Jesus was the Son of God, Muslims ask, why did He say He was the Son of Man (Matthew 20:18; 24:30)? There is no contradiction here, for Jesus was both the Son of God *and* the Son of Man. Help your Muslim friend understand that even if the phrase "Son of Man" were solely a reference to Jesus' humanity, it does not constitute a denial of His deity. In becoming a human being, Jesus did not thereby cease to be God. The incarnation of Christ did not involve the *subtraction* of deity, but the *addition* of humanity. Jesus clearly asserted His deity on many occasions (Matthew 16:16-17; John 8:58; 10:30). But besides being divine, He had a human nature as a result of the incarnation (see Philippians 2:6-8). He thus had two natures (divine *and* human) conjoined in one person.

Further, Scripture itself indicates Jesus was not denying He was God when He referred to Himself as the Son of Man. It is highly revealing that the term "Son of Man" is used of Christ in contexts where His deity is quite evident. For example, the Bible indicates that only God has the prerogative of forgiving sins (Isaiah 43:25), but Jesus as the "Son of Man" exercised this prerogative (Mark 2:7-10). Likewise, at the second coming, Christ will return to earth as the "Son of Man" in clouds of glory to reign on earth (Matthew 26:63-64). In this passage, Jesus is alluding to Daniel 7:13, where the Messiah is described as the "Ancient of Days," a phrase used to indicate His deity (see Daniel 7:9). So, Jesus as the Son of Man is the divine Messiah.

## _____ *Ask...* _____

- Did you know the term "Son of Man" is used in reference to Jesus' deity in the New Testament? Can I show you where?

---

### Jesus Was Absolute Deity

Muslims say the Bible has been corrupted. For this reason, a large part of your apologetic will have to focus on defending the Bible as the reliable Word of God. Once you have done this (see chapters 12 and 13), you can proceed to show the Muslim what the Bible truly says about Jesus' deity. There is more on this issue than I can share in one chapter, but I will provide some highlights in what follows.

### Jesus Is Creator and Savior

A comparison of the Old and New Testaments provides powerful testimony to Jesus' identity as Yahweh (God Almighty). For example, a study of the Old Testament indicates that it is *only* God who saves. In Isaiah 43:11, God asserts, "I, even I, am the LORD [Yahweh], and *apart from me there is no savior*" (emphasis added). This is an extremely important verse, for it indicates that 1) a claim to be Savior is, in itself, a claim to deity; and 2) there is only one Savior—God. Against this backdrop, it is truly revealing of Christ's divine nature that the New Testament refers to Jesus as the Savior. Following the birth of Christ, an angel appeared to some neighboring shepherds and said, "Today in the town of David a Savior has been born to you; he is Christ the Lord" (Luke 2:11).

Likewise, God says in Isaiah 44:24: "I, the LORD [Yahweh], am the maker of all things, stretching out the heavens *by Myself,* and spreading out the earth *all alone*" (NASB, emphasis added). The fact that Yahweh is the "maker of all things" who stretched out the heavens "by Myself" and spread out the earth "all alone"—and the accompanying fact that Christ is the Creator of "all things" (John 1:3; Colossians 1:16; Hebrews 1:2)—proves that Christ is God Almighty.

## _____ Ask... _____

- Since, in Isaiah 44:24, God is said to have created all things, how do you think this relates to the New Testament teaching that Jesus created all things (John 1:3)?

- Since God is said to be the only Savior in Isaiah 43:11, how do you think this relates to the New Testament teaching that Jesus is the Savior (Luke 2:11)?

### The Old Testament Scriptures Were Applied to Jesus

It is highly revealing that Old Testament passages about Yahweh were directly applied to Jesus in the New Testament. For instance, Isaiah 40:3 says, "In the desert prepare the way for the LORD [Yahweh]; make straight in the wilderness a highway for our God [Elohim]." Mark's Gospel tells us that Isaiah's words were fulfilled in the ministry of John the Baptist, who prepared the way for Jesus (Mark 1:2-4).

Still another illustration is Isaiah 6:1-5, where the prophet recounts his vision of Yahweh "seated on a throne high and exalted" (verse 1). He said, "Holy, holy, holy is the LORD [Yahweh] Almighty; the whole earth is full of his glory" (verse 3). Isaiah also quotes Yahweh as saying: "I am the LORD; that is my name! I will not give my glory to another" (42:8). Later, the apostle John—under the inspiration of the Holy Spirit—wrote that Isaiah "saw Jesus' glory" (John 12:41). Yahweh's glory and Jesus' glory are equated.

## ____ Ask... _____

- In view of how numerous Old Testament passages about God Almighty are directly applied to Jesus in the New Testament, what does this tell you about Jesus' identity?

---

Christ's deity is confirmed for us in that many of the actions of Yahweh in the Old Testament are performed by Christ in the New Testament. For example, in Psalm 119 we are told about a dozen times that it is Yahweh who gives and preserves life. But in the New Testament, Jesus claims this power for Himself: "Just as the Father raises the dead and gives them life, even so the Son gives life to whom he is pleased to give it" (John 5:21).

In the Old Testament the voice of Yahweh was said to be "like the roar of rushing waters" (Ezekiel 43:2). Likewise, we read of the glorified Jesus in heaven: "His feet were like bronze glowing in a furnace, and his voice was like the sound of rushing waters" (Revelation 1:15). What is true of Yahweh is just as true of Jesus.

### Divine Names Are Ascribed to Jesus

Certainly a clear indicator of Jesus' deity is the fact that divine names are consistently ascribed to Him in the Bible. We have seen that Jesus is equated with the Yahweh of the Old Testament. But the New Testament equivalent of "Yahweh" is *Kurios*. Like "Yahweh," *Kurios* means "Lord" and usually carries the idea of a sovereign being who exercises absolute authority. (The word *can* be used of a human being, as in Colossians 3:22, where it means "master." But on the occasions where the word is used in the New Testament of Christ, it is clearly intended to be taken in an absolute sense—as a parallel to the name "Yahweh" in the Old Testament.)

*The Interpreter's Dictionary of the Bible* tells us that "to an early Christian accustomed to reading the Old Testament, the word 'Lord,' when used of Jesus, would suggest His identification with the God of the Old Testament."[3] Theologian William G.T. Shedd likewise suggests that "any Jew who publicly confessed that Jesus of Nazareth was 'Lord,' would be understood to ascribe the divine nature and attributes to Him."[4] Hence, the statement that "Jesus is Lord" *(Kurios)* constitutes a clear affirmation that Jesus is *Yahweh* (see Romans 10:9; 1 Corinthians 12:3; Philippians 2:11).

The apostle Paul points us to the close relationship between "Yahweh" and *Kurios* in Philippians 2. He tells us that Christ was given a name above every name, "that at the name of Jesus every knee should bow, in heaven and on earth and under the earth, and every tongue confess that Jesus Christ is Lord *[Kurios]*" (verses 9-11). Paul, an Old Testament scholar par excellence, is alluding to Isaiah 45:22-24: "I am God, and there is no other. By myself I have sworn, my mouth has uttered in all integrity a word that will not be revoked: Before me every knee will bow; by me every tongue will swear." Paul was drawing on his vast knowledge of the Old Testament to make the point that Jesus Christ is Yahweh, the Lord *(Kurios)* of all mankind. Jesus is absolute deity just as the Father is absolute deity (see Chapter 7, which contains a discussion of the Trinity).

## Jesus Displayed Divine Love

Some Muslims who have converted to Christ say that one thing that proved to them that Christ was God was the divine love He showed to others (Luke 23:34). I think this is a powerful point that can be used in witnessing to Muslims. Da'ud Rahbar, a Muslim who converted to Christianity, wrote,

> When I read the New Testament and discovered how Jesus loved and forgave His killers from the cross, I could not fail to recognize that the love He had for men is the only kind of love worthy of the Eternal God....If the innocent Jesus, who forgave and loved His crucifiers from the cross,

was not the Creator-God Himself, then the Creator-God is proven to be inferior to Jesus. And this cannot be. The Creator-God and Jesus are one and the same being. May all men know that truly divine love.[5]

## ___ *Ask...* ___

- Have you considered the wonderful love of Jesus?

- Have you considered the possibility that if the innocent Jesus, who forgave and loved His crucifiers from the cross, was not the Creator-God Himself, then the Creator-God is proven to be inferior to Jesus?

  *(If the Muslim argues that Jesus was not crucified, see the information later in this chapter regarding how to answer this claim.)*

---

### Jesus Accepted Worship

What about the Muslim claim that Jesus never instructed His followers to worship Him? The reality is that Jesus was worshiped on many occasions in the New Testament, and He *always accepted such worship as perfectly appropriate.* Jesus accepted worship from Thomas (John 20:28), the angels (Hebrews 1:6), some wise men (Matthew 2:11), a leper (Matthew 8:2), a ruler (Matthew 9:18), a blind man (John 9:38), an anonymous woman (Matthew 15:25), Mary Magdalene (Matthew 28:9), and the disciples (Matthew 28:17). In the book of Revelation, Jesus receives the same worship given to the Father (see Revelation 4:10; 5:11-14).

## _____ *Ask...* _____

• What does it say about Jesus' true identity that in the book
of Revelation, God the Father and Jesus are clearly seen as
receiving the same worship?

___

The fact that Jesus *willingly received* (and *condoned*) worship
on various occasions says a lot about His true identity, for it is the
consistent testimony of Scripture that only God may be worshiped. Exodus 34:14 tells us, "Do not worship any other god,
for the LORD, whose name is Jealous, is a jealous God" (compare
with Deuteronomy 6:13; Matthew 4:10). In view of this, the fact
that Jesus was worshiped on numerous occasions shows that He
is in fact God.

### Jesus the Divine Word of God

In John 1:1 Jesus is called "the Word." The Greek noun for
"Word" in this verse is *Logos*. Its importance lies in the fact that
Christ the *Logos* is portrayed as a preexistent, eternal Being.
Indeed, John even says the *Logos* is God. The *Logos* is also said
to be the Creator of the universe, for "through him all things
were made; without him nothing was made that has been made"
(John 1:3).

The Jewish Targums (simplified paraphrases of the Old Testament Scriptures) reveal that the ancient Jews, out of reverence
for God, sometimes substituted the phrase "the Word of God" in
place of the word "Yahweh." The Jews were fearful of breaking
the third commandment: "You shall not misuse the name of the
LORD your God, for the LORD will not hold anyone guiltless who
misuses his name" (Exodus 20:7). New Testament scholar Leon
Morris explains:

> These Targums were produced at a time when,
> from motives of reverence and from a fear of

breaking the third commandment, Jews had ceased to pronounce the divine name. When they came to this name in the original the readers and translators substituted some other expression they thought more reverent, such as "the Holy One" or "the Name." Sometimes they said "the Word (Memra)." For example, where our Bible says, "And Moses brought forth the people out of the camp to meet God" (Exod. 19:17), the Targum reads, "to meet the Word of God."[6]

When we come to John's Gospel, we find out that the "Word" is a divine person (Jesus) who has come into the world to reveal *another* person (the Father) to the world. *This* "Word" was the source of all life (John 1:3). *This* "Word" was nothing less than God Himself: "The Word was with God, and the Word was God" (John 1:1).

I must stress the significance of John's making such an assertion in view of his monotheistic background. The belief in monotheism was not an optional doctrine for the Jews. It was a conviction to be clung to and defended with fierce tenacity. John's background was one that recognized with an unshakable certainty the existence of only one true God. It is against this backdrop that John unflinchingly asserted that Christ the *Logos* (Word) is God.

When John said, "In the beginning was the Word" (John 1:1), the verb "was" in this verse is an imperfect tense in the Greek, indicating continued existence. When the time–space universe came into being, Christ the divine Word was already existing in a loving, intimate relationship with the Father and the Holy Spirit. The imperfect tense "reaches back indefinitely beyond the instant of the beginning."[7] The verb "was" is most naturally understood as indicating the eternal existence of the Word: "The Word continually was."[8] Thus, the *Logos* did not come into being at a specific point in eternity past, but at that point at which all else began to be, He already was.

## Jesus Possessed the Same Glory as the Father

Because Christ is the eternal *Logos,* all that can be said of God can be said of Jesus Christ. Indeed, in John 1:1 "John is not merely saying that there is something divine about Jesus. He is affirming that He is God, and doing so emphatically."[9]

Later in John 1, we are told that "the Word became flesh and made his dwelling among us" (John 1:14). In this verse John was drawing from his knowledge of the Old Testament. The phrase, "made his dwelling among us," literally means "to pitch one's tent."[10] Bible scholar F.F. Bruce elaborates on the significance of this phrase:

> The statement that the incarnate Word "pitched his tabernacle (Greek: *eskenosen*) among us" harks back to the tabernacle (Greek: *skene*) of Israel's wilderness wanderings. The tabernacle was erected by God's command in order that his dwelling-place might be established with his people: "let them make me a sanctuary," he said, "that I may dwell in their midst" (Ex. 25:8). So, it is implied, as God formerly manifested his presence among his people in the tent which Moses pitched, now in a fuller sense he has taken up residence on earth in the Word made flesh.[11]

John's use of the Greek word *eskenosen* ("pitched his tabernacle") becomes even more significant when we realize that the glory that resulted from the immediate presence of the Lord in the tabernacle came to be associated with the *shekinah,* a word that refers to "the radiance, glory, or presence of God dwelling in the midst of his people."[12] When the *Logos* became flesh (John 1:14), the glorious presence of God was fully embodied in Him, for He is the true Shekinah.[13] Bible expositor J. Dwight Pentecost thus writes, "The same glory that Moses beheld in the tabernacle in Exodus 40:34-38 and that the priest saw in the temple in 1 Kings

8:10-11 was revealed in the person of Jesus Christ on the Mount of Transfiguration. Peter testified to this in 2 Peter 1:16-18."[14]

The true temple of God was therefore not the edifice in Jerusalem, but the very body of Jesus. It was in Him that the glory of God shone. As Benjamin Warfield put it, "the flesh of our Lord became…the Temple of God on earth (cf. Jn. 2:19), and the glory of the Lord filled the house of the Lord."[15] For this reason, John testified, "We have seen his glory" (John 1:14)—no doubt a reference to the transfiguration, in which Jesus, toward the end of His three-year ministry, pulled back the veil from His glory so that "His face shone like the sun, and his clothes became as white as the light" (Matthew 17:2).

In view of such astounding factors, the Muslim concept of "the Word of God" referring to Jesus being created in Mary's womb by a divine command is found to be woefully off the mark. Biblically, Jesus "the Word" is *absolute deity.*

## ____ *Ask…* ____

- What meaning do you attach to Jesus being "the Word of God"?

- Can I share with you what the Bible means when it says Jesus is the "Word of God"?

---

### Examining Bible Verses That Muslims Cite to Disprove Jesus' Deity

#### JOHN 10:30—*Jesus and the Father Are "One"*

Muslims argue that in John 10:30 Jesus was saying He was "one" with the Father in purpose only, not in His deity. Such a view is not faithful to the biblical data. While the Greek word for "one" *(hen)* by itself does not have to refer to more than unity of purpose, the context of John 10 makes it clear that much more than this is meant. We know this by observing the Jews' response to Jesus' affirmation that "I and the Father are one." They immediately picked up stones to put Him to death. They understood that Jesus was claiming to be God in an unqualified sense. Indeed, according to verse 33, the Jews said, "For a good work we do not stone You, but for blasphemy; and because *You, being a man, make Yourself out to be God*" (NASB, emphasis added). The penalty for blasphemy, according to Old Testament law, is death by stoning.

Notice that Jesus did not respond by saying, "Oh, no, you've got it all wrong. I was not claiming to be God. I'm just claiming unity of purpose with Him." Jesus did not offer a correction because the Jews understood Him *exactly as He had intended* to be understood. Jesus was affirming His deity. The Jews would never have stoned Jesus for claiming to have unity of purpose with God, for even the Jews themselves claimed to have this.

## _____ *Ask...* _____

- Why would the Jews—who themselves believed they had unity of purpose with the Father—try to kill Jesus for affirming unity of purpose with the Father?

- If Jesus was merely affirming His unity of purpose with the Father, why did the Jews understand His words to be an affirmation that He was God (John 10:33)?

### JOHN 14:28—*The Father Is "Greater" than Jesus*

Muslims argue that because Jesus said the Father is "greater" than Him, He was denying He was God. However, Jesus is not speaking in this verse about His nature or His essential being (He had earlier said "I and the Father are one" in this regard—John 10:30), but is rather speaking of His lowly position in the incarnation. The Athanasian Creed affirms that Christ is "equal to the

Father as touching his Godhood and inferior to the Father as touching his manhood." The Father was seated upon the throne of highest majesty in heaven; the brightness of His glory was uneclipsed as He was surrounded by hosts of holy beings perpetually worshiping Him with uninterrupted praise. Far different it was with His incarnate Son—despised and rejected by men, surrounded by implacable enemies, and soon to be nailed to a criminal's cross. It was from this lowly perspective that Jesus could say that the Father was "greater" than Him.

## ___ *Ask...* _____

- Is the President of the United States intrinsically greater than us by nature, or is it more correct to say his *position* is greater than ours?

- Did you know that in John 14:28 Jesus is speaking of the Father's higher *position* and not higher *nature?*

_____

### MARK 10:18—*Does Jesus Lack "Goodness"?*

In Mark 10:17, a young ruler called Jesus "good teacher." Muslims argue that because Jesus responded that no one is good except God alone, Jesus was admitting He was not God. However, in this passage Jesus was not claiming He was not "good." Nor was He denying He was God to the young ruler. Rather, Jesus was asking the man to examine the implications of what he was saying. In effect, Jesus said, "Do you realize what you are saying when you call Me good? Are you saying I am God?" Jesus' response was not a denial of His deity but was rather a veiled claim to it.

## ___ *Ask...* _____

- Where in the text does Jesus explicitly say that He is not good?

- Is it not clear from the context that what Jesus was really saying is, "You have given me a title that belongs only to God. Do you understand and mean it?"

---

### JOHN 20:28—*Jesus as Lord and God*

In John 20:28, doubting Thomas witnessed the resurrected Jesus and said to Him, "My Lord and my God!" Muslims argue that Thomas was merely uttering an exclamation—"My God!"

However, if Thomas had said "My God!" as an exclamation of surprise, Jesus would have rebuked him for taking God's name in vain. Not only did Jesus not rebuke Thomas, He *commended* him for recognizing Jesus' true identity as "Lord" and "God" (John 20:29). Moreover, Thomas's acknowledgment of Jesus as God is consistent with what we are told elsewhere in John's Gospel about Jesus (see John 1:1; 8:58; 10:30).

## ___ *Ask...* ___

- If Thomas was just uttering an exclamation—"My God!" —wouldn't his words be equivalent to taking God's name in vain?

- If Thomas had taken God's name in vain in the presence of Jesus, don't you think Jesus would have rebuked him?

- Why do you think Jesus commended Thomas instead of rebuking him?

---

### MARK 13:32—*Is Jesus Omniscient?*

Jesus said of His second coming in Mark 13:32, "No one knows about that day or hour, not even the angels in heaven, nor the Son, but only the Father." Muslims thus argue that Jesus is not God, for He does not have the attribute of omniscience.

The Muslim view is incorrect. However, the proper understanding of this verse requires a little theological background. Though it is a bit complex to explain, the eternal Son of God was, prior to the incarnation, one in person and in nature (wholly divine). In the incarnation, He became *two in nature* (divine and human) while remaining *one person*. Thus Christ at the same moment in time had what seem to be contradictory qualities. He was finite and yet infinite, weak and yet omnipotent, increasing in knowledge and yet omniscient, limited to being in one place at one time and yet omnipresent. It was only from His humanity that Christ could say He did not know the day or hour of His return. In His humanity, Jesus was not omniscient but was limited in understanding just as all human beings are. If Jesus had been speaking from the perspective of His divinity, He would not have said the same thing.

Scripture is abundantly clear that in His divine nature, Jesus *is* omniscient—just as omniscient as the Father is. The apostle John said that Jesus "did not need man's testimony about man, for he knew what was in a man" (John 2:25). Jesus' disciples said to Him, "Now we can see that you know all things" (16:30). After the resurrection, when Jesus asked Peter for the third time whether Peter loved Him, Peter responded, "Lord, you know all things; you know that I love you" (21:17). Jesus knew just where the fish were in the water (Luke 5:4,6; John 21:6-11), and He knew just which fish contained the coin (Matthew 17:27). He knows the Father as the Father knows Him (Matthew 11:27; John 7:29; 8:55; 10:15; 17:25). Though Christ is omniscient, part of His "self-emptying" in the incarnation (Philippians 2:5-11) involved His voluntarily choosing not to use some of His divine attributes on some occasions, so that He could properly fulfill His mediatorial mission as assigned by the Father. Mark 13:32 is an example of this.

## _____ *Ask...* _____

- Can anyone other than God have the attribute of omniscience?

- Can I share some verses with you that show Jesus is omniscient?

---

### MARK 14:50—*No Eyewitnesses to the Crucifixion?*

Muslims argue that, since Jesus' disciples deserted Him and fled upon His arrest (Mark 14:50), there were no eyewitnesses to the events that followed, including the crucifixion (and hence there is no evidence the crucifixion ever occurred). Though it is true that all the disciples *initially* fled because they were fearful, the verses that immediately follow Mark 14:50 indicate that Peter returned and followed at a distance. He even sat with the guards and warmed himself at the fire (Mark 14:51-54). The parallel account in John 18:15-16 tells us that another disciple accompanied Peter. Further, at the crucifixion of Jesus, we are told that Jesus' own mother and His beloved disciple John were both there at the foot of the cross (John 19:25-27). We are also told that other acquaintances of His stood and watched the crucifixion from a distance (Luke 23:49). The claim that there were no eyewitnesses to the crucifixion does not hold up to the facts.

## _____ *Ask...* _____

- Did you know that Jesus' mother and His beloved disciple John were eyewitnesses to Jesus' crucifixion (John 19:25-27)?

---

### MATTHEW 16:20—*Keeping Quiet About "the Christ"*

Muslims say that, because Jesus in Matthew 16:20 warned His disciples not to tell anyone He was the Christ, He was obviously reacting against any suggestion that He was deity. Contrary to the Muslim view, the reason for Jesus' warning was rooted in the popular misunderstandings that were floating around during that time about the Messiah (or "Christ"). There was a very high expectation to the effect that when the Messiah came, He would deliver the Jews from Roman domination. The people were expecting a political Messiah–deliverer.

So, for news that Jesus truly was the Messiah to circulate at this early point in His ministry would immediately excite people's preconceived ideas about what this Messiah-figure was supposed to do. The Romans might very well subsequently mark Him as a rebel leader. Seeking to avoid an erroneous popular response to His words and deeds, Jesus issued instructions to His disciples to not tell anyone He was the Christ. He did not want anyone prematurely speaking of His actual identity until He had had sufficient opportunity to make the character of His mission clear to the masses. As time passed, Christ's identity became increasingly clear to those who came into contact with Him.

# 10

## *The Biblical View of Jesus, Part Two*

As we have seen, Muslims believe that Jesus was one of the greatest prophets sent from Allah. They even believe that He was sinless and that He performed supernatural acts by Allah's power. However, they disagree with what the Bible says about the meaning of those miracles.

### Jesus' Miracles *Do* Prove His True Identity

Though Muslims say that Jesus' miracles do not prove His divine identity, the Bible says that His miracles *do* signify His identity. Scripture often refers to the miracles of Jesus as "signs." This word emphasizes the *significance* of the action rather than the marvel of it (see John 4:54; 6:14; 9:16). These signs were strategically performed by Jesus to signify His true identity and glory as the divine Messiah.

This is illustrated in the account of John the Baptist being put in jail. After being locked up, John sent his disciples to ask Jesus, "Are you the one who was to come, or should we expect someone else?" (Matthew 11:3). As I noted in the previous chapter, it was the common viewpoint among the Jews of that time that when the Messiah came, He would set up His glorious kingdom. There were very high messianic expectations in the first century, and even John himself probably expected the soon emergence of the kingdom that he had been preaching about.

But now something unexpected happened—*John was imprisoned*. Instead of experiencing the kingdom, which (it was commonly thought) would be characterized by such things as liberty and freedom, John now found himself locked up in jail and in danger of execution. So—what was he to make of this development? John may have expected that Jesus would use coercive powers as the Messiah–deliverer of Israel. He thus decided to send messengers to ask Jesus, "Are you the one who was to come, or should we expect someone else?" (Luke 7:20).

Jesus' response is extremely significant. Instead of merely giving John verbal assurance that He was the divine Messiah, He pointed to His miraculous acts, including giving sight to the blind, enabling the lame to walk, and opening deaf ears (Luke 7:22). Why did Jesus do this? Because these were the precise miracles prophesied to be performed by the divine Messiah when He came (see Isaiah 29:18-21; 35:5-6; 61:1-2). The miraculous deeds alone ("signs") were more than enough proof that Jesus was the promised Messiah. These specific prophesied miracles were Jesus' divine credentials—His divine "ID card," so to speak.

John's Gospel tells us that Jesus' signs were performed in the presence of His disciples to ensure there was adequate witness to the events that transpired (John 20:30). "Witness" is a pivotal concept in this Gospel. The noun "witness" is used 14 times and the verb "testify" 33 times, and the reason for this is clear. *The signs performed by Jesus are thoroughly attested.* There were many witnesses. Therefore, the signs cannot simply be dismissed or explained away!

Thirty-five separate miracles performed by Christ are recorded in the Gospels. Of these, Matthew mentions 20; Mark, 18; Luke, 20; and John, seven. But these are only a selection from among many that He did (Matthew 4:23-24; 11:4-5; 21:14). The miracles or signs that are recorded in Scripture are presented "that you may believe that Jesus is the Christ, the Son of God" (John 20:31).

John's Gospel goes on to tell us that "Jesus did many other things as well. If every one of them were written down, I suppose that even the whole world would not have room for the books that would be written" (John 21:25). Among the many miracles attributed to Jesus in the New Testament are changing water into wine (John 2:7-9); healing Peter's mother-in-law (Matthew 8:15; Mark 1:31; Luke 4:39); causing the disciples to catch a great number of fish (Luke 5:5-6); healing a leper (Matthew 8:3; Mark 1:41); healing a paralytic (Matthew 9:2; Mark 2:5; Luke 5:20); calming a stormy sea (Matthew 8:26; Mark 4:39; Luke 8:24); healing an invalid (John 5:8); feeding 5000 men and their families (Matthew 14:19; Mark 6:41; Luke 9:16; John 6:11); walking on the sea (Matthew 14:25; Mark 6:48; John 6:19); feeding 4000 men and their families (Matthew 15:36; Mark 8:6); healing a blind man (Mark 8:25); healing another man born blind (John 9:7); healing a demoniac boy (Matthew 17:18; Mark 9:25; Luke 9:42); causing Peter to catch a fish with a coin in its mouth (Matthew 17:27); healing ten lepers (Luke 17:11-19); and raising Lazarus from the dead (John 11:43-44). No wonder Peter would later preach to the Jews that Jesus was "a man attested to you by God with miracles and wonders and signs which God performed through him in your midst" (Acts 2:22 NASB).

## Distinguishing Between Divine Miracles and Satanic Miracles

I noted in chapter 8 that some Muslim apologists assert that, because false Christs and false prophets can do miracles that are inspired by the devil, then Christ's miracles have no value in proving His alleged identity as God. Is such a claim valid? Is there no way to distinguish between a miracle from God and one inspired by the devil?

Although Satan has great spiritual powers, there is a gigantic difference between the power of the devil and the power of God. God is infinite in power (omnipotent); the devil (like demons) is finite and limited. Moreover, only God can create life (Genesis 1:1,21; Deuteronomy 32:39); the devil cannot (see Exodus 8:19). Only God can truly raise the dead (John 10:18; Revelation 1:18); the devil cannot, though he will one day give "breath" (animation) to the idolatrous image of the Antichrist (Revelation 13:15).

The devil has great power to deceive people (Revelation 12:9), to oppress those who yield to him, and even to possess them (Acts 16:16). He is a master magician and a super scientist. And with His vast knowledge of God, man, and the universe, he is able to perform *"counterfeit* miracles, signs and wonders" (2 Thessalonians 2:9, emphasis added; see also Revelation 13:13-14). Simon the sorcerer in the city of Samaria amazed people with his Satan-inspired magic (Acts 8:9-11), but the miracles accomplished through Philip were much, much greater (Acts 8:13). The devil's *counterfeit* miracles do not compete with God's *true* miracles.

Perhaps the best illustration of Satan's counterfeit wonders is found in the Exodus account. In Exodus 7:10, for example, we read that Moses' rod was turned into a snake by the power of God. Then, according to verse 11, Pharaoh "summoned wise men and sorcerers, and the Egyptian magicians also did the same things by their secret arts." The purpose of these acts, of course, was to convince Pharaoh that his magicians possessed as much power as Moses and Aaron, and that it was not necessary for Pharaoh to yield to their request to let Israel go. It worked, at least for the first three encounters (Aaron's rod, the plague of blood, and the plague of frogs). However, when Moses and Aaron, by the power of God, brought forth living lice from the sand, the magicians were not able to counterfeit this miracle. They could only exclaim, "This is the finger of God" (Exodus 8:19).

The Scriptural evidence is undeniably clear that heavy-duty, "Grade-A" miracles can be performed *only* by God. Only God can fully control and supersede the natural laws He Himself created. As the account of Job illustrates, all the power the devil has is granted him by God and is *carefully limited and monitored* (see Job 1:10-12). In other words, Satan is "on a leash." Satan's *finite* power is under the control of God's *infinite* power.

It is interesting to observe that, when a serious question arose in biblical days as to which events were of God and which were of the devil, a contest would often ensue in which God's power triumphed over that of the devil. For instance, God was clearly the victor in the contest between Him and the magicians of Egypt (recall, for example, that Moses' snake swallowed that of the Egyptian sorcerers, Exodus 7:11-12). Likewise, Elijah was triumphant over Baal's prophets on Mount Carmel, when fire came down from heaven and consumed the sacrifices (1 Kings 18).[1]

## _____ *Ask...* _____

- Did you know that the Old Testament prophesied that when the divine Messiah came, He would perform specific miracles like opening deaf ears, giving sight to the blind, and enabling the lame to walk (Isaiah 29:18-21; 35:5-6; 61:1-2)?

- Since Jesus fulfilled these very specific prophecies, is it not clear that Jesus is the divine Messiah, not just a prophet? *(Emphasize the divine nature of the Messiah. Also emphasize that only Jesus did these miracles, not false Christs inspired by the devil.)*

- Why didn't Muhammad do the kinds of miracles Jesus did, if Muhammad was truly greater than Jesus?

---

## Jesus Was the Divine Messiah Prophesied in the Old Testament

From the book of Genesis to the book of Malachi, the Old Testament abounds with anticipations of the divine Messiah. Numerous predictions—fulfilled to the "crossing of the t" and the "dotting of the i" in the New Testament—relate to His birth, life, ministry, death, resurrection, and glory.

God's ability to foretell future events is one thing that separates Him from all the false gods. Addressing the polytheism of Isaiah's time, God said,

- "Who then is like me? Let him proclaim it. Let him declare and lay out before me what has happened since I established my ancient people, and what is yet to come—yes, let him foretell what will come" (Isaiah 44:7).

- "Who foretold this long ago, who declared it from the distant past? Was it not I, the LORD? And there is no God apart from me" (Isaiah 45:21).

- "I foretold the former things long ago, my mouth announced them and I made them known; then suddenly I acted, and they came to pass....Therefore I told you these things long ago; before they happened I announced them to you so that you could not say, 'My idols did them; my wooden image and metal god ordained them'" (Isaiah 48:3,5).

Of course, anyone can *make* predictions—that is easy. But having them *fulfilled* is another story altogether. The more statements one makes about the future and the greater the detail, the better the chances are that one will be proven wrong.[2] But *God was never wrong;* all the messianic prophecies in the Old Testament were fulfilled specifically and precisely in the person of Jesus.

## Prophecies Fulfilled by Jesus

Jesus often indicated to listeners that He was the specific fulfillment of messianic prophecy. For example, He made the following comments on different occasions:

- "Do not think that I have come to abolish the Law or the Prophets; I have not come to abolish them but to fulfill them" (Matthew 5:17).

- "This has all taken place that the writings of the prophets might be fulfilled" (Matthew 26:56).

- "Beginning with Moses and all the Prophets, he explained to them what was said in all the Scriptures concerning himself" (Luke 24:27).

- "This is what I told you while I was still with you: Everything must be fulfilled that is written about me in the Law of Moses, the Prophets and the Psalms" (Luke 24:44).

- "You diligently study the Scriptures because you think that by them you possess eternal life. These are the Scriptures that testify about me, yet you refuse to come to me to have life" (John 5:39-40).

- "If you believed Moses, you would believe me, for he wrote about me. But since you do not believe what he wrote, how are you going to believe what I say?" (John 5:46-47).

- "He rolled up the scroll, gave it back to the attendant and sat down. The eyes of everyone in the synagogue were fastened on him, and he began by saying to them, 'Today this scripture is fulfilled in your hearing'" (Luke 4:20-21).

An in-depth study of the messianic prophecies in the Old Testament is beyond the scope of this chapter. However, the chart on the next page lists just a few of the more important messianic prophecies that were directly fulfilled by Jesus Christ.

Any reasonable person who examines these Old Testament prophecies in an objective manner must conclude that Jesus was the promised divine Messiah. If these prophecies were written hundreds of years before they were fulfilled, and if they couldn't have been foreseen and depended upon factors outside human control for their fulfillment, and if all of these prophecies perfectly fit Jesus Christ, then Jesus had to be the Messiah.[3]

Christ on three different occasions directly claimed to be the "Christ" or divine Messiah. (Note that the word "Christ" is the Greek equivalent of the Hebrew word "Messiah.") For example,

# MESSIANIC PROPHECIES FULFILLED BY JESUS CHRIST

| Topic | Old Testament Prophecy | New Testament Fulfillment in Christ |
|---|---|---|
| From the line of Abraham | Genesis 12:2 | Matthew 1:1 |
| From the line of David | 2 Samuel 7:12-16 | Matthew 1:1 |
| Virgin Birth | Isaiah 7:14 | Matthew 1:23 |
| Birthplace: Bethlehem | Micah 5:2 | Matthew 2:6 |
| Forerunner: John | Isaiah 40:3; Malachi 3:1 | Matthew 3:3 |
| Escape into Egypt | Hosea 11:1 | Matthew 2:14 |
| King | Psalm 2:6 | Matthew 21:5 |
| Prophet | Deuteronomy 18:15-18 | Acts 3:22-23 |
| Priest | Psalm 110:4 | Hebrews 5:6-10 |
| Judge | Isaiah 33:22 | John 5:30 |
| Called "Lord" | Psalm 110:1 | Luke 2:11 |
| Called "Immanuel" | Isaiah 7:14 | Matthew 1:23 |
| Anointed by Holy Spirit | Isaiah 11:2 | Matthew 3:16-17 |
| Ministry of miracles | Isaiah 35:5-6 | Matthew 9:35 |
| Forsaken by God | Psalm 22:1 | Matthew 27:46 |
| Rejected by own people | Isaiah 53:3 | John 7:5,48 |
| Sold for 30 shekels | Zechariah 11:12 | Matthew 26:15 |
| Forsaken by disciples | Zechariah 13:7 | Mark 14:50 |
| Silent before accusers | Isaiah 53:7 | Matthew 27:12-19 |
| Hands and feet pierced | Psalm 22:16 | John 20:25 |
| Crucified with thieves | Isaiah 53:9,12 | Matthew 27:38 |
| No bones broken | Psalm 34:20 | John 19:33-36 |
| Scourging and death | Isaiah 53:5 | John 19:1,18 |
| Resurrection | Psalm 16:10; 22:22 | Matthew 28:6 |
| Ascension | Psalm 68:18 | Luke 24:50-53 |
| At the right hand of God | Psalm 110:1 | Hebrews 1:3 |

in John 4:25-26 Jesus encountered a Samaritan woman who said to Him, "I know that Messiah (called Christ) is coming." To which Jesus replied, "I who speak to you am he." Later, in His high priestly prayer to the Father, Jesus referred to Himself in the third person as "Jesus Christ, whom you have sent" (John 17:3). In Mark 14:61-62 we find the high priest asking Jesus, "Are you the Christ, the Son of the Blessed One?" To which Jesus declared unequivocally, "I am."

Others recognized that Jesus was the prophesied Messiah. In response to Jesus' inquiry concerning His disciples' under-standing of Him, Peter confessed, "You are the Christ" (Matthew 16:16). When Jesus said to Martha, "I am the resurrection and the life. He who believes in me will live, even though he dies; and whoever lives and believes in me will never die. Do you believe this?" Martha answered, "Yes, Lord....I believe that you are the Christ" (John 11:25-27).

## Jesus Was a Prophet—But *Much More* than a Prophet

It is true that one of Jesus' offices was that of prophet. In fact, Jesus called Himself a prophet in Matthew 13:53-57. As a prophet, Jesus communicated the Father's message to humankind (John 14:10). Further, Jesus, not Muhammad, was the *greatest* of all prophets, for He not only communicated the Father's message to humankind, He also revealed God bodily in His life and person (John 1:14-18; Colossians 2:9). Jesus was indeed a prophet, but He was much more than a prophet. He is also the supreme High Priest (Psalm 110:4; Hebrews 7:17-28) and a messianic King (Psalm 2:6-9; Psalm 110:1; Isaiah 9:6-7). God became incarnate in Jesus Christ, exercising the three offices of Prophet, Priest, and King, and being the mighty Redeemer of God's elect.

It is interesting to observe that, as a prophet, Jesus always pre-sented His teachings as being ultimate and final. He never wavered in this. Jesus unflinchingly placed His teachings above those of Moses and the prophets—and in the Jewish culture at that!

Jesus always spoke from His own authority. He never said, "Thus saith the Lord…" as did the prophets (or "Allah says," as did Muhammad); He always said, "Verily, verily, *I* say unto you…" He never retracted anything He said, never guessed or spoke with uncertainty, never made revisions, never contradicted Himself, never resorted to abrogations, and never apologized for what He said. He even asserted that "heaven and earth will pass away, but my words will never pass away" (Mark 13:31), thus elevating His words directly to the realm of heaven.

# ____ *Ask…* _____

• Whereas Muhammad always spoke in the authority of Allah, what do you think the significance is of Jesus' always speaking from *His own* authority?

Jesus' teachings had a profound effect on people. His listeners always seemed to sense that His words were not the words of an ordinary man. When Jesus taught in Capernaum on the Sabbath, the people "were amazed at his teaching, because his message had authority" (Luke 4:32). After the sermon on the mount, "the crowds were amazed at his teaching, because he taught as one who had authority, and not as their teachers of the law" (Matthew 7:28-29). When some Jewish leaders asked the temple guards why they hadn't arrested Jesus when He spoke, they responded, "No one ever spoke the way this man does" (John 7:46).

## Jesus' Words Had Divine Authority

One cannot read the Gospels for long before recognizing that Jesus regarded Himself and His message as inseparable. The reason Jesus' teachings had ultimate authority was because He was (is) God. The words of Jesus were the very words of God!

Indeed, what mere *human* teacher would dare speak words like this to his peers?

- "If anyone is thirsty, let him come to me and drink. Whoever believes in me, as the Scripture has said, streams of living water will flow from within him" (John 7:37-38).

- "Peace I leave with you; My peace I give to you; not as the world gives do I give to you" (John 14:27 NASB).

- "I am the bread of life; he who comes to Me will not hunger, and he who believes in Me will never thirst" (John 6:35 NASB).

- "Come to Me, all who are weary and heavy-laden, and I will give you rest" (Matthew 11:28 NASB).

- "I came that they may have life, and have it abundantly" (John 10:10 NASB).

To confirm the divine authority of His words, Jesus often performed a miracle immediately following a teaching. For example, after telling the paralytic that his sins were forgiven, Jesus healed him to prove He had the divine authority to forgive sins (Mark 2:1-12). After telling Martha that He was "the resurrection and the life," He raised her brother Lazarus from the dead—thereby proving the veracity and authority of His words. After rebuking the disciples in the boat for having too little faith, He stilled a raging storm to show they had good reason to place their faith in Him (Matthew 8:23-27). Muhammad never did any such miracle to confirm the authority of his teachings!

While I am on the topic of Jesus as a prophet, I want to mention that Jesus was not just a prophet to *Israel,* as Muslims claim, but His words were intended for the whole world. In His great commission to the disciples, Jesus said, "All authority in heaven and *on earth* has been given to me. Therefore go and make disciples of *all nations,* baptizing them in the name of the Father and of the Son and of the Holy Spirit, and teaching them to obey everything I have commanded you. And surely I am with you always, to the very end of the age" (Matthew 28:18-20, emphasis added).

## _____ *Ask...* _____

- Did you know Jesus' words were intended not just for Israel but for the whole world? Can I read you a Scripture verse on this? *(Matthew 28:18-20.)*

Further, contrary to the Muslim claim that each prophet's truth abrogates revelation from previous prophets, Jesus *denied* that He abrogated revelations from earlier prophets. Indeed, He said in Matthew 5:17-18, "Do not think that I have come to abolish the Law or the Prophets; I have not come to abolish them but to fulfill them. I tell you the truth, until heaven and earth disappear, not the smallest letter, not the least stroke of a pen, will by any means disappear from the Law until everything is accomplished."

## _____ *Ask...* _____

- Did you know Jesus claimed His words did not abrogate the revelation of previous prophets, as Muslims claim? Can I read to you from Scripture? *(Matthew 5:17-18.)*

Jesus also indicated that His own words would never, ever be abrogated. Jesus flatly asserted, "Heaven and earth will pass away, but *my words will never pass away*" (Matthew 24:35, emphasis added). This means that nothing Muhammad said could ever abrogate or do away with Jesus' words. Jesus' words are *final and authoritative* because He Himself is God.

## Jesus Truly *Did* Die on the Cross

When you hear a Muslim charge that Jesus did not die on the cross, one of the first things you will want to do is ask for historical proof to back up this claim. He will not be able to provide it. He will simply repeat what he has read or heard from the Quran. You can then take the opportunity to explain the substantial evidence in support of the fact that Jesus did die on the cross.

In scripturally proving your case for Jesus' death on the cross, the following points may prove helpful:[4]

- There are numerous predictions in the Old Testament that Jesus would die (Isaiah 53:5-10; Psalm 22:16; Daniel 9:26; Zechariah 12:10).

- There are many predictions in the Bible that Jesus would be resurrected (see Psalm 16:10; Isaiah 26:19; Daniel 12:2; John 2:19-21; Matthew 12:40; 17:22-23), but one cannot be resurrected *unless one has first died.*

- Jesus often spoke of the fact that He was going to die for the sins of humankind (John 2:19-21; 10:10-11; Matthew 12:40; Mark 8:31).

- Jesus' own mother and His beloved disciple John were eyewitnesses of His crucifixion (John 19:25-27).

- Jesus was beaten beyond recognition by Roman guards, given a crown of thorns, and then crucified. He bled from large wounds to His hands and feet, losing a phenomenal amount of blood. He was stabbed in the side with a spear; from the spear wound came "blood and water" (John 19:34). The accumulation of such wounds yields *100-percent nonsurvival.*

- At the last moment of life, Jesus gave up His spirit to the Father (Luke 23:46-49).

- Pilate checked to make sure Jesus was dead (Mark 15:44-45).

- Ancient non-Christian historians recorded Christ's death as a fact. This includes such notables as the Roman historian Cornelius Tacitus and the Jewish historian Flavius Josephus. And early Christian writers like Polycarp affirmed Christ's death.

## ____ *Ask...* ____

- Did you know there are numerous predictions in the Old Testament that Jesus would die (Isaiah 53:5-10; Psalm 22:16; Daniel 9:26; Zechariah 12:10)?

- Did you know there are many predictions in the Bible that Jesus would be resurrected from the dead (see Psalm 16:10; Isaiah 26:19; Daniel 12:2; John 2:19-21; Matthew 12:40; 17:22-23)? Before a person can be resurrected, he first must be dead, right?

- Are you aware of Jesus' own testimony about Himself and His death? Can I read you His own words in Matthew 20:28?

- Did you know that non-Christian historians such as the Roman historian Cornelius Tacitus and the Jewish historian Flavius Josephus documented Jesus' death?

- How could Jesus have survived what was inflicted upon Him? He bled from large wounds to his hands and feet and was stabbed in the side with a spear, from which came "blood and water" (John 19:34).

## God the Father *Allowed* Jesus to Die

Muslims believe Allah would never have allowed one of his own prophets to be dishonored and suffer a humiliating death on a cross. The crucifixion, we are told, is simply incompatible with Allah's absolute sovereignty.

Contrary to this view, the Bible is clear that God Himself *allowed* Jesus to die on the cross for the salvation of humankind (Romans 8:3-4; 1 Peter 1:18-20). It is also clear that God *often* allows His servants (whether prophets, apostles, or His own Son) to suffer. There is no incompatibility between God's sovereignty and His allowance of certain events that, from our limited perspective, seem unfair or bad. The story of Job is a great example (read chapters 1–3). Even Muhammad suffered to some extent. Indeed, some accounts indicate he died from poison given to him by one of his wives, a Jewess.[5]

Besides, who is to say that God did not rescue Jesus from His enemies? Norman Geisler and Abdul Saleeb make the keen observation that "even if Muslims assume that God will deliver his prophets from their enemies, it is wrong to conclude that he did not deliver Christ from his enemies. Indeed, this is precisely what the resurrection is."[6]

One thing your Muslim acquaintance may not have thought of relates to Jesus' submission. As noted earlier in the book, "Islam" means "submission." "Muslim" means "one who submits." Jesus, too, was one who submitted. Indeed, He submitted in obedience to God *all the way to the cross* (Hebrews 5:7ff.). Muslims should therefore honor Jesus for this great act of submission, for by it He attained the salvation of humankind.

While Jesus' dying on the cross will be a stumbling block to Muslims at first, eventually, through your patient witness, they may become attracted to Jesus as they come to understand the true significance of the cross. Once they finally grasp that Jesus' work on the cross makes it possible for them to have an eternal relationship with God, they may indeed turn to Christ as Savior, as many Muslims in the past have done.

## ____ *Ask...* _____

- Are you aware of the evidence that even Muhammad suffered during his life? Tradition says he may have even died from poison given to him by one of his wives.

- Have you considered that Jesus' suffering may be viewed as an evidence of His submission all the way to the cross (Hebrews 5:7ff.)? Is not such submission worthy of honor?

- Even if we assume that God will deliver His prophets from their enemies, isn't it wrong to conclude that God did not deliver Jesus from *His* enemies? Have you considered the possibility that that is precisely what the resurrection is?

### Explaining Christ's Death to a Muslim

Many evangelists to Muslims have noted that it is sometimes difficult to explain *why* Jesus had to die as a sacrifice. From Islam's vantage point, no man can bear the sins of another (Sura 39:7). Moreover, many Muslims may not even think they are sinners in need of salvation. Help them to understand we're *all* sinners.

## ____ *Ask...* _____

- Why is the world in such a sad state of affairs? How do you explain the fact that there are many wars with brutal killing; there are terrorists blowing up buildings and killing innocent people; the crime rate is escalating out of control? Have you considered the possibility that such factors constitute empirical proof of the reality of human sin?

  *(Explain that the reason Jesus was sacrificed on the cross was to deal with this problem of human sin.)*

In explaining Jesus' sacrifice, you might focus attention on Abraham's sacrifice in the Old Testament as described in Genesis 22. (Remember, Muslims have great respect for Abraham.) This event is even recorded in the Quran (Sura 37:102-7):

> Then, when (the son) reached (the age of) (serious) work with him, he said: "O my son! I see in vision that I offer thee in sacrifice: Now see what is thy view!" (The son) said: "O my father! Do as thou art commanded: thou will find me, if God so wills one practicing Patience and Constancy!" So when they had both submitted their wills (to God), and he had laid him prostrate on his forehead (for sacrifice), We called out to him "O Abraham! Thou hast already fulfilled the vision!" Thus indeed do We reward those who do right. For this was obviously a trial—And We ransomed him with a momentous sacrifice.

Notice the two key words—*ransom* and *sacrifice*. These are the same words that describe what Jesus did at the cross:

- "The Son of Man did not come to be served, but to serve, and to give his life as a ransom for many" (Matthew 20:28).

- "There is one God and one mediator between God and men, the man Christ Jesus, who gave himself as a ransom for all men" (1 Timothy 2:5-6).

- "He has died as a ransom to set them free from the sins committed under the first covenant" (Hebrews 9:15).

- "Christ, our Passover lamb, has been sacrificed" (1 Corinthians 5:7).

178 • The Biblical View of Jesus, Part Two

- "Unlike the other high priests, he does not need to offer sacrifices day after day, first for his own sins, and then for the sins of the people. He sacrificed for their sins once for all when he offered himself" (Hebrews 7:27).

- "Christ was sacrificed once to take away the sins of many people" (Hebrews 9:28).

In view of this, the sacrificial death of Christ is not necessarily un-Quranic. Use Abraham's story as a way of illustrating the need of a sacrifice to take another's place. Jesus as the Lamb of God took our place as a sacrifice so that we could be saved (John 1:29,36)! You might want to read through Isaiah 53 with your Muslim friend and emphasize how Jesus' sacrifice benefits us personally—including dealing with our sorrows, our sins, our crimes, our well-being, and our healing!

*Warning:* Most Muslims believe it was Ishmael, not Isaac, that was to be sacrificed by Abraham. For the time being, I would avoid even raising the issue, and focus most attention on the issues of sacrifice and ransom.[7] You can correct the minor error on Ishmael later.

## _Ask..._

- I notice the Quran includes the story of Abraham offering his son in sacrifice (Sura 37:102-7). According to this passage, wasn't Abraham's son "ransomed" from death by an animal "sacrifice"? Didn't the animal take the son's place?

- Did you know that these two words—*ransom* and *sacrifice*—are the exact words that describe what Jesus did for us at the cross? Can I read you a few verses? *(Read from Matthew 20:28; 1 Corinthians 5:7; 1 Timothy 2:5-6; Hebrews 7:27; 9:15,28.)*

## Jesus Physically Rose from the Dead and Ascended to Heaven

Contrary to the Muslim claim that Jesus did not rise from the dead (since He didn't die) and ascend into heaven, the biblical testimony is that both of these events were realities. Jesus not only rose from the dead, but He also provided powerful evidence for the resurrection before many witnesses. Scripture tells us that Jesus first attested to His resurrection by appearing to Mary Magdalene (John 20:1)—a fact which, to me, is a highly significant indicator of the authenticity and reliability of the resurrection account. If the resurrection story were a fabrication by the disciples, *no one in the first-century Jewish culture would have invented it this way*. The fact is that in Jewish law a woman's testimony was unacceptable in any court of law except in a very few circumstances. A fabricator would have been much more likely to place Peter or one of the other male disciples at the resurrection tomb. But the biblical text tells us that the Lord appeared first to Mary because *that was the way it actually happened*.

Following this, Mary promptly told the disciples the glorious news. That evening, the disciples had gathered in a room with the doors shut for fear of the Jews (John 20:19). This fear was well-founded, for after Jesus had been arrested, Annas the high priest specifically asked Jesus about the disciples (18:19). Jesus had also previously warned the disciples in the upper room, "If they persecuted me, they will persecute you also" (15:20). These facts no doubt lingered in their minds after Jesus was brutally crucified.

But then their gloom turned to joy. The risen Christ appeared in their midst and said to them, "Peace be with you" (John 20:19). This phrase was a common Hebrew greeting (1 Samuel 25:6 NASB). But on this occasion there was added significance to Jesus' words. After their conduct on Good Friday (they had all scattered like a bunch of spineless cowards after Jesus' arrest), the disciples may well have expected a rebuke from Jesus. Instead, He displayed compassion by pronouncing peace upon them.

Jesus immediately showed the disciples His hands and His side (John 20:20). The risen Lord wanted them to see that it was truly He. The wounds showed that He did not have another body, but the *same* body. He was dead, but now He is alive forevermore.

Now, consider this: By all accounts, the disciples came away from the crucifixion frightened and full of doubt. And yet, following Jesus' resurrection appearance to them, their lives were transformed. *The cowards became bulwarks of courage, fearless defenders of the faith.* The only thing that could account for this incredible transformation was the resurrection.

As the days passed, Jesus continued to make many appearances, proving that He had indeed truly risen from the dead. Acts 1:3 says, "He showed himself to these men and gave many convincing proofs that he was alive. He appeared to them over a period of forty days and spoke about the kingdom of God." Moreover, "He appeared to more than five hundred of the brothers at the same time, most of whom are still living" (1 Corinthians 15:6).

## Falsification of the Gospel Accounts?

Some Muslim critics have called into question the Gospel accounts of Matthew, Mark, Luke, and John, saying that early Christians allegedly altered some of what was in the Bible, inserting such things as the resurrection of Christ. The folly of this view is that these witnesses gave up their lives defending the truth of the resurrection and Christianity. Doubters would expect us to believe that not only did the apostles suffer incredibly during their lives but also ended up laying down their very lives, *all for the sake of an elaborate lie.* I think it takes more faith to believe *that* theory than it does the actual resurrection account.

## _____ *Ask...* _____

- If New Testament writers merely made up the story of the resurrection, why would they have given up their lives in defending Christianity?

Another point that bears consideration is that if Jesus' followers had concocted events like the resurrection, wouldn't Jesus' critics have then immediately come forward to debunk these lies and put an end to Christianity once and for all? As noted previously, Paul said the resurrected Christ appeared to more than 500 people at a single time, "most of whom are still alive" (1 Corinthians 15:6). If Paul had misrepresented the facts, wouldn't one of these 500 have come forward to dispute his claims? But no one came forward to dispute anything because the resurrection *really occurred.*

## The "Swoon Theory"

Some Muslim apologists have tried to argue that Jesus was indeed crucified on the cross, but He did not die—He merely swooned. This theory is highly imaginative. Consider its claims:

- Jesus went through six trials and was beaten beyond description.

- He was so weak that He could not even carry the wooden cross bar.

- Huge spikes were driven through His wrists and feet, resulting in heavy blood loss.

- A Roman soldier thrust a spear into His side so that blood and water came out.

- Four Roman executioners (who had many years of experience in their line of work) erred and mistakenly pronounced Jesus dead.

- Close to a hundred pounds of gummy spices were applied to Jesus' body, and during this process, no one saw Jesus breathing.

- A large stone weighing several tons was rolled against the tomb; Roman guards were placed there; and a seal was wrapped across the entrance.

- Despite heavy blood loss, Jesus awoke in the cool tomb, split off the grave wrappings, pushed away a stone of several tons, fought off the Roman guards, and appeared to the disciples. *Such a scenario is impossible to believe.*

## _____ *Ask...* _____

- How could the swoon theory be true? Can I explain to you why I can't believe this theory?

### Other Assertions by Muslims

What about Muslim apologist Ahmed Deedat's argument against the death and resurrection of Christ from Luke 24:39: "Look at my hands and my feet. It is I myself! Touch me and see; a ghost does not have flesh and bones, as you see I have"? Deedat believes Jesus was telling the disciples they should touch Him and handle Him so they could see He had not died, but was still physically alive and in their midst. The folly of this view becomes evident when we realize that immediately following His words in Luke 24:39, Jesus goes on to explain that He has indeed risen from the dead in fulfillment of the Scriptures: "This is what is written: The Christ will suffer and rise from the dead on the third day, and repentance and forgiveness of sins will be preached in his name to all nations, beginning at Jerusalem" (Luke 24:46-47). Deedat is ripping verses out of context in a futile attempt to prove a point.

Deedat is also wrong in his claim that "nowhere in the 27 books of the New Testament did Jesus ever say He was 'dead and now alive.'" Early on in Luke's Gospel, Jesus declared that "the Son of Man must suffer many things and be rejected by the elders, chief priests and teachers of the law, and he must be killed and on the third day be raised to life" (Luke 9:22). Jesus later told His disciples, "This is what is written: The Christ will suffer and rise from the dead on the third day" (Luke 24:46). Further, in the book of Revelation, the resurrected Christ stated, "I am the Living One; I was dead, and behold I am alive for ever and ever!" (Revelation 1:18).

Deedat is wrong again when he asserts that not a single author of the canonical Gospels recorded a single word about the ascension of Christ. In John 20:17, we read Christ's own words: "I am ascending to my Father and to your Father, to my God and to your God." In John 7:33 Jesus said, "I am with you for only a short time, and then I go to the one who sent me." "Now I am going to him who sent me" (John 16:5). "I am going to the Father, where you can see me no longer" (John 16:10). In Acts 1:9, recorded by Luke (the same author who wrote the Gospel of Luke), we read, "He was taken up before their very eyes, and a cloud hid him from their sight."

In view of the way some Muslim apologists—even well-respected ones like Ahmed Deedat—boldly make erroneous claims about the Bible, I urge you to *never take their word* for what the Bible says; always open up your Bible and check it out for yourself. Otherwise, the Muslim may win an argument because you did not check the facts.

I close with the observation that, although Muslims have offered some futile arguments against the resurrection and ascension of Jesus Christ, the reality is this: Jesus is missing from His tomb, while Muhammad's tomb at a mosque in Medina is still occupied.[8] In terms of eternal salvation, Muslims would do well to place their faith in "the Living One" who "was dead" but is now "alive for ever and ever!" (Revelation 1:18).

## _Ask..._

- Could I ask you to read through the Gospel of Luke over the next few weeks and then give me your honest estimate of Jesus?

  *(Many Muslims, as a result of reading one of the Gospels, have observed the wide chasm between Jesus and Muhammad.)*

# 11

## *The Muslim View of the Bible*

Muslims face a dilemma when dealing with the Christian Bible. According to the Quran, believers in Allah are not supposed to reject any of Allah's Scriptures. If they obey the Quran, they are forbidden from accepting *only a part* of Allah's revelation to humankind (a revelation that includes the Bible—see Sura 4:136). Muslims are even commanded to consult the Hebrew and Greek Scriptures for confirmation of Muhammad's revelations (Sura 10:94). However, if they accept what the Bible teaches—including such doctrines as Jesus being the Son of God, Jesus being God in human flesh, God being a Trinity, salvation being by faith in Christ, and so forth—then they *must* reject what the Quran teaches. In that case, they would no longer be Muslims. How, then, can Muslims solve this dilemma?

### The Bible Has Been Corrupted

Muslims claim that the original Bible was the Word of God (apparently still pure during the time of Muhammad[1]), but that it then became *corrupted* by Jews and Christians. The Bible of today has been mingled with many "untruths." These untruths relate particularly to areas where the Bible disagrees with the Quran. World religion scholar Stephen Neill observes that "it is well known that at many points the Quran does not agree with the Jewish and Christian Scriptures. Therefore, from the Muslim point of view, it follows of necessity that the Scriptures must have been corrupted."[2]

Muslim apologist Ajijola thus asserts,

> The first five books of the Old Testament do not constitute the original Torah, but parts of the Torah have been mingled up with other narratives written by human beings and the original guidance of the Lord is lost in that quagmire. Similarly the four Gospels of Christ are not the original Gospels as they came from the prophet Jesus.…The original and the fictitious, the divine and human are so intermingled that the grain cannot be separated from the chaff. The fact is that the original Word of God is preserved neither with the Jews nor with the Christians.[3]

Muslims believe, then, that what used to be the Word of God in the Bible has been so adulterated by human hands that it is now hardly distinguishable from the word of man. In some verses there may be a remaining glimmer of the truth Jesus taught, but these are few and far between in "the jungles of interpolations and contradictions with which the Bible is dense."[4]

Muslims say the Jews inserted many things into the Old Testament that served to personally benefit them. Muslim apologist Maurice Bucaille, for example, declares that "a revelation is mingled in all these writings, but all we possess today is what men have seen fit to leave us. These men manipulated the texts to please themselves, according to the circumstances they were in and the necessities they had to meet."[5]

This is illustrated in the Muslim assertion that, though *they* are the rightful heirs to the promises made to Abraham through Ishmael (his firstborn son), the Jews, for personal gain, concocted a story (and inserted it into the Old Testament) to the effect that Isaac became Abraham's heir, and that the inheritance from Abraham includes possession of the land of Palestine. In this Jewish version, Ishmael and his descendants became outcasts.[6] The *original* Old Testament, we are told, did not have this concocted story. Hence, we cannot trust the Old Testament Scriptures.

In the New Testament, Muslims say that Christians inserted such doctrines as the Trinity and Jesus being the Son of God. The original New Testament did not contain such ideas, we are told. The original Jesus presented Himself as nothing more than a prophet of Allah. Christians then took it upon themselves to deify this prophet. Today's New Testament, then, is not viewed as containing the actual words of Jesus, but rather words that were "put into His mouth" by Christians. The New Testament is corrupted.

Muslims claim that Jesus' original gospel was lost by the early church, and hence certain men—Matthew, Mark, Luke, and John—set out to *reconstruct* the written life of Christ. But these accounts all contradict each other and hence are entirely unreliable. Muslims do not want man-made versions of the gospel; they want the original gospel handed down to the prophet Jesus.[7] (These Muslims do not explain how their negative view of Matthew, Mark, Luke, and John relates to the fact that Muhammad commended the reading of the Christian Bible of his day—including Matthew, Mark, Luke, and John—see Sura 10:94.)

Amazingly, Muslim apologist Ahmed Deedat has argued that "out of over four thousand differing manuscripts the Christians boast about, the church fathers just selected four which tallied with their prejudices and called them Gospels of Matthew, Mark, Luke and John."[8] Further, Muslim apologists argue that none of the New Testament Gospel writers were eyewitnesses to what happened. Bucaille writes, "We do not in fact have an eyewitness

188 • The Muslim View of the Bible

account from the life of Jesus, contrary to what many Christians imagine."[9]

## A Defective Document

Muslims also argue that there are innumerable variants (mistakes) among the various manuscript copies of the Bible. For example, one Muslim writer says "it is admitted by the most learned men in the Hebrew language, that the present English version of the Old Testament contains at least 100,000 errors (this would amount to approximately three errors in every verse)."[10] Hence, it is asked, how can we trust the Bible?

Some Muslim writers believe that the Bible even admits it is a defective document. After all, in John 20:30 we read, "Jesus did many other miraculous signs in the presence of his disciples, *which are not recorded in this book*" (emphasis added). Likewise, in John 21:25 we read, "Jesus did many other things as well. If every one of them were written down, I suppose that even the whole world would not have room for the books that would be written." These verses constitute open admissions that the Bible is defective in its recording of revelation.[11]

Still further, we are told that the Bible of today is obviously corrupted because it uses language about God that is completely inappropriate. For example, the Bible speaks of God having a face, hands, eyes, and other body parts (for example, Exodus 33:11). God is *not* a physical being, and hence the Bible is simply wrong. As well, the Bible speaks of God "repenting" (for example, Genesis 6:6 KJV). Such unbefitting ideas were surely not a part of the original Bible.[12]

Additionally, we are told that there is only *one* version of the Quran, whereas there are many different versions of the Bible today (NASB, NIV, KJV, and so forth). We have one Quran but many Bibles. Muslims thus charge that while we can trust the Quran, we surely cannot trust the Bible.

## Contradictions and Problems
## in the Biblical Text

In recent years, Muslim apologists have argued for the corruption of the Bible by focusing attention on alleged contradictions and problems in the text. Though it is far beyond the scope
of a single chapter to include a discussion of every verse Muslims
cite, I will focus below on some representative verses they cite
that demonstrate their approach to discrediting the Bible. (I will
respond to these alleged contradictions in chapter 13.)

*Genesis 1–2—Man or animals created first?* In Genesis 1 and
2 we find an account of His creation of the heavens and the earth,
including God's creation of man and the animals. Bucaille claims
that in Genesis 1 the animals are portrayed as being created before
man, whereas in Genesis 2 man is portrayed as being created
before the animals. Hence, this is a clear contradiction in the
Bible.[13]

*Genesis 2:17—Did Adam die the day he sinned?* Muslims
often point out that in Genesis 2:17 it says Adam would die the
same day he ate of the forbidden fruit. In Genesis 5:5, however,
we are told that Adam lived to the age of 930 years. Hence, this
is a contradiction.

*Genesis 6:3—Man's life span 120 years?* In Genesis 6:3 we
read, "My Spirit will not contend with man for ever, for he is
mortal; his days will be a hundred and twenty years." Muslim
apologists argue that in Genesis 6:3, God just before the flood
limited man's life span to 120 years, but Genesis 11:10-32 indicates the ten descendants of Noah had life spans ranging from
148 to 600 years. The contradiction between these two passages
is obvious.[14]

*Genesis 7–8—The source of the flood waters.* Bucaille notes
that Genesis 7:4 says the floodwaters came from rain, whereas
Genesis 8:2 says the floodwaters came from rain *and* the waters

of the earth. This is clearly a contradiction. Bucaille also comments that there are conflicting reports regarding the length of time for the flood—Genesis 7:4 says 40 days, while Genesis 7:24 says 150 days. Genesis 7–8 is thus riddled with contradictions.[15]

***Exodus 33:11—Can man see God?*** Muslims argue that some verses portray human beings seeing God, such as Exodus 33:11, where Moses speaks to God "face to face." Yet other verses say that no man has ever seen God (John 1:18). Muslims say these accounts cannot be reconciled.[16]

***2 Samuel 24:1—Did God or the devil incite David?*** In 2 Samuel 24:1 we read that it was the Lord who incited David to number Israel. Yet in 1 Chronicles 21:1 we are told that Satan incited David to do so. Deedat thus asks, "How could the Almighty God have been the source of these contradictory 'Inspirations'?"[17]

***Matthew 1:1-17—Conflicting genealogies.*** Muslim apologists often argue that there are many contradictions in the Gospel accounts. We are told that the Gospel writers "provide us with descriptions which contradict other authors' narrations." Indeed, "Christians are very often astonished at the existence of such contradictions between the Gospels—if they ever discover them."[18]

An example is that the genealogy of Jesus contained in Matthew's Gospel (1:1-17) contradicts that found in Luke's Gospel (3:23-38). Bucaille says "the two genealogies contained in Matthew's and Luke's Gospels give rise to problems.... These problems are a source of great embarrassment to Christian commentators because the latter refuse to see in them what is very obviously the product of human imagination."[19]

***Matthew 11:14—Was John the Baptist the Elijah to come?*** Here Jesus is reported as saying that John the Baptist is the Elijah who was to come. Yet in John 1:19-21 John the Baptist denies he is the Elijah who was to come. This is yet another contradiction.[20]

***Matthew 12:40—Jesus wasn't in the earth "three days and three nights."*** In this verse we read Jesus' prophecy of His death and resurrection: "As Jonah was three days and three nights in the belly of a huge fish, so the Son of Man will be three days and three nights in the heart of the earth." Ahmed Deedat argues that, when one adds up the amount of time Jesus was actually in the tomb, "the greatest mathematician in Christendom will fail to obtain the desired result—THREE days and THREE nights."[21] After all, Jesus is said to have been crucified Friday evening and resurrected Sunday morning, which is hardly three days and three nights.

***Matthew 16:28—A false prophecy?*** Matthew records Jesus as saying, "I tell you the truth, some who are standing here will not taste death before they see the Son of Man coming in his kingdom." The problem is, Jesus has still not come in His kingdom, and hence the people standing with Jesus at the time of His prediction all died before seeing Him come in His kingdom. This is a false prophecy that was put into Jesus' mouth.[22]

***Matthew 20:29-34—Contradictory gospel accounts of a healing.*** Matthew reports that Jesus healed two blind men as He left Jericho. Mark 10:46-52 and Luke 18:35-43 say Jesus healed one man as He entered Jericho. Muslims say there is no way to reconcile these accounts.[23]

***Matthew 24:34—Another false prophecy?*** Here Jesus declared, "I tell you the truth, this generation will certainly not pass away until all these things have happened." The problem is, Jesus' generation passed away without the events He described coming to pass. Hence, a false prophecy was again put into the mouth of Jesus.[24]

***Matthew 27:5—How did Judas die?*** Matthew tells us that Judas died by hanging himself. Yet in Acts 1:18 we are told that

Judas died by falling headlong in a field; his abdomen burst open so that his intestines spilled out. Here is yet another contradiction.

*Mark 16:17-18—Prove your faith by drinking poison.* Some Muslims argue that Mark 16 contains verses that were not a part of the original Bible. Some even issue a challenge to make their point: "Prove your faith by drinking poison or taking up a deadly serpent" (see verse 18).[25]

*James 2:14-26—Is salvation by works or by faith?* Muslims contend that some verses in the Bible say that works cannot save a person, but rather only faith in Christ can (Romans 3:20; Galatians 2:16). But other verses, such as James 2:14-26, say that people are justified by works. Muslims say that such verses are irreconcilable.[26]

## The Gospel of Barnabas

Besides attacking the canonical gospels (Matthew, Mark, Luke, and John), many Muslims point to the Gospel of Barnabas as being the most reliable and accurate gospel. One reason Muslims like this gospel so much is that some of it seems to agree with Muslim doctrine. Here are some examples:

*The Gospel of Barnabas teaches that the Bible has been corrupted.* "Then said the disciples: 'Clear is the deception of our doctors: therefore tell us thou the truth, because we know that thou art sent from God.' Then answered Jesus: 'Verily I say unto you, that Satan ever seeketh to annul the laws of God; and therefore he with his followers, hypocrites and evil-doers, the former with false doctrine, the latter with lewd living, today have contaminated all things, so that scarcely is the truth found'" (chapter 44).

*The Gospel of Barnabas teaches that Jesus was not the Son of God.* "Dearly beloved, the great and wonderful God hath during these past days visited us by his Prophet Jesus Christ in great mercy of teaching and miracles, by reason whereof many, being deceived by Satan, under pretense of piety, are preaching most impious doctrine, calling Jesus son of God, repudiating the circumcision ordained of God forever, and permitting every unclean meat: among whom also Paul hath been deceived" (Prologue).

***The Gospel of Barnabas teaches that the line of promise comes through Ishmael.*** "If the messenger of God whom ye call Messiah were son of David, how should David call him Lord? Believe me, for verily I say to you, that the promise was made in Ishmael, not in Isaac" (Chapter 43).

If Muslims had their way, the Gospel of Barnabas would be spliced into the Bible, and Matthew, Mark, Luke, and John would be excised. One Muslim writer commented that no other Gospel comes even close to the Gospel of Barnabas.[27]

In view of the issues addressed in this chapter, many modern Muslim apologists have concluded that the Bible is merely a human book—"the handiwork of man."[28] They don't bother trying to reconcile their view with Muhammad's commendation of the Bible of his time (Sura 10:94). Indeed, one must wonder whether they even realize they're contradicting Muhammad when they argue so stringently against the Bible.

# 12

## *A Defense of the Bible, Part One*

The authenticity and reliability of the Bible is one of the most important foundations to establish when discussing issues and debating with Muslims. In responding to Muslim claims about the Bible, it is necessary to both answer their objections and criticisms of the Bible, *and* set forth a positive statement of the trustworthiness of the Bible. In what follows I shall do both.

### Require Proof That the Bible Has Been Changed

It is one thing to claim that the Bible has been corrupted. It is another thing entirely to prove it. One of the first things to do when a Muslim tells you that the Bible has been corrupted is to ask for indisputable historical proof for such claims.

## ___ *Ask...* _____

- Can you show me historical evidence to back up your claim that the Bible has been corrupted?

- Was the Bible changed before or after the time of Muhammad?

- If it was changed before the time of Muhammad, why does the Quran commend the Bible's reading (Suras 5:69; 10:94)?

- If it was changed before the time of Muhammad, wouldn't that amount to saying Muhammad was a false teacher, since he commended the reading of the Bible?

- If the Bible was changed *after* Muhammad's time, how do you explain the fact that we have numerous biblical manuscripts predating Muhammad that prove that the Bible we have today is the *same* as the Bible from before Muhammad's time? *(More on this shortly.)*

---

## Demonstrate the Impossibility of the Changes That Muslims Argue For

Help your Muslim acquaintance understand how unreasonable it is to say that the Bible became corrupted during or after Muhammad's time. Relevant points include the following:

- By Muhammad's time there were hundreds of thousands of copies of the Bible dispersed over a large part of the world. To successfully corrupt the Bible, all these copies would have had to be meticulously gathered (assuming people around the world would be willing to surrender them, an impossible-to-believe scenario), and then the changes would have had to be made.

- Another scenario is that hundreds of thousands of Bible-owning people from around the world met together and *colluded* to make the changes. But since most of these people were true believers, is it likely they would tamper with a book upon which they were basing their eternal salvation? Would such collusion even be physically possible?

- Hundreds of years before Muhammad was even born, the Bible had already been translated into a number of languages. Would Muslims have us believe that these various translations were identically altered all over the world so they would have a uniform corruption?

- It is impossible to believe that both Jews *and* Christians were involved in corrupting the Bible, as Muslims claim. The reality is that the Jews and Christians of those centuries were hostile to one another, and if either party had tried to alter the biblical text, the other party would have cried "foul" and exposed the misdeed by producing the original.[1] Further, during this time there were many dissenting Christian sects. An alteration of the biblical text by any one of these sects would have brought immediate condemnation by the others.

- Scholar William J. Saal raises the point that if the Jews had corrupted their Scriptures, wouldn't they have at least changed all the horrible things we read about them in the Torah (such as their total unfaithfulness during the wilderness sojourn and their participation in idolatry)?[2] Likewise, if Christians had corrupted the New Testament, wouldn't unflattering episodes about Christians have been removed from the New Testament (like Peter denying Christ three times, and the disciples scattering like a bunch of faithless cowards when Christ was arrested)?

- Is it likely the almighty and sovereign God of the universe would allow His Word to have become corrupted like this?

## *Ask...*

- Did you know that by Muhammad's time there were hundreds of thousands of copies of the Bible dispersed over a large part of the world? Doesn't it seem rather unlikely that all these copies were meticulously gathered and then collectively corrupted?

- Do you really think hundreds of thousands of Christians would go along with corrupting a book upon which they were basing their eternal salvation?

- Since the Bible had already been translated into a number of languages before Muhammad was even born, is it your contention that these various translations were identically altered all over the world so they would have a uniform corruption? How likely is that?

- Don't you think that if Jews had corrupted the biblical text, Christians would have detected and exposed the misdeed by producing the originals?

- Don't you think that if the Jews had corrupted their Scriptures, they at least would have changed some of the horrible things we read about them in the Torah?

- Is it likely that the almighty and sovereign God of the universe would allow His Word to have become corrupted like this? Does not Sura 6:34 say, "There is none that can alter the words (and decrees) of God"?

---

It is also important to understand that the early Jews had meticulous rules to ensure that their scribes accurately copied the text of the Hebrew Scriptures. Later on, this text was handed down to the Massoretes. Scholar L. Bevan Jones writes,

> The Massoretes, in turn, numbered the verses, words, and letters of every book. They calculated

the middle word and the middle letter of each. They enumerated verses which contained all the letters of the alphabet, or a certain number of them; and so on. These trivialities, as we might rightly consider them, had yet the effect of securing minute attention to the precise transmission of the text; and they are but an excessive manifestation of a respect for the sacred Scriptures which in itself deserves nothing but praise. The Massoretes were indeed anxious that not one jot or tittle—not one smallest letter nor one tiny part of a letter—of the Law should pass away or be lost.[3]

## The Quran Indicates That God's Word Cannot Be Changed

In Sura 2:75 the Bible is called "the word of God." We are then told in Sura 6:115, "None can change His [Allah's] words" (insert added). An important issue to raise with your Muslim acquaintance is that, if the Bible is God's Word, as the Quran says, and if God's Word *cannot be changed,* then how can Muslims charge that the Bible has been corrupted without disagreeing with the Quran? Though Muslims assert that there are contradictions in the Bible, they need to explain *their own* contradiction in saying that the Bible has been changed when the Quran says God's Word *cannot* be changed.[4]

## ____ *Ask...* ____

- Since the Quran calls the Bible "the word of God" in Sura 2:75, and since the Quran teaches that no one can change Allah's words (Sura 6:115), then how can Muslims charge that the Bible has been corrupted without disagreeing with the Quran?

- If you reject the Bible, aren't you at the same time rejecting what the Quran says about the Bible?

---

## The Bible Itself Argues Against the Possibility of Its Corruption

The charge that the Bible has been corrupted not only goes against what the Quran says, but it also contradicts what the Bible itself teaches. After all, in Isaiah 40:8 we read, "The grass withers and the flowers fall, but the word of our God stands for ever." Likewise, in the New Testament Jesus says, "Heaven and earth will pass away, but my words will never pass away" (Matthew 24:35).

In my view, the almighty God who had the power and sovereign control to inspire the Scriptures in the first place is surely going to continue to exercise His power and sovereign control in the *preservation* of Scripture. Further, God's preservational work is illustrated in the very text of the Bible. By examining how Christ viewed the Old Testament (keeping in mind that Jesus did not have in His possession the original books penned by the Old Testament writers, but only copies), we see that He had full confidence that the Scriptures He used had been faithfully preserved through the centuries.

Bible scholar Greg Bahnsen writes, "Because Christ raised no doubts about the adequacy of the Scripture as His contemporaries knew them, we can safely assume that the first-century text of the Old Testament was a wholly adequate representation of the divine word originally given. Jesus regarded the extant copies of His day as so approximate to the originals in their message that He appealed to those copies as authoritative."[5] The respect Jesus and His apostles held for the Old Testament text of their day is an expression of their confidence that God had providentially preserved these copies and translations so that they were substantially identical with the inspired originals. We can deduce that the same is true regarding the New Testament and God's preservation of the entire Bible since Jesus' time.

Another important point to note is this: In Revelation 22:18-19 we read, "I warn everyone who hears the words of the prophecy of this book: If anyone adds anything to them, God will add to him the plagues described in this book. And if anyone takes words away from this book of prophecy, God will take away from him his share in the tree of life and in the holy city, which are described in this book." The Jews were also given similar commands in the Old Testament. Deuteronomy 4:2 says, "Do not add to what I command you and do not subtract from it, but keep the commands of the LORD your God that I give you." Deuteronomy 12:32 says, "See that you do all I command you; do not add to it or take away from it." Proverbs 30:5-6 says, "Every word of God is flawless; he is a shield to those who take refuge in him. Do not add to his words, or he will rebuke you and prove you a liar."

In view of such verses, one must ask how reasonable it is to suggest that Old Testament–believing Jews and Bible-believing Christians would choose to corrupt and change God's Word. Such individuals would not only be damning themselves before God, but also *misleading all their descendants* (their children and their children's children), who would read the very Scriptures they corrupted. How likely is that?

## ____ *Ask...* ____

- Would you mind if I read a few Bible verses to you? *(Read Revelation 22:18-19; Deuteronomy 4:2; 12:32; and Proverbs 30:5-6.)*

- In view of these verses, do you really think it is reasonable to think that Old Testament–believing Jews and Bible-believing Christians would choose to corrupt and change God's Word?

- Wouldn't these individuals not only be damning themselves before God, but also misleading *all their descendants* (their children and their children's children), who
would read the very Scriptures they corrupted? Do you
really believe they did that?

## Muslims Are Inconsistent in Their View of the Bible

It is noteworthy that even though Muslims go to great lengths
to argue for the corruption of the biblical text, whenever they
come upon a Bible text they feel lends support to *their* viewpoint,
they immediately accept that verse's authenticity. For example,
Muslims argue from Deuteronomy 18 that Muhammad is the fulfillment of the prediction of a great prophet to come. Muslims
argue from John 14 that Muhammad is the fulfillment of the
"Comforter" of which Jesus spoke. Ask your Muslim acquaintance whether he or she thinks it is fair and consistent to accept
Bible verses that Muslims think lend support to Islam while
rejecting all the verses that do not lend support to Islam.

## _____ *Ask...* _____

- Why do Muslims uniformly argue against the reliability
of the Bible, except in cases where they think the Bible
lends support for Islamic views? Is that fair and consistent?

## Manuscript Evidence Proves the Bible to be Trustworthy

It is quite clear from the Quran that Muhammad commended
the reading of the Bible of his day (Suras 5:69; 10:94). In view of
this, an important point to make is that Muslims should accept the

Bible *of today* because abundant manuscript evidence proves it is
the same Bible that existed in (and before) Muhammad's day.
Indeed, there are more than 5000 partial and complete early manuscript copies of the New Testament. These manuscript copies
are very ancient; they are also available for inspection right now,
in our day. Following are some of the most prominent from
among these copies:

- The Chester Beatty papyrus (P45) dates to the third
  century A.D. and contains the four Gospels and chapters 4–17 of the Book of Acts. (P = papyrus.)

- The Chester Beatty papyrus (P46) dates to about
  A.D. 200 and contains ten Pauline epistles (all but
  the pastorals) and the book of Hebrews.

- The Chester Beatty papyrus (P47) dates to the third
  century A.D. and contains Revelation 9:10–17:2.

- The Bodmer Papyrus (P66) dates to about A.D. 200
  and contains the Gospel of John.

- The Bodmer Papyrus (P75) dates to the early third
  century and contains Luke and John.

- The Sinaiticus uncial manuscript dates to the fourth
  century and contains the entire New Testament.

- The Vaticanus uncial manuscript dates to the fourth
  century and contains most of the New Testament (it
  lacks Hebrews 9:14ff., the pastoral epistles,
  Philemon, and Revelation).

- The Washingtonianus uncial manuscript dates to the
  early fifth century and contains the Gospels.

- The Alexandrinus uncial manuscript dates to the
  fifth century and contains most of the New Testament.

- The Ephraemi Rescriptus uncial manuscript dates to the fifth century and contains portions of every book except 2 Thessalonians and 2 John.

- The Bezae/Cantabrigiensis uncial manuscript dates to the fifth century and contains the Gospels and Acts.

- The Claromontanus uncial manuscript dates to the sixth century and contains the Pauline epistles and Hebrews.

- The Itala version (versions were translations that were prepared for missionary purposes) dates to the third century.

- The Vulgate (Latin) version dates to the fourth century and later.

- The Syriac version dates to the second to sixth centuries.

- The Coptic version dates to the third and fourth centuries.

- The Armenian version dates to the fifth century.

- The Georgian version dates to the fifth century.[6]

What all this means is that *before Muhammad was even born* there was massive manuscript evidence for the New Testament—and since our Bible translations of today are based on these early manuscripts, the Muslim charge of corruption since Muhammad's time is shown to be completely false.

## _____ *Ask...* _____

- Did you know that scholars possess manuscripts in support of the New Testament text that date to the second century? Can I tell you about some of them?

- Since a great number of New Testament manuscripts pre-date Muhammad, and since our Bibles today are based on these early manuscripts, how can it be charged that the Bible has been corrupted since Muhammad's time?

From these early centuries, there are also some 86,000 quotations of the New Testament from the early church fathers and several thousand lectionaries (church-service books containing Scripture quotations used in the early centuries of Christianity). In fact, there are enough quotations, from the early church fathers that, even if we did not have a single manuscript copy of the Bible, scholars could still reconstruct all but 11 verses of the New Testament from material written within 150 to 200 years after the time of Christ.

## EARLY PATRISTIC QUOTATIONS OF THE NEW TESTAMENT[7]

| Writer | Gospels | Acts | Pauline Epistles | General Epistles | Revelation | Totals |
|---|---|---|---|---|---|---|
| Justin Martyr | 268 | 10 | 43 | 6 | 3 | 330 |
| Irenaeus | 1,038 | 194 | 499 | 23 | 65 | 1,819 |
| Clement of Alexandria | 1,017 | 44 | 1,127 | 207 | 11 | 2,406 |
| Origen | 9,231 | 349 | 7,778 | 399 | 165 | 17,922 |
| Tertullian | 3,822 | 502 | 2,609 | 120 | 205 | 7,258 |
| Hippolytus | 734 | 42 | 387 | 27 | 188 | 1,378 |
| Eusebius | 3,258 | 211 | 1,592 | 88 | 27 | 5,176 |
| Grand Totals | 19,368 | 1,352 | 14,035 | 870 | 664 | 36,289 |

As this chart indicates, we have more than 36,000 quotations from just seven of the church fathers alone. Can any other ancient document boast of such widespread and reliable support? Such overwhelming support for the New Testament text deals a death-blow to the Muslim claim of corruption.

## ____ *Ask...* ____

- Did you know that, even if we did not have a single man-uscript copy of the New Testament, we could reconstruct all but 11 verses of the New Testament from material written within 150 to 200 years after the time of Christ by the church fathers?

- Since this is the case, how can it be charged that the Bible of today is different from the Bible of Muhammad's time? After all, our Bible today is based on manuscripts that pre-date Muhammad.

---

## What About the Variants?

### The New Testament

In the previous chapter, I noted that Muslim apologists often argue that there are innumerable mistakes in the manuscripts of the Bible. It is true to say that in the thousands of manuscript copies we possess of the New Testament, scholars have discov-ered that there are some 200,000 "variants." This may seem like a staggering figure to the uninformed mind, but to people who study the issue, the number of variants is nowhere near so damning as it may initially appear. Indeed, a look at the hard evi-dence shows that the New Testament manuscripts are amazingly accurate and trustworthy.

To begin, I must emphasize that out of these 200,000 variants, more than 99 percent hold virtually no significance whatsoever. Many of these variants simply involve a missing letter in a word; some involve reversing the order of two words (such as "Christ

Jesus" instead of "Jesus Christ"); some may involve the absence of one or more insignificant words. Really, when all the facts are put on the table, only about 40 of the variants have any real significance—and even then, no doctrine of the Christian faith or any moral commandment is affected by them. In more than 99 percent of these cases, the original text can be reconstructed to a practical certainty.

By practicing the science of textual criticism—comparing all the available manuscripts with each other—we can come to an assurance regarding what the original document must have said. Perhaps an illustration will be helpful.

Let us suppose we have five manuscript copies of an original document that no longer exists. Each of the manuscript copies is different. Our goal is to compare the manuscript copies and ascertain what the original must have said. Here are the five copies:

- *Manuscript #1:* Jesus Christ is the Savior of the whole world.

- *Manuscript #2:* Christ Jesus is the Savior of the whole world.

- *Manuscript #3:* Jesus Christ the Savior of the whole world.

- *Manuscript #4:* Jesus is Savior of the whle world.

- *Manuscript #5:* Jesus Christ is the Savor of the wrld.

Could you, by comparing the manuscript copies, ascertain what the original document said with a high degree of certainty that you were correct? Of course you could.

This illustration may be simplistic, but a great majority of the 200,000 variants are reconciled by the above methodology. By comparing the various manuscripts, most of which contain relatively minor differences like the above, it becomes fairly clear what the original must have said. Further, I must emphasize that the sheer volume of manuscripts we possess greatly narrows the margin of doubt regarding what the original biblical document said.

Bible scholar Winfried Corduan has pointed out that, if someone in the past had burned all the textual variants of the Bible, like Caliph Uthman burned all the Quran variants, we would have a single manuscript of the Bible, in the same way as there was an "authoritative manuscript" of the Quran. Corduan notes that "the very existence of so many variant readings allows us to recover what the original must have said with a great degree of confidence. By contrast, it is impossible to restore the Quran to what existed prior to Uthman, since we now have only one version of the Quran—the one Uthman wanted us to have."[8]

## The Old Testament

Because Muslims often attack the Old Testament as being untrustworthy, I want to make mention of the Dead Sea scrolls in this regard. In these scrolls, discovered at Qumran (on the northwest shore of the Dead Sea) in 1947, we have Old Testament manuscripts that date to about a thousand years earlier (150 B.C.) than the Old Testament manuscripts previously in our possession (which dated to no earlier than about A.D. 980). The significant thing is that when one compares the two sets of manuscripts, it is clear that they are essentially the same, with very few changes. The fact that manuscripts separated by a thousand years are essentially the same indicates the incredible accuracy of the Old Testament's manuscript transmission.

The copy of the book of Isaiah discovered at Qumran illustrates this. Dr. Gleason Archer, who personally examined both the A.D. 980 and 150 B.C. copies of Isaiah, comments:

> Even though the two copies of Isaiah discovered in 1947 in Qumran Cave 1, near the Dead Sea, were a thousand years earlier than the oldest dated manuscript previously known (A.D. 980), they proved to be *word for word identical* with

our standard Hebrew Bible in more than 95 percent of the text. The 5 percent of variation con-
sisted chiefly of obvious slips of the pen and
variations in spelling.[9]

The Dead Sea scrolls *prove* that the copyists of biblical manuscripts took great care in going about their work. These copyists
knew they were duplicating God's Word. Hence they went to
incredible lengths to insure that no error crept into their work.
The scribes carefully counted every line, word, syllable, and letter
to guarantee accuracy.[10]

What this ultimately means is that Muslim apologists like
Ahmed Deedat and Maurice Bucaille, in their attempt to prove
corruption in the Bible, are arguing against the same Bible that
existed in the time of Muhammad, which *Muhammad and the
Quran indicated was trustworthy.* Would Deedat and Bucaille say
Muhammad was wrong? Would they say the Quran was in error?

## ____ *Ask...* _____

- Did you know that, in the Dead Sea scrolls discovered at
  Qumran in 1947, we have Old Testament manuscripts that
  date to about a thousand years earlier (150 B.C., far predating Muhammad) than the Old Testament manuscripts
  previously in our possession (which date to about A.D.
  980)?

- Did you know that, when one compares the two sets of
  manuscripts, it is clear that they are essentially the same,
  with very few changes?

- What does that say to you about claims of corruption in the
  biblical text?

## Early Literary Evidence in Support of the New Testament

Support for the authenticity and reliability of the New Testament Gospels is found in many quotations from both Christian *and* secular sources that date very close to the time of Christ.

### Christian Sources

Christian leaders who lived between A.D. 95 and 170 consistently point to the reliability of the Gospels. Following is a sampling.

- *Clement* was a leading elder in the church at Rome. In his epistle to the Corinthians (A.D. 95), he cites portions of Matthew, Mark, and Luke, and introduces them as the actual words of Jesus.[11]

- *Papias*, the bishop of Hierapolis in Phrygia and author of *Exposition of Oracles of the Lord* (about A.D. 130), cites the Gospels of Matthew, Mark, Luke, and John, presumably as canonical. He specifically refers to John's Gospel as containing the words of Jesus.[12]

- *Justin Martyr*, foremost apologist of the second century (active about A.D. 140), considered all four Gospels to be Scripture.[13]

- *The Didache*, an ancient manual of Christianity that dates from about the end of the first century, cites portions of the three synoptic Gospels and refers to them as the words of Jesus. This manual quotes extensively from Matthew's gospel.[14]

- *Polycarp*, a disciple of the apostle John, quotes portions of Matthew, Mark, and Luke, and refers to them as the words of Jesus (about A.D. 150).[15]

- *Irenaeus*, a disciple of Polycarp (about A.D. 170), quoted from 23 of the 27 New Testament books, omitting only Philemon, James, 2 Peter, and 3 John.[16]

Clearly, there are numerous early sources from between A.D. 95 and 150 that refer to Matthew, Mark, Luke, and John as containing the actual words of Christ. History is therefore on the side of the Gospels and argues against the Muslim claim that they are unreliable.

## Non-Christian Sources

Besides Christian witnesses in the early centuries of Christianity, there were also non-Christian sources living close to the time of Christ that corroborate the evidence of Christ as a historical figure. For example, Jewish historian Flavius Josephus (born A.D. 37) made reference to "Jesus, the so-called Christ." Roman historian Cornelius Tacitus (born A.D. 52) wrote of "Christus," who was "put to death by Pontius Pilate" (contrary to the Muslim claim that Jesus did not die). Pliny the Younger (in about A.D. 112) spoke of the "sect of Christians." Suetonius (in about A.D. 120) spoke of disturbances over "Chrestus" (Christ).[17] All in all, the external evidence for the reliability of the Bible is quite impressive.

## Muhammad Did Not Understand the Bible

There are two pivotal and undeniable facts before us:

First, the Quran teaches there is one God named Allah, who is not a Trinity and who cannot have a "son," since this would associate partners with him. Jesus was merely a prophet—not God, and not the Son of God. He did not die for man's sins. Salvation is attained through submission and obedience to Allah.

Second, the Bible teaches that God's name is Yahweh and that He is a Trinity. The second person of the Godhead is Jesus, and He is known as the "Son of God." Jesus is eternal God, and through the incarnation became God in human flesh. Salvation is attained by placing personal faith in Jesus, who died on the cross for man's sins.

In view of the above two paragraphs, what are we to make of Muhammad's commending of the Bible of his day (Suras 5:69; 10:94)? We know that the Bible of his day is the same as the Bible of our day, so only one conclusion is possible: *Muhammad really did not understand the essential teachings of Christianity, else he wouldn't have commended the Bible.* I presented evidence in Chapters 2 and 3 that the versions of Christianity Muhammad was exposed to were those of the Nestorians and Ebionites, both followers of heretical perversions of Christianity. Since the prophet of the Quran was ignorant regarding the nature of true Christianity, this means that the Quran itself is in error in commending the Bible, which in turn serves to undermine it as a true revelation from God. If it were a true revelation from God, it would have recognized the true nature of Christianity to begin with.[18]

## _Ask..._

*After sharing the above information, ask this question.*

• If Muhammad was wrong about the true nature of Christianity, doesn't this undermine the Quran as a true revelation from God, since a true revelation from God would not err about the nature of Christianity?

## The "Many Versions" of the Bible

The argument that there are many versions of the Bible but only one version of the Quran is hollow because the argument does not accurately reflect the facts. We do not have different "versions" of the Bible in the sense of having *different Bibles* (with different books, chapters, and verses); rather we have *different English translations* (as well as various translations in other languages) from the same basic set of Hebrew and Greek manuscripts in our possession. Such translations include the New American Standard Version, The New International Version, and the King James Version.

It is worth noting that there are a number of English translations of the Quran, but no one says that there are "different versions" of the Quran because of that. Likewise, we have different translations of the Bible, but they are all translations using the same body of Hebrew and Greek manuscripts.[19]

## There Never Were More Than "Four Thousand Different Gospels"

I noted in the previous chapter that Muslim apologist Ahmed Deedat argues that "out of over four thousand differing manuscripts the Christians boast about, the church fathers just selected four which tallied with their prejudices and called them Gospels of Matthew, Mark, Luke and John."[20] Deedat completely misunderstands the nature of the biblical manuscripts. The reality is that, as we have seen, the thousands of manuscripts we possess are copies of *all 27 books* of the New Testament. Many of these manuscripts are copies of the four canonical Gospels. Such an embarrassing misunderstanding on Deedat's part shows he has not really examined the evidence nearly as well as he represents the case to be.

## Eyewitness Testimony in the New Testament

Contrary to the claim of Muslim apologist Maurice Bucaille that "we do not in fact have an eyewitness account from the life of Jesus,"[21] the New Testament is most definitely based on eyewitness testimony. For example, John, who wrote the Gospel of John, said in his first epistle, "That which was from the beginning, which we have heard, which we have seen with our eyes, which we have looked at and our hands have touched—this we proclaim concerning the Word of life" (1 John 1:1). John was with Jesus' mother Mary at the foot of the cross as Jesus was dying (John 19:25-27). Peter, though not an author of a Gospel, was nevertheless an eyewitness. He wrote in one of his epistles, "We did not follow cleverly invented stories when we told you about the power and coming of our Lord Jesus Christ, but we were eyewitnesses of his majesty" (2 Peter 1:16).

# 13

## *A Defense of the Bible, Part Two*

Muslims declare that, in addition to the fact that the Bible is generally filled with errors and variants, it also contains numerous specific contradictions. In chapter 11 I listed some of the most typical of these arguments. Following are some general observations on the issue of contradictions in the Bible, as well as answers to specific charges made by Muslims.

### Apparent Contradictions Do Not Equate to Bible Corruption

There are several points to make regarding the Muslim claim about contradictions. First, while the Gospels may have some *apparent* contradictions, I do not believe they have *genuine* contradictions. There are differences, yes, but actual contradictions, no.

Second, and foundationally, it is important to keep in mind that inspiration (the fact that Scripture is "God-breathed"— 2 Timothy 3:16) and inerrancy are, strictly speaking, ascribed only to the original autographs of Scripture. Certainly I believe the copies we have of the original autographs are extremely accurate. But theologians have been very careful to say that the Scriptures—*in their original autographs and properly interpreted*—will be shown to be wholly true in everything they teach.

Third, if all four Gospels were the same, with no differences, Muslim critics would be vehemently accusing Christians of collusion. The fact that the Gospels have differences shows that there was no collusion; rather, they represent four different (but inspired) accounts of the same events.

Finally, one should not assume that a *partial* account in a biblical book is a *faulty* account. One book might provide certain details about an event, and another book might provide other, different details regarding the event. But just because they provide different details does not mean the accounts are faulty.

## A Response to Alleged Bible Contradictions

### GENESIS 1–2—*Man or Animals Created First?*

Muslim apologists argue that in Genesis 1 the animals are portrayed as being created before man, whereas in Genesis 2 man is portrayed as being created before the animals.[1] However, there is no real contradiction since Genesis 2 does not report precisely *when* God created the animals. All it says is that God brought the animals to Adam so Adam might name them. The proper way to understand Genesis 2, then, is that God brought the animals *He had formerly created* to Adam so Adam could name them.[2]

### GENESIS 2:17—*Did Adam Die the Day He Sinned?*

Muslims point out that Genesis 2:17 says Adam would die the same day he ate of the forbidden fruit, but Genesis 5:5 says Adam lived to the age of 930 years. There is no real contradiction, however, since Adam and Eve *did* die the day they ate the fruit. They did not die that day *physically*, but they did die *spiritually*.

The word "death" carries the idea of separation. Physical death involves the separation of the soul or spirit from the body. Spiritual death involves the separation of the human being from God. When Adam and Eve partook of the forbidden fruit, they were immediately separated from God *in a spiritual sense*. (Their consequent action of trying to hide from God in the Garden of Eden indicates their awareness of this spiritual separation.) The moment of their sin, they became "dead in...transgressions and sins" (Ephesians 2:1-3). Their spiritual separation from God eventually led to their physical deaths.

### GENESIS 6:3—*Man's Life Span 120 Years?*
Muslim apologists argue that according to this verse, God limited man's life span to 120 years, but then people following this time lived 148 to 600 years.[3] There is no real contradiction, however, since the context indicates that the 120 years refers not to man's life span, but to the time God would allow before He sent the flood upon humankind. God thus provided plenty of time for humans to repent before sending judgment.

### GENESIS 6:6—*Inappropriate Language About God?*
Muslims assert that the Bible of today is corrupted because it uses language about God that is inappropriate. For example, Genesis 6:6 (KJV) indicates that God repented.

This is not inappropriate language for God, because God does not repent in the human sense of turning from sin. Rather, the word "repentance," when used of God, generally refers to a change in God's course of action because of something man has done. For example, God promised to judge the Ninevites, but then God changed His mind and withheld judgment after the entire city repented (see the book of Jonah). Many people fail to realize that God has what you might call a "built-in repentance clause" to His promises of judgment. This clause is found in Jeremiah 18:7-10:

> If at any time I announce that a nation or kingdom is to be uprooted, torn down and

> destroyed, and if that nation I warned repents of
> its evil, then I will relent and not inflict on it the
> disaster I had planned. And if at another time I
> announce that a nation or kingdom is to be built
> up and planted, and if it does evil in my sight and
> does not obey me, then I will reconsider the good
> I had intended to do for it.

What we see here is that God changes His policy toward man when He beholds a change in the actions of man. God is a God of mercy. And when He sees repentance, He responds with mercy and grace.

If Muslims are going to criticize the Bible because it occasionally portrays God as "repenting," then the Quran is open to the same criticism, for Allah is often found to be annulling or abrogating certain verses in the Quran (something the Bible never does). Further, one of Allah's "most excellent names" is "He that is continually repenting." It is not fair for Muslims to criticize the Bible for portraying God as "repenting" when the Quran does the same thing.

## GENESIS 7–8—*The Source of the Floodwaters*

Muslims point out that one verse in Genesis says the floodwaters came from rain, while another says the floodwaters came from rain *and* the waters of the earth (see Genesis 7:4; 8:2). Further, in this passage there are alleged conflicting reports of the length of time for the Flood—some verses say 40 days, while others say 150 days (Genesis 7:4,12,17,24).[4] Correctly interpreted, however, there is no real contradiction among these verses. There would be a contradiction if one verse said rain would be the *only* source of water, but it does not say that. Taken together, these are complementary verses. *A partial statement is not a false statement*; it simply provides part of the picture. When we take these verses together, we have the whole picture.

As to the claim that the Bible provides different and contradictory lengths of time for the flood, Muslims are simply misinterpreting the passage. Scripture indicates that it *rained* for 40 days (Genesis 7:12), but the floodwaters *"prevailed"* on the earth for 150 days (7:24 NASB), after which time the waters decreased (8:3).[5]

## Exodus 33:11—*Can God Be Seen?*

Some verses indicate that people have seen God "face to face" (Exodus 33:11), while other verses say no one has ever seen God (John 1:18). Muslims say this is a contradiction. What are we to make of this?

Foundationally, Paul tells us that God the Father is invisible (Colossians 1:15; 1 Timothy 1:17) and "lives in unapproachable light, whom no one has seen or can see" (1 Timothy 6:16). John's Gospel likewise tells us that "no one has ever seen God [the Father], but God the One and Only [Jesus Christ], who is at the Father's side, has made him known" (John 1:18, inserts added). John 5:37 similarly tells us that no one has ever seen God the Father's form.

Does the fact that Moses spoke to God "face to face" mean that God has a physical body that Moses beheld (Exodus 33:11)? No. The phrase "face to face" is simply a figurative way of indicating "personally," "directly," or "intimately." Moses was in the direct presence of God and interacted with Him on a personal and intimate basis. The word "face," when used of God, is an *anthropomorphism*—that is, it is a word used to figuratively describe God in human terms. Seen in this light, there is no contradiction in the Bible here.

## 2 Samuel 24:1—*Did God or the Devil Incite David?*

Muslims point out that 2 Samuel 24:1 says that the Lord incited David to number Israel, while 1 Chronicles 21:1 says Satan incited David to do so.[6] However, these are not *contradictory* accounts; they are *complementary* accounts. Both are true, but each reflects a different aspect of a larger truth.

Satan was the actual instrument used to incite David to number Israel (1 Chronicles 21:1), but God permitted Satan to do this. In the Hebrew mind-set, whatever God *permits*, God *commits*. By allowing this census-taking, God is viewed in 2 Samuel 24:1 as having brought about the act Himself. (Keep in mind that the Hebrews were not too concerned about "first causes" and "secondary causes.") Satan did what he did because he wanted to destroy David and the people of God. God's purpose, however, was simply to humble David and teach him and his people a valuable spiritual lesson.

The same is true of Job's sufferings. It was Satan that directly caused the suffering of Job. But as the text of Scripture clearly indicates, God permitted Satan to do this.

### MATTHEW 1:1-17—*A Contradictory Genealogy?*

Muslims say the genealogy contained in Matthew's Gospel (1:1-17) contradicts that found in Luke's Gospel (3:23-38).[7] Christians respond that the genealogies are different, but not contradictory. Up to David, the two genealogies are very similar, practically the same. In fact, they share some 18 or 19 common names, depending on whether Matthan and Matthat are the same person. From David on, they are very different. Almost none of the names from David to Joseph coincide. (In fact, only two of the names—Shealtiel and Zerubbabel—coincide.) Why are they different?

Matthew's genealogy traces Joseph's line of descendants, and deals with the passing down of the legal title to the throne of David (David → Solomon → Coniah → Joseph → Jesus). As Joseph's adopted son, Jesus became his legal heir so far as his inheritance was concerned. The word "whom" in the phrase "of whom was born Jesus" (Matthew 1:16) is a *feminine* relative pronoun, clearly indicating that Jesus was the physical child of Mary and that Joseph was not His physical father.

Matthew traced the line from Abraham and David in 41 links to Joseph. He obviously did not list every individual in the genealogy. Jewish reckoning did not require every name in order to construct a satisfactory genealogy.

Abraham and David were the central figures of the two uncon-
ditional covenants pertaining to the Messiah. Matthew's Gospel
was written to Jews, so Matthew wanted to prove to Jews that
Jesus was the promised Messiah. This would demand a fulfillment of the Abrahamic Covenant (Genesis 12) and the Davidic
Covenant (2 Samuel 7). Matthew was calling attention to the fact
that Jesus came to fulfill the covenants made with Israel's fore-
fathers.

Luke's genealogy traces Mary's lineage, and carries it all the
way back beyond the time of Abraham to Adam and the com-
mencement of the human race. Whereas Matthew's genealogy
pointed to Jesus as the Jewish Messiah, Luke's genealogy points
to Jesus as the Son of Man, a name often used of Jesus in Luke's
Gospel. Whereas Matthew's genealogy was concerned with the
Messiah as related to the Jews, Luke's genealogy was concerned
with the Messiah as related to the entire human race and as the
"offspring" of the woman (Eve)—the one who would "crush" the
head of the serpent (Genesis 3:15).

## MATTHEW 11:14—*Was John the Baptist the Elijah to Come?*

In Matthew 11:14 Jesus is reported as saying that John the
Baptist is the Elijah who was to come, while in John 1:19-21 John
the Baptist denies this. Properly interpreted, however, these
verses show no real contradiction. Luke 1:17 clarifies any possible confusion on the proper interpretation of Matthew 11:14 by
pointing out that the ministry of John the Baptist was carried out
"in the spirit and power of Elijah." So, though John the Baptist
was not *actually* Elijah, he did carry out his ministry *in the spirit
and power* of Elijah. Seen in this light, Jesus and John did not
contradict each other.

## MATTHEW 12:40—*In the Tomb Three Days and Three Nights*

Muslim apologists argue that Matthew 12:40 is in error in
saying Jesus was in the tomb for three days and three nights.[8] The

Gospel accounts are clear that Jesus was crucified and buried on Friday, sometime before sundown. This means that Jesus was in the grave for part of Friday, the entire Sabbath (Saturday), and part of Sunday. In other words, He was in the tomb for two full nights, one full day, and part of two days. How do we reconcile this with Jesus' words in Matthew 12:40: "As Jonah was three days and three nights in the belly of a huge fish, so the Son of Man will be three days and three nights in the heart of the earth"?

In the Jewish mind-set, any *part* of a day was reckoned as a *complete* day. The Babylonian Talmud (a set of Jewish commentaries) tells us that "the portion of a day is as the whole of it." Hence, though Jesus was really in the tomb for part of Friday, all of Saturday, and part of Sunday, in Jewish reckoning He was in the tomb for "three days and three nights." Seen in this light, this verse poses no problem for the veracity of the Bible.

### MATTHEW 16:28—A False Prophecy?

In this verse Jesus said, "I tell you the truth, some who are standing here will not taste death before they see the Son of Man coming in his kingdom." Muslims point out that Jesus has not yet come in His kingdom, and hence the people standing with Jesus all died before seeing Him come.[9]

Christians respond that there was a sense in which Christ's contemporaries saw "the Son of Man coming in his kingdom." It is likely that when Jesus said this He had in mind the transfiguration, which happened precisely one week later. In fact, in Matthew's account, the transfiguration (17:1-13) immediately follows the prediction itself (16:28). If this interpretation is correct, as the context seems to indicate, the transfiguration served as a *preview* or *foretaste* of the kingdom in which the divine Messiah would appear in a state of glory. More specifically, in the transfiguration the power and the glory within Jesus broke through the veil of his flesh and shone out, to the point that His very clothing kindled with the dazzling brightness of the light. This is the very same glory that will be revealed to the world when Christ comes to this earth again to set up His kingdom (see Matthew 24:30; 25:31).

## MATTHEW 20:30—*Contradictory Accounts of a Healing?*

Muslims note that Matthew 20:29-34 says Jesus healed *two* blind men as He left Jericho, while Mark 10:46-52 and Luke 18:35-43 say Jesus healed *one* man as He entered Jericho. Properly interpreted, however, this is not a contradiction. There are several possible explanations. One is that the healing took place as Jesus was leaving *old* Jericho and was nearing *new* Jericho (there were two Jerichos in those days). If Jesus were at a place between the two Jerichos, then, depending on one's perspective, He could be viewed as "leaving" one Jericho or "entering" the other Jericho. Now, there were apparently two blind men in need of healing, but of the two, Bartimaeus was the more aggressive, and hence two of the Gospel accounts (Mark and Luke) mention only him. If the blind men were healed between the two Jerichos, this would clear up the apparent contradiction.

Another possible explanation is that the blind men pled with Jesus as He entered (either the old or the new) Jericho, but they did not receive their actual healings until Jesus was leaving the city. It is also possible that Jesus healed one blind man as He was entering the city, and healed two other blind men as he was leaving. Clearly, there are a number of ways of reconciling the Gospel accounts.

## MATTHEW 24:34—*Another False Prophecy?*

Matthew records Jesus' words as follows: "I tell you the truth, this generation will certainly not pass away until all these things have happened." The problem, Muslims say, is that Jesus' generation passed away without the occurrence of the events He described.

Evangelical Christians have generally held to one of two interpretations of Matthew 24:34. One is that Christ is simply saying that those people who witness the signs stated earlier in Matthew 24 (all of which deal with the future tribulation period) will see the coming of Jesus Christ within that very generation. In other words, the generation that is alive when such events as the abomination of desolation (verse 15) and the great tribulation (verse 21) begin to come to pass will still be alive when these prophetic judgments are completed. Since the tribulation is a period of seven years (Daniel 9:27; Revelation 11:2), Jesus was saying that the generation alive at the *beginning* of the Tribulation will still be alive at the *end* of it, at which time the second coming of Christ occurs.

Other evangelicals say the word generation in this verse is to be taken in its secondary meaning of "race, kindred, family, stock, or breed." Jesus' statement could mean that the Jewish race would not pass away until all things are fulfilled. Since many divine promises were made to Israel—including the eternal inheritance of the land of Palestine (Genesis 12; 14–15; 17) and the Davidic kingdom (2 Samuel 7)—then Jesus could be referring to God's preservation of the nation of Israel in order to fulfill His promises to the nation. Indeed, Paul speaks of a future of the nation of Israel when the Jews will be reinstated in God's covenantal promises (Romans 11:11-26).

Whichever interpretation is correct, the verse does not involve an irreconcilable contradiction, as Muslims claim.

### MATTHEW 27:5—*How Did Judas Die?*

Muslim apologists point out that Matthew 27:5 says Judas died by hanging himself, while Acts 1:18 says Judas died by falling headlong in a field and bursting open. Properly interpreted, however, there is no real contradiction. Apparently Judas first hanged himself. Then, at some point, the rope either broke or loosened so that his body slipped from it and fell, perhaps to rocks below, and burst open. Neither account is complete. Taken together, we have a full picture of what happened to Judas.

### MARK 16:17-18—*Snakes and Poison*

In their effort to prove that Mark 16 contains verses that were not a part of the original Bible, some Muslims challenge Christians,

"Prove your faith by drinking poison or taking up a deadly serpent" (verse 18).[10] This passage actually says: "These signs will accompany those who believe: In my name they will drive out demons; they will speak in new tongues; they will pick up snakes with their hands; and when they drink deadly poison, it will not hurt them at all; they will place their hands on sick people, and they will get well."

Certainly we find ample evidence for some of these activities in New Testament times. Indeed, in the New Testament we witness the casting out of demons (Acts 8:7; 16:18; 19:15-16), speaking in tongues (Acts 2:4-11; 10:46; 19:6; 1 Corinthians 12:10; 14:1-24), and even protection from a poisonous snake (Acts 28:3-5). A few observations are in order, however.

First, the construction of the verse in the original Greek of verse 18 uses "conditional clauses." The verse carries this idea: "And if they should be compelled to pick up snakes with their hands, and if they should be compelled to drink deadly poison, it shall by no means harm them." What this means is that if some non-Christian authority or persecutor forced a Christian to do such things (a real possibility in the early church), God would supernaturally protect that believer. Understood in context, this verse certainly gives no justification for voluntarily drinking poison or handling snakes to prove faith. We see no such activity in the early church. (Note that Paul's encounter with the snake at Malta was completely unintentional—Acts 28:3-5.)

Having said this, it is correct to say that Mark 16:9-20 is absent from two of the oldest Greek manuscripts presently in our possession—Codex Alexandrinus and Codex Sinaiticus. As well, these verses are absent from the Old Latin manuscripts, the Sinaitic Syriac manuscript, about 100 Armenian manuscripts, and the two oldest Georgian manuscripts. Understandably, then, many Christian scholars believe that Mark 16:9-20 does not belong in the Bible. But this fact does not undermine the veracity of the rest of the Bible, for the rest of the Bible enjoys powerful manuscript support.

## JOHN 20:30; 21:25—*The Bible Does Not Admit Defectiveness*

Muslim writers believe that the Bible itself admits it is a defective document. After all, in John 20:30 we read, "Jesus did many other miraculous signs in the presence of his disciples, *which are not recorded in this book*" (emphasis added). Likewise, in John 21:25 we read, "Jesus did many other things as well. If every one of them were written down, I suppose that even the whole world would not have room for the books that would be written."

In response, all John 20:30 is saying is that, while Jesus' ministry was characterized by miracles from beginning to end, it is not necessary to record each one in order to establish that Jesus is in fact the promised Messiah. Some 35 different miracles are recorded in the four Gospels, but John selected only seven for special consideration so that people might come to believe that Jesus is the Christ, the promised Messiah. It was not necessary to provide "overkill" evidence by including every single miracle. John was satisfied to provide *massive* evidence for Jesus' identity instead of *overwhelming* evidence. This being the case, it is illegitimate to cite this verse as proof of the claim that the Bible admits its own defectiveness.

What about John 21:25? John's only point in this verse is that Jesus' ministry was so wonderful, so miraculous, so beyond the ability of human words to fully capture that the Gospel account he wrote reflects *only a portion* of the wonder of Jesus. John's sense is that he had but dipped a cup in the ocean of wonder that is Jesus Christ. Someone has calculated that one can read the accounts of Jesus in the Gospels in about three hours. If all that Jesus said and did during His *full three-year* ministry were considered, then surely John's expression is reasonable. It is thus illegitimate as well to cite this verse as proof of the claim that the Bible admits its own defectiveness.

## JAMES 2:14-26—*Is Salvation by Works or Faith?*

Muslims argue that some verses in the Bible say that faith in Christ alone brings salvation (Romans 3:20; Galatians 2:16), whereas other verses, such as James 2:14-26, say that people are justified by works.[11] Properly interpreted, however, there is no contradiction.

The passage in James merely declares that faith without works is dead. Martin Luther explained that James 2 is not teaching that a person is saved by works. Rather a person is "justified" (declared righteous before God) by faith alone, but *not by a faith that is alone*. In other words, genuine faith will always result in good works in the saved person's life.

James is writing to Jewish Christians ("to the twelve tribes"— James 1:1) who were in danger of giving nothing but lip service to Jesus. His intent, therefore, is to distinguish true faith from false faith. He shows that true faith results in works, which are visible evidences of faith's invisible presence. In other words, good works are the "vital signs" indicating that faith is alive. Apparently some of these Jewish Christians had made a false claim of faith. It is the counterfeit boast of faith that James condemned. Merely claiming to have faith is not enough. Genuine faith is evidenced by works.

## Dealing with Alleged Contradictions

Above I have examined just a few of the alleged contradictions that sometimes come up in discussions with Muslims. As we have seen, in every case there is a viable explanation that shows there is no *real* contradiction, only a different or a partial account. But I can promise you that there will be other verses that come up in your discussions with Muslims. For this reason, I urge you to make use of some of the other excellent resources that are available for answering assertions about Bible contradictions, which I have listed in appendix C.

## The Gospel of Barnabas Is Untrustworthy

In chapter 11, I noted that Muslims often say that the Gospel of Barnabas is the most accurate and reliable Gospel. This "Gospel" teaches such things as the corruption of the Bible, that

Jesus is not the Son of God, and that God's covenant with Abraham was fulfilled through the line of Ishmael, not Isaac. But the evidence is quite convincing that this "Gospel" is a fake.

- The "Gospel" shows virtually no familiarity with the world of the first century.[12]

- There is not a single manuscript known for the Gospel of Barnabas prior to the 1500s (some 1400 years after Barnabas' time).

- From the first to the fifteenth centuries, not a single church father or teacher ever quoted from the Gospel of Barnabas.

- Internal evidence in the "Gospel" indicates a medieval origin. For example, the author mentions a year of jubilee coming every 100 years, while God commanded that the Old Testament jubilees be celebrated every *fifty* years (Leviticus 25:11). The author of Barnabas may have been drawing his information from Pope Boniface VIII, who in A.D. 1300 decreed that the next jubilee would be held after a hundred years, not fifty.[13]

- This "Gospel" seems to draw some of its phraseology (terms like "false and lying gods" and "circles of hell") from Dante's *Inferno* and *Paradiso*. (Dante lived in the early fourteenth century.) Such terms are never found in the Bible (or even the Quran).[14]

- It is odd that Muslims cite the Gospel of Barnabas in support of Islam, for it flatly denies that Jesus is the Messiah (Sections 42, 48). By contrast, the Quran—held to be absolutely authoritative by Muslims—says that Jesus *is* the Messiah (Sura 5:75). If the Gospel of Barnabas is so accurate, as Muslims claim, why does the Quran disagree with it?

- The Gospel of Barnabas has a number of obvious historical mistakes.[15] For example, it says that Jesus sailed to Nazareth. (Nazareth is not on a shoreline.) It also reports that Jesus was born when Pilate was governor of Judea. However, Pilate did not become governor until about A.D. 26, when Jesus was already an adult.[16]

## Tests of Canonicity

Muslims often argue that it was just human opinion that determined which books made it into the Bible. They question how anyone can know which books were truly inspired and which weren't. In what follows I will briefly summarize the five primary canonical tests that were applied to books. Here they are, listed in question format:

1. *Was the book written or backed by a prophet or apostle of God?* This is the single most important test. The reasoning here is that the *Word* of God, which is inspired by the *Spirit* of God for the *people* of God must be communicated through a *man* of God.[17] Deuteronomy 18:18 informs us that only a prophet of God will speak the Word of God. Second Peter 1:20-21 assures us that Scripture is only written by men of God. In Galatians 1, the apostle Paul argued support for the book of Galatians by appealing to the fact that he was an authorized messenger of God, an apostle.

2. *Is the book authoritative?* In other words, can the same authority be recognized in this book as was recognized in Jesus: "The people were amazed at his teaching, because he taught them as one who had authority, not as the teachers of the law" (Mark 1:22)? Put another way, does this book ring with the sense of "Thus saith the Lord"?

3. ***Does the book tell the truth about God and doctrine as it is already known by previous revelation?*** The Bereans searched the Old Testament Scriptures to see whether Paul's teaching was true (Acts 17:11). They knew that if Paul's teaching did not accord with the Old Testament canon, it could not be of God. Agreement with all earlier revelation is essential (Galatians 1:8).

4. ***Does the book give evidence of having the power of God?*** The reasoning here is that any writing that does not exhibit the transforming power of God in the lives of its readers could not have come from God. Scripture says that the Word of God is "living and active" (Hebrews 4:12). Second Timothy 3:16-17 indicates that God's Word has a transforming effect. If the book in question did not have the power to change a life, then, it was reasoned, the book could not have come from God.

5. ***Was the book accepted by the people of God?*** In Old Testament times, Moses' scrolls were placed immediately into the Ark of the Covenant (Deuteronomy 31:24-26). Joshua's writings were added in the same fashion (Joshua 24:26). In the New Testament, the apostle Paul thanked the Thessalonians for receiving his message as the Word of God (1 Thessalonians 2:13). Paul's letters were circulated among the churches (Colossians 4:16; 1 Thessalonians 5:27). It is the norm that God's people—that is, the majority of them and not simply a faction—will initially receive God's Word as such.

Many of the New Testament books were recognized as Scripture right during the general time they were written. It is highly revealing that in 1 Timothy 5:18, the apostle Paul joined an Old Testament reference and a New Testament reference and called them *both* (collectively) "Scripture" (Deuteronomy 25:4 and Luke 10:7). It would not have been unusual in the context of first-century Judaism for an Old Testament passage to be called

"Scripture." But for a New Testament book to be called "Scripture" so soon after it was written says volumes about Paul's view of the authority of contemporary New Testament books.

More specifically, only three years had elapsed between the writing of Luke's Gospel and the writing of 1 Timothy (Luke was written around A.D. 60; 1 Timothy was written around the year 63). Despite this, Paul (himself a Jew—a "Hebrew of Hebrews") does not hesitate to place Luke on the same level of authority as the Old Testament book of Deuteronomy.

Further, the writings of the apostle Paul were recognized as Scripture by the apostle Peter (2 Peter 3:16). Paul, too, understood that his own writings were inspired by God and therefore authoritative (1 Corinthians 14:37; 1 Thessalonians 2:13). Paul, of course, wrote over half the New Testament.

Help your Muslim acquaintance see that *God* determined the canon, and that many people living in biblical times recognized that the individual books written by the prophets and apostles were indeed Scripture. God *determines* the canon, human beings *discover* the canon; God *regulates* the canon, human beings *recognize* the canon.[18]

## _____ *Ask...* _____

- Since Muhammad did not question the validity of which books had been accepted in the Bible (see Suras 5:69; 10:94), why are you doing so? Are you disagreeing with Muhammad's assessment of the Bible? If Muhammad was wrong on *this* issue, are there *other* issues he was wrong on as well? What does this say about his being a true prophet?

# 14

## Sin and Salvation in Islam

The purpose of man, according to orthodox Islam, is not to know God and become more conformed to His character. Rather, man's purpose is simply to understand God's will and become more obedient to his commands. Salvation is found in complete surrender to Allah. This is in keeping with the meaning of "Islam" ("submission") and "Muslim" ("one who submits"). Salvation, then, is ultimately based on works.

Before we can properly understand the Muslim view of salvation, however, we first need to understand what Islam teaches about sin. It has long been said among Christian theologians that a weak view of sin will always lead to a weak view of salvation. If one does not recognize a serious sin problem for human beings, then one will generally minimize any need for an atonement. This is illustrated in the religion of Islam.

### The Muslim View of Sin

Islam minimizes the reality of human sin. Muslim's firmly deny the Christian doctrine of original sin that is rooted in the fall of Adam.

To be sure, Muslims do concede that Adam disobeyed God and was expelled from the Garden of Eden. When Adam sinned, however, his nature did not change at all. He did not suddenly gain a "sin nature" that would in the future lure him into new sinful activity. Adam was the same after his fall as he was before. He was still perfectly able to obey God.

Muslims also believe that Adam's fall had no effect on his descendants. Like Adam himself, his descendants have always been able to obey God so long as they understand what God requires of them. This is why Allah has sent so many prophets to humankind throughout history.

Muslim writer Badru Kateregga affirms that all people are born innocent, pure, and free. "There is no single act which has warped the human will."[1] Muslim tradition records what Muhammad allegedly said on this subject: "No child is born except in the state of natural purity (fitra) and then his parents make him Jewish, Christian, or Magian."[2] Another Muslim writer notes that "people are born innocent and remain so until each makes him or herself guilty by a guilty deed. Islam does not believe in 'original sin'; and its Scripture interprets Adam's disobedience as his own personal misdeed—a misdeed for which he repented and which God forgave."[3] Hence, whereas Christians view Adam's sin as a monumental event that introduced him and his progeny to a new nature of sin, Muslims view Adam's act as a minor slip-up that was quickly forgotten after he repented; the episode affected no one.

A key argument Muslims offer in support of the idea that Adam did not commit a major sin is that he was a prophet of Allah, and Allah's prophets simply do not engage in major sin. God would never entrust important revelation to one who was an evildoer. Instead of saying that Adam engaged in a major sin, Muslims say Adam just made a mistake, for he had forgotten God's command not to eat of the tree. He erred, but then he repented, and all was well.

All of this is not to say that Muslims have no doctrine of sin at all. They do believe that sin exists, but they believe people commit sins not because they have a sin nature, but because of human weakness and forgetfulness (Sura 4:28). Human beings are easily led astray. They have an inherent feebleness. That is why people need Allah's laws. If sin emerges as a result of forgetfulness and feebleness, then Allah's law serves as a constant reminder of what is expected of humankind.

## An Atonement Is Unnecessary

Muslims believe that people are able, in their own strength, to free themselves from bondage to sin and choose to follow the path of Allah. Accordingly, an atonement for sin is utterly unnecessary. Muslims do not believe that human beings need to be redeemed by a divine Redeemer and hence see no need for the sacrificial death of a Savior (Jesus Christ). Man is viewed as fundamentally good, and the Muslim hope is anchored in the belief that Allah will forgive those who seek to obey His will.[4]

Another reason an atonement is unnecessary in Muslim theology is that Allah makes arbitrary decisions on matters of salvation. According to the Quran, Allah may lead people on the correct path, or he may lead people astray. Allah can show mercy to people if he wants, or he may show cruelty to them. He is answerable to no one. Because Allah can forgive whomever he wants, and condemn whomever he wants, an atonement is entirely unnecessary. Since God makes an arbitrary decision in these matters, he has no need to satisfy his own justice.

## Good Works Are Enough (It Is Hoped)

The Quran teaches that if a person has any hope of salvation, it will be based on pleasing Allah by good works. We read in Sura 23:102-3: "In the day of judgment, they whose balances shall be heavy with good works, shall be happy; but they, whose balances shall be light, are those who shall lose their souls, and shall remain in hell forever." Salvation is based upon one's own merit, for one's good deeds must outweigh one's bad deeds.

Muslims generally believe that one stands the best chance of salvation by copying the sayings and actions of Muhammad, the greatest of all humans. After all, Muhammad was pleasing to Allah, and if a Muslim can do and say what Muhammad did, then perhaps he or she will end up in paradise. This is one reason Muslim tradition is so important, for it is within tradition that one finds a record of what Muhammad did and said in various circumstances.

Many Muslims seem all too aware that they fall short of what might be expected of them on the Day of Judgment. They accordingly seek to engage in extra works so that, perhaps, they can tip the scales in their favor. Such individuals recite extra prayers, observe extra fasts, make more gifts to charity, repeat the 99 most beautiful names of Allah, go on pilgrimages not just to Mecca but to other Muslim places as well, and perform other good works—all in order to gain merit before Allah.

## No Assurance of Salvation

Even for the one who engages in all these extra good works, there is still no guarantee—indeed, no assurance—of salvation. When a Muslim dies, he does not know whether he will go to paradise or to hell. Ultimately, as noted above, it is all based on the arbitrary will of Allah, and no one can predict what Allah's decision will be.[5]

The one exception to this is that anyone who dies in service to Allah—whether he is good or evil—is assured a place in paradise. This explains why radical Islamic terrorists are all too happy to give up their lives attacking "infidels."

# A CHRISTIAN CRITIQUE OF THE MUSLIM VIEW OF SIN AND SALVATION

## The Bible Teaches Original Sin

Contrary to the Muslim view, when Adam and Eve sinned it did not just affect them in a minimal way. In fact, Scripture teaches that Adam and Eve spiritually died the day they partook of the forbidden fruit.

The word "death" in the Bible carries the idea of separation. *Physical* death involves the separation of the soul or spirit from the body. *Spiritual* death involves the separation of the human being from God. When Adam and Eve partook of the forbidden fruit, they were immediately separated from God in a spiritual sense. The moment of their sin, they became "dead in...transgressions and sins" (Ephesians 2:1-3). Their spiritual separation from God eventually led to their physical deaths.

## Sin Is Universal

Also contrary to the Muslim view, Adam and Eve's sin did not affect them in an isolated way, but affected the entire human race. In fact, ever since then, every human being born into the world has been born in a state of sin. The apostle Paul said, "Just as sin entered the world through one man, and death through sin...in this way death came to all men, because all sinned" (Romans 5:12). We also read in Romans 5:19: "Through the disobedience of the one man the many were made sinners." First Corinthians 15:21-22 likewise tells us that "death came through a man" and "in Adam all die."

In keeping with this, David said in Psalm 51:5, "Surely I was sinful at birth, sinful from the time my mother conceived me" (see also Psalm 53:1-3 and Genesis 8:21). According to this verse, human beings are born into the world in a state of sin. The sin nature is passed on *from conception*. This is why Ephesians 2:3 says we are "*by nature* objects of wrath" (emphasis added).

As we continue to examine Scripture, the universality of the sin problem bears witness to the reality of original sin. In Ecclesiastes 7:20 we read, "There is not a righteous man on earth who does what is right and never sins." Isaiah 64:6 declares, "All of us have become like one who is unclean, and all our righteous acts are like filthy rags; we all shrivel up like a leaf, and like the wind our sins sweep us away." In Job 15:14-16 we read, "What is man, that he could be pure, or one born of woman, that he could be righteous? If God places no trust in his holy ones, if even the heavens are not pure in his eyes, how much less man, who is vile and corrupt, who drinks up evil like water!" The apostle John tells us in 1 John 1:8, "If we claim to be without sin, we deceive ourselves and the truth is not in us." There is no doubt that all of humanity is fallen in sin as a result of the initial sin of our first parents, and it has affected us in a dreadful, awful way. In fact, it is fair to say that a prime manifestation of this sin in the human heart is the Muslim denial that there is a sin problem at all.

## _____ *Ask...* _____

- Did you know the Bible says we are only deceiving ourselves if we say we have no sin (1 John 1:8)?

- Have you considered the possibility that a prime manifestation of sin in the human heart is the denial that there is a sin problem at all?

- One thing that has gotten my attention is Charles Spurgeon's comment, "He who doubts human depravity had better study himself."[6] I know there is sin in me. Do you think there is sin in you?

- May I share a few verses from the Bible on the universality of sin in our world? *(Read from Romans 5:12,19; Psalm 51:5; Ecclesiastes 7:20; and Isaiah 64:6.)*

## Sin Is Everywhere

A reasonable look at the empirical evidence in the world around us seems to support the Christian teaching on man's depravity and fallenness rather than the idea of man's alleged innate goodness. John Ankerberg and John Weldon have observed that "since 3600 B.C. the world has known only 292 years of peace. In that period, stretching more than 55 centuries, there have been an incredible 14,531 wars in which over 3.6 billion people have been killed."[7] In this same vein, Christian missionary to Muslims David Shenk writes,

> Did you hear the radio today? Did you listen to the news? Perhaps the radio told about fighting. Maybe you heard about hunger or floods or accidents. Perhaps you heard about trouble in London, Nairobi, Cairo, or New York. Was most of the news good news, or news about trouble? Probably most of the news was about trouble.
>
> When God made the world, he said that it was very good. But now much that we hear and see in the world is not good. What has gone wrong? Why is there trouble in the world? Why is there hunger? What is the cause of all this trouble?
>
> The prophets have written that trouble comes when people turn away from God. Sin is turning away from God.[8]

## _Ask..._

- Have you noticed that most of the news reported in newspapers and the evening news on TV is *bad* news?

- Doesn't it seem like there is plenty of evidence that humans are fallen in sin?

## The Quran Acknowledges the Sin Problem

Though Muslims deny the doctrine of original sin, there is plenty of evidence from the pages of the Quran that man has a sin problem:

- "The (human) soul is certainly prone to evil" (Sura 12:53).

- "Verily man was created anxious, fretful when evil touches him but mean-spirited when good reaches him" (Sura 70:19-21).

- "Man is given up to injustice and ingratitude" (Sura 14:34).

- "Man was created weak" (Sura 4:28).

- "(Man) becomes an open disputer" (Sura 16:4).

- "Man doth transgress all bounds" (Sura 96:6).

- "If God were to punish men for their wrongdoing, He would not leave, on the (earth), a single living creature" (Sura 16:61).

## _____ *Ask...* _____

- Since the Quran admits man has a serious sin problem, would you mind if I shared with you what the Bible says about this? *(Read from Romans 5:12,19; Psalm 51:5; Ecclesiastes 7:20; and Isaiah 64:6.)*

---

## Sin Is Not Just Human
## Feebleness and Forgetfulness

Contrary to the Muslim view that sin involves mere human feebleness and forgetfulness, Scripture indicates that sin involves active rebellion against a holy God and a violation of His holy law, and that we are *all* guilty. A key meaning of sin in the Bible is "to miss the target." Sin is failure to live up to God's standards. All of us miss the target. There is not one person who is capable of fulfilling all of God's laws at all times.

The apostle Paul thus stressed that *all* human beings fall short of God's glory (Romans 3:23). The words "fall short" are a single word in the Greek, which is a present tense. This indicates continuing action. Human beings *perpetually* fall short of God's glory. The word "glory" here refers not just to God's splendor but to the outward manifestation of His attributes—including His righteousness, justice, and holiness. Human beings fall short of God in these and other areas.

Human sin always shows up clearly in the presence of God's holiness. In the "light" of His holiness, the "dirt" of sin shows up crystal clear. Remember what happened to the prophet Isaiah? Here was a relatively righteous man. But when he beheld God in His infinite holiness, his own personal sin came into clear focus and he could only say, "Woe to me!...I am ruined! For I am a man of unclean lips, and I live among a people of unclean lips" (Isaiah 6:5).

When we measure ourselves against other human beings, we may come out looking okay. In fact, to measure ourselves against other human beings might lead us to believe that we are fairly righteous in and of ourselves. But other human beings are not our moral measuring stick. God is. And as we measure ourselves against God in His infinite holiness and righteousness, our sin shows up in all of its ugliness.

Billy Graham once told a story that well illustrates how human sin shows up best in the light of God's holiness. Consider his words:

> Several years ago I was to be interviewed at my home for a well-known television show and, knowing that it would appear on nationwide television, my wife took great pains to see that everything looked nice. She had vacuumed and

dusted and tidied up the whole house and had gone over the living room with a fine-tooth comb since that was where the interview would be filmed.

When the film crew arrived with all the lights and cameras, she felt that everything in that living room was spic and span. We were in place along with the interviewer when suddenly the television lights were turned on and we saw cobwebs and dust where we had never seen them before. In the words of my wife: "That room was festooned with dust and cobwebs which simply did not show up under ordinary light."

The point is, of course, that no matter how well we clean up our lives and think we have them all in order, when we see ourselves in the light of God's Word, in the light of God's holiness, all the cobwebs and all the dust do show up.[9]

## _____ *Ask...* _____

- Would you agree with me that if we were to just compare ourselves to other people, we wouldn't come out looking that bad?

- What if we were to compare ourselves to an infinitely holy God? How do you think we would fare?

- May I tell you a story? *(Tell the story of Billy Graham above.)*

---

### Jesus' Words About Sin

The seriousness of man's sin problem comes into clearest focus in the teachings of Jesus Christ. Jesus taught that as a result of the fall human beings are evil (Matthew 12:34) and that man is capable of great wickedness (Mark 7:20-23). Moreover, He said that man is lost (Luke 19:10), that he is a sinner (Luke 15:10), and that he is in need of repentance before a holy God (Mark 1:15).

Jesus often spoke of sin in metaphors that illustrate the havoc sin can wreak in one's life. He described sin as blindness (Matthew 23:16-26), sickness (Matthew 9:12), being enslaved in bondage (John 8:34), and living in darkness (John 8:12; 12:35-46). Moreover, Jesus taught that this is a universal condition and that all people are guilty before God (Luke 7:37-48).

## _____ *Ask...* _____

*After sharing the above, ask the following question.*

• If Jesus is right regarding how serious sin is, doesn't that call for a serious solution to the sin problem? *(Be ready to talk about Jesus' sacrificial death. See below.)*

---

Based on the above, it seems clear that sin is not just forgetfulness and feebleness. Consider the case of Adam. As noted previously, Muslims believe Adam just made a mistake, for he had forgotten God's command not to eat of the tree. This explanation stretches credibility in view of the fact that the Quran says Satan *reminded* Adam of God's command as he was tempting Adam to eat of the fruit. We read, "Then began Satan to whisper suggestions to them, bringing openly before their minds all their shame that was hidden from them (before): he said: 'Your Lord only forbade you this tree, lest ye should become angels or such beings as live for ever'" (Sura 7:20).

## ___ *Ask...* ___

- Am I right in saying that most Muslims believe Adam did not commit a bad sin, but merely forgot about God's command that he not eat the forbidden fruit?

- How can this view be reconciled with the Quran, which in Sura 7:20 says that Satan *reminded* Adam of God's command as he was tempting Adam to eat the fruit?

---

### Sin Is an Inner Reality

Jesus taught that both inner thoughts and external acts render a person guilty. Indeed, He asserted in Matthew 5:28 that "anyone who looks at a woman lustfully has already committed adultery with her in his heart." Likewise, He taught that from within the human heart come evil thoughts, sexual immorality, theft, murder, adultery, greed, malice, deceit, envy, slander, arrogance, and folly (Mark 7:21-23). Moreover, He affirmed that God is fully aware of every person's sins, both external acts and inner thoughts; *nothing escapes His notice* (Matthew 22:18; Luke 6:8; John 4:17-19). This means that at the future judgment of humanity, human beings will be required to give an account not just of their external deeds, with good deeds being weighed against bad deeds on a scale of justice; we will have to give an account of what went on in our hearts as well.

To be sure, our external actions will be judged (Psalm 62:12; see also Matthew 16:27; Ephesians 6:7-8). But we will *also* be judged for what goes on in our hearts and minds. The Lord "will bring to light what is hidden in darkness and will expose the motives of men's hearts" (1 Corinthians 4:5). The Lord is the One "who searches hearts and minds" (Revelation 2:23).

## ___ *Ask...* ___

- Did you know that Jesus taught that from within the human heart come such things as evil thoughts, sexual immorality, theft, murder, adultery, and greed (Mark 7:21-23)?

- Did you know that Jesus affirmed that God is fully aware of every person's sins, both external acts and inner thoughts, with *nothing escaping His notice* (Matthew 22:18; Luke 6:8; John 4:17-19)?

- I am certainly aware of the sin inside me. Can I share with you how I've been liberated from the sin problem? *(Give your testimony of how Jesus set you free and saved you.)*

---

### Good Works Are Not Enough to Save

Contrary to the works salvation taught by Islam, God has revealed in the Bible that works do not save. The apostle Paul declared, "We maintain that a man is justified by faith apart from observing the law" (Romans 3:28). He further said, "a man is not justified by observing the law, but by faith in Jesus Christ," for "by observing the law no one will be justified" (Galatians 2:16). "It is by grace you have been saved, through faith—and this not from yourselves, it is the gift of God—not by works, so that no one can boast" (Ephesians 2:8-9). God "has saved us and called us to a holy life—not because of anything we have done but because of his own purpose and grace" (2 Timothy 1:9).

Paul, who wrote the above verses under the inspiration of the Holy Spirit, was formerly a Jew who had sought to earn his relationship with God by observing the law, just like any good Jew. But Paul discovered what we must all discover—good works cannot bring one into God's favor, for even our best works fall far short of the magnificent holiness of God. We are told that "no one is good—except God alone" (Mark 10:18). Indeed, "all our righteous deeds are like a filthy garment" (Isaiah 64:6 NASB). Our best efforts fail.

This is not to say that Christians give no place at all to good works in daily life, but these works play no role in our *salvation*. Salvation comes about through faith (Romans 4; Galatians 3:6-14). Good works are a *by-product* of salvation (Matthew 7:15-23; 1 Timothy 5:10,25) and should result from the changed purpose for living that salvation brings (1 Corinthians 3).

Help your Muslim friend understand that, while Islam seeks to take forgetful and feeble people and make them better (by reminding them of Allah's law), Christianity seeks to take *dead* people and make them *spiritually alive* (John 3:1-5,16-17). We are all born into this world spiritually *dead* (separated from God because of sin). By trusting in Christ, we are made spiritually *alive*.

## _____ *Ask...* _____

- Did you know that according to Jesus, our problem is not mere forgetfulness or feebleness, but that we are *spiritually dead,* separated from God because of our sin?

- Would you like to know how to become spiritually alive? *(Share the information found in the rest of this chapter.)*

A good story to share with your Muslim acquaintance is that of the thief on the cross next to Jesus' cross. Jesus promised this thief—who had no chance of going out and doing any good works—that he would be with Jesus that day in paradise (Luke 23:43). Such a story may be welcome news to the Muslim who has spent his life apart from God and who is aware of his shortcomings.

## God's Declaration of Righteousness

The wonderful good news of salvation involves a theological word: *justification*. Justification is a singular and instantaneous event in which God declares the believing sinner to be righteous. Justification viewed in this way is a judicial term in which God makes a *legal declaration*. It is not based on performance of good works. It involves God's pardoning of sinners and declaring them absolutely righteous at the moment they trust in Christ for salvation (Romans 3:25,28,30; 8:33-34; Galatians 4:21–5:12; 1 John 1:7–2:2).

Here is the theological backdrop: Humankind's dilemma of falling short of God's glory (Romans 3:23) points to the need for a solution. Man's sin—his utter unrighteousness—is such that there is no way of his coming into a relationship with God on his own. Humankind is guilty before a holy God, and this guilt of sin puts a barrier between man and God.

The solution is found in justification. Negatively, this word means that one is once-for-all pronounced not guilty before God. Positively, the word means that one is once-for-all pronounced righteous before God. The very righteousness of Christ is imputed ("credited" or "transferred") to the believer's life. From the moment a person places faith in Christ the Savior, God sees that person through the lens of Christ's righteousness.

Note that this declaration is something *external* to humans. It does not hinge on man's personal level of righteousness. It does not hinge on anything man does. It hinges solely on God's declaration. It is a once-for-all judicial pronouncement that takes place the moment a sinner places faith in Christ. Even while the person is still a sinner and is experientially not righteous, he or she is nevertheless righteous *in God's sight* because of justification.

Romans 3:24 tells us that God's "declaration of righteousness" is given to believers "freely by his grace." The word *grace* literally means "unmerited favor." It is because of God's unmerited favor that believers can freely be "declared righteous" before God. This cannot be earned.

A key blessing that results from our being declared righteous is that we now have peace with God (Romans 5:1). The Father sees believers through the lens of Jesus Christ. And because there is peace between the Father and Jesus Christ, there is also peace between the Father and believers, since believers are "in Christ."

If one were to look through a piece of red glass, everything would appear red. If one were to look through a piece of blue glass, everything would appear blue. If one were to look through a piece of yellow glass, everything would appear yellow, and so on. Likewise, when we believe in Jesus Christ as our Savior, God looks at us *through the Lord Jesus Christ*. He sees us in all the pure white holiness of His Son. Our sins are imputed to the account of Christ, and Christ's righteousness is imputed to our account. For this reason, the Scriptures indicate that there is now no condemnation—literally, *no punishment*—for those who are in Christ Jesus (Romans 8:1).

## _____ *Ask...* _____

- May I share with you what it's like to know that all your sins are forgiven? *(Give a brief testimony.)*

- Wouldn't *you* like to be able to know that all your sins have been forgiven? *(Talk about the wonderful doctrine of justification, made possible by Christ's death.)*

---

## An Atonement for Sin Is Absolutely Necessary

God did not just subjectively or arbitrarily decide to overlook man's sin or wink at his unrighteousness. Contrary to the Muslim denial of a need for an atonement, Scripture says an atonement was necessary in order to make justification possible. Jesus died on the cross for us. He died in our stead. He paid for our sins. Jesus *ransomed* us from death by His own death on the cross (2 Corinthians 5:21).

Jesus Himself defines for us the nature of the atonement (if anyone would know, it would be Him). The biblical Jesus taught that His mission was to provide a substitutionary atonement on the cross. By so doing, He provided a salvation for human beings that they had no hope of procuring for themselves. His atonement made justification possible.

Jesus affirmed that it was for the very purpose of dying that He came into the world (John 12:27). Moreover, He indicated that His death was a sacrificial offering for the sins of humanity (He said His blood "is poured out for many for the forgiveness of sins"—Matthew 26:26-28). Jesus took His sacrificial mission with utmost seriousness, for He knew that without Him, humanity would certainly perish (Matthew 16:25; John 3:16) and spend eternity apart from God in a place of great suffering (Matthew 10:28; 11:23; 23:33; 25:41; Luke 16:22-28).

Jesus therefore described His mission this way: "The Son of Man did not come to be served, but to serve, and to give his life as a ransom for many" (Matthew 20:28). "The Son of Man came to seek and to save what was lost" (Luke 19:10), for "God did not send his Son into the world to condemn the world, but to save the world through him" (John 3:17).

In John 10, Jesus compares Himself to a good shepherd who not only gives His life to save the sheep (John 10:11) but lays His life down of His own accord (John 10:18). This is precisely what Jesus did at the cross (Matthew 26:53-54)—He laid His life down to atone for the sins of humanity.

Certainly this is how others perceived His mission. At the beginning of His three-year ministry, when Jesus approached John the Baptist at the Jordan River, John said, "Look, the Lamb of God, who takes away the sin of the world!" (John 1:29). John's portrayal of Christ as the Lamb of God is a graphic affirmation that Jesus Himself would be the sacrifice that would atone for the sins of humanity (see Isaiah 53:4-7).

In Romans 3:25 we read, "God presented him as a sacrifice of atonement." The Greek word for "sacrifice of atonement" is rendered more literally *propitiation*. This word communicates the idea that Jesus' sacrificial death on the cross provided full satisfaction of God's holy demands against a sinful people, thereby averting His just wrath against them (Romans 1:18; 2:5,8; 3:5). Because of this propitiation, we can freely and *justly* be "declared righteous" (that is, justified).

## Illustrating the Need for Atonement

Earlier in the book, I advised that in explaining Jesus' atoning sacrifice, it might be wise to focus attention on Abraham's sacrifice of his son in the Old Testament (Genesis 22). This is so important that it bears repeating. Recall that in the Quran's depiction of this event, we are told that Abraham's son was "ransomed" from death by an animal "sacrifice" (Sura 37:102-7). These are the *same words* that describe what Jesus did at the cross (Matthew 20:28; 1 Corinthians 5:7; 1 Timothy 2:5-6; Hebrews 7:27; 9:15,28).

In view of this, the atoning sacrificial death of Christ is not necessarily un-Quranic. Use Abraham's story as a way of illustrating the need for a sacrifice to take another's place and allow that person to be spared. Jesus as the Lamb of God took *our* place as a sacrifice so that we could be saved (John 1:29,36)! You might want to read through Isaiah 53 with your Muslim friend and emphasize how Jesus' sacrifice benefits us personally—including dealing with our sorrows, our sins, our crimes, our well-being, and our healing!

*Warning:* Do not forget that most Muslims believe it was Ishmael, not Isaac, that was to be sacrificed. For the time being, I would simply avoid this issue and focus the major attention on the issues of sacrifice and ransom.[10] You can correct the minor error on Ishmael later.

## _Ask..._

- According to Sura 37:102-7, wasn't Abraham's son "ransomed" from death by an animal "sacrifice"? Didn't the animal take the son's place?

- Did you know that these two words—"ransom" and "sacrifice"—are the exact words that describe what Jesus did for us at the cross? Can I read you a few verses? *(Read from Matthew 20:28; 1 Corinthians 5:7; 1 Timothy 2:5-6; Hebrews 7:27; 9:15,28.)*

---

## The Marvel of Atonement

It is very important to present what the Bible says about the necessity of the atonement, for in Islam there *is* no atonement, and hence there is *no objective basis for Allah to decide to forgive someone*. Because there is no atonement in Islam, this ultimately means that Allah is being unrighteous and unjust when he arbitrarily decides to forgive someone. Gleason Archer notes that only through the cross could God remain just *and* the justifier of sinners who trust in Jesus. "To suppose that God can righteously forgive without requiring any atonement is to impute immorality to God and make him a protector of sin rather than its condemner."[11]

## _Ask..._

- May I talk to you about how Jesus' death on the cross provides an objective basis for God to forgive the sins of human beings?

---

Christ's work of atonement is marvelous indeed, for it makes possible the forgiveness of sins for all who trust in Him for salvation. Here are just a few wonderful verses that speak of this forgiveness.

- Hebrews 10:17-18—" 'Their sins and lawless acts I will remember no more.' And where these have been forgiven, there is no longer any sacrifice for sin."

- Psalm 32:1-2—"Blessed is he whose transgressions are forgiven, whose sins are covered. Blessed is the man whose sin the LORD does not count against him and in whose spirit is no deceit."

- Ephesians 1:7—"In him we have redemption through his blood, the forgiveness of sins, in accordance with the riches of God's grace."

- Micah 7:19—"You will again have compassion on us; you will tread our sins underfoot and hurl all our iniquities into the depths of the sea."

- Psalm 103:11-12—"As high as the heavens are above the earth, so great is his love for those who fear him; as far as the east is from the west, so far has he removed our transgressions from us."

## *Ask...*

- Wouldn't you like to experience the joy of knowing that all of your sins have been forgiven by God?

- Can I tell you how to receive this forgiveness by believing in Jesus? *(Be ready to share the gospel.)*

---

### Adopted into God's Family

One of the wonderful results of Christ's atonement, provided to us by the grace of God, is that by believing in Jesus Christ we are adopted into God's family. Contrary to the enslavement to sin that leads to fear, the believer has received the "Spirit of sonship" from God (Romans 8:15).

This is significant, for in New Testament times an adopted son enjoyed all the rights and privileges of a natural-born son. Hence, we need not be fearful about approaching God but can boldly approach His throne and say, "Abba, Father" (Romans 8:15). "Abba" is an Aramaic term of affection and intimacy—similar to the English word "daddy."

Believers are also called "God's children" (Romans 8:16). Believers are God's children by the new birth (John 1:12; 1 John 3:1-2). Because of this new relationship with God, believers are called "heirs of God" and "co-heirs with Christ" (Romans 8:17). In a typical family, each child in the family receives a share in the parents' estate. This makes each child an "heir," and the children as a group are "co-heirs." As God's children we are "heirs," and together we are "co-heirs" with Christ (see Galatians 4:7).

Believers inherit "every spiritual blessing in Christ" (Ephesians 1:3). And upon entering glory, believers will inherit all the riches of God's glorious kingdom (1 Corinthians 3:21-23).

Help your Muslim friend understand this wonderful truth. I am aware of Muslims who became Christians precisely because they came to view God as a wonderful heavenly Father who can adopt believers into His eternal family. And all this has been made possible because of Jesus.

## _____ *Ask*... _____

- Did you know the Bible teaches we can actually become a part of God's family and share in an inheritance? May I tell you how? *(Share the gospel.)*

### The Certainty of Salvation

Contrary to Islam's teaching that a Muslim can have no assurance of salvation, the Bible indicates that once a person becomes a part of the family of God by trusting in Christ, he or she is absolutely secure. Scripture affirms this: "These whom He predestined, He also called; and these whom He called, He also justified; and these whom He justified, these He also glorified" (Romans 8:30 NASB). Here there is an unbroken chain of events from predestination to glorification in heaven, and past tenses are used to emphasize the certainty of our final glorification. We are promised that "the gifts and the calling of God are irrevocable" (Romans 11:29 NASB). Scripture declares, "God has given us eternal life, and this life is in His Son. He who has the Son has the life; he who does not have the Son of God does not have the life. These things I have written to you who believe in the name of the Son of God, *so that you may know* that you have eternal life" (1 John 5:11-13 NASB, emphasis added).

Ephesians 4:30 indicates that believers are sealed for the day of redemption by the Holy Spirit (see also Ephesians 1:13). This seal—which indicates ownership, authority, and security—cannot be broken (even by the believer himself). The seal guarantees our entry into heaven. In ancient times, a Roman emperor would seal his letter with wax and then stamp it with his own personal seal. That seal would guarantee that the letter would make it to its final destination. Anyone who opened the letter before it arrived at its destination would be put to death. The believer in Jesus is like a letter destined for heaven, and the Holy Spirit (God Himself) is our "seal," guaranteeing that we will make it to our final destination.

Besides this, we are told that the Father keeps us in His sovereign hands, and no one can take us out of those hands (John 10:28-30). God has us in His firm grip. And that grip will never let us go.

Not only that, but the Lord Jesus Himself continually intercedes and prays for us (Hebrews 7:25). His work of intercession as our divine High Priest is necessary because of our weaknesses, our helplessness, and our immaturity as children of God. He knows our limitations, and He knows the power and the strategy of the foe with whom we have to contend—Satan. He is therefore faithful in making intercession for us—*and His prayers are always answered.*

# 15

## *The Muslim View of the Afterlife*

The Quran speaks about death, resurrection, the future Day of Judgment, heaven, and hell. Though it may not tell us as much as we would like to know on these subjects, there is enough data within its pages to construct a picture of the Muslim expectation about the afterlife.

Foundationally, the Quran recognizes that every human being dies. We read, "Every soul shall have a taste of death" (Sura 3:185). Indeed, at death "the angels stretch forth their hands, (saying), 'Yield up your souls'" (Sura 6:93). Following this, the Muslim faces a future day of resurrection and the judgment, and because there is no assurance of salvation among Muslims, this can be a frightening prospect. The death of unbelievers is especially frightful: "If thou couldst see, when the angels take the souls of the Unbelievers (at death), (How) they smite their faces and their backs, (saying): 'Taste the penalty of the blazing Fire'" (Sura 8:50).

Of course, there is one group of people that is guaranteed direct entrance into paradise (heaven), and that is martyrs who die in the service of Allah. All other believers must await the future day of resurrection. Between death and resurrection, people are in a very deep sleep. One will not know until one awakens on the day of resurrection whether one is to go to hell or to paradise.[1]

## ____ *Ask...* ____

- Are you sure you are going to paradise?

- Can I tell you why I am sure I'm going to heaven, and why it's the most exciting thing in the world to me?

## The Muslim View of Resurrection and Judgment

Muslims believe that Allah will one day resurrect all who have died. The day and the hour are not known to mortals. At the last day, Allah will sound a trumpet, the earth will be split, and the bodies of human beings will rejoin their souls. Allah will recreate each individual's body and rejoin his or her soul to it. In the Quran we read: "See they not that God, who created the heavens and the earth…is able to give life to the dead? Yea, clearly he has the power over all things" (Sura 46:33). While many Muslims believe this to be a physical resurrection, others believe in only a spiritual resurrection.

Following the resurrection, human beings will be judged. They will be face-to-face with Allah and will have to give an account for all their actions. The Quran teaches that "only on the day of judgment shall you be paid your full recompense" (Sura 3:185).

Allah will judge people on the scale of absolute justice. The scale is used to balance one's good deeds against bad deeds. One's good deeds will be placed in one pan of the balance, and evil deeds in the other. If the good deeds are heavier, so that the scale is tipped, the person will go to paradise (subject to Allah's arbitrary decision). If, however, the evil deeds are heavier, he or she will be cast into the fires of hell. The Quran declares, "Then those whose balance (of good deeds) is heavy, they will attain salvation: But those whose balance is light, will be those who have lost their souls, in Hell will they abide" (Sura 23:102-103). This essentially means that one must be at least 51 percent good to get into paradise.[2] This judgment will be based on the records of two recording angels who keep track of one's good and bad deeds throughout one's life.

One Muslim writer describes the route to one's eternal destiny this way: "When the trial of judgment is over, those destined to Hell or Paradise will be made to pass over a narrow bridge to their respective destinations. The bridge is so fashioned that the favored will cross with ease and facility while the condemned will tumble off into Hell."[3]

## The Muslim View of Heaven

The Muslim who makes it to heaven, as a result of his good deeds outweighing his bad deeds, will enjoy a place of unimaginable delight. Heaven is pictured as a beautiful green garden of bliss, with flowing water and shade. Believers receive whatever their hearts desire. Faithful men are even promised the companionship of young and beautiful women. The faithful will lie on soft silken couches, and "will enjoy gentle speech, pleasant shade, and every available fruit, as well as all the cool drink and meat they desire. They will drink from a shining stream of delicious wine, from which they will suffer no intoxicating aftereffects" (Sura 37:45-47). This means the wine of heaven does not disturb one's senses, nor does it leave one with a hangover.

Apparently the Muslim heaven is a place of massive dimensions. We are told there is a tree in paradise so big that a rider can travel in its shade for a hundred years without passing out of it.[4] Muslims can take leisurely walks anywhere in paradise, and on all sides the view is spectacular, including fountains, pavilions, and rivers.[5]

## The Muslim View of Hell

Hell is for those whose evil deeds outweigh their good deeds on the scale of absolute justice. Muslims view hell as a place of unimaginable suffering. It is a place of scalding winds and black smoke.[6] The Quran teaches that there will be "a fierce blast of fire and boiling water, and in the shades of black smoke" (Sura 56:42-43). The boiling water is said to melt one's skin. Then the scorched skin is immediately replaced with new skin so the person can taste the torment of hell anew. The Quran says, "When they are cast, bound together, into a constricted place therein, they will plead for destruction there and then" (Sura 25:13). The person suffering such a destiny can neither escape nor perish.[7] While some Muslims interpret the horrible descriptions of hell spiritually, the majority take them quite literally.[8]

Some Muslims view hell as a kind of Islamic purgatory. They believe Muslims will have to spend time in hell to pay for their sins before being granted the privilege of entering paradise. The amount of time each Muslim must stay in hell depends on the gravity and degree to which he or she has sinned. It is believed that one group of people that will remain in hell forever are religious hypocrites, that is, people who claim to be Muslim but are not.[9] Phil Parshall reports that "hypocrisy carries with it an extreme penalty. With intestines protruding outward, the sinner is made to go around hell confessing to people that he held to a double standard in life."[10]

Some Muslim traditions allude to the voices of dead people that one can hear as one walks through a cemetery. The dead are said to be crying out in torment as a result of their suffering in hell. In one tradition, we read that a person is being punished in hell because he neglected to engage in ritual cleansing following urination. Muhammad categorized this as a major sin.[11] This reflects the strict legalism of Islam.

# THE CHRISTIAN VIEW OF THE AFTERLIFE

In your discussions with Muslims, the doctrine of the afterlife is not nearly as important as the doctrines of the Bible, God, Jesus, and the gospel of salvation. I recommend that you spend most of your time talking about these other issues. However, should the issue of the afterlife come up, it is important that you have a good working knowledge of what the Bible teaches on the subject. The following summary should prove helpful.

## The Christian View of Judgment

Though there are some similarities between the Muslim and Christian views of the afterlife, there are notable differences as well. One key difference is that Muslims believe the purpose of the judgment is to determine whether or not a person is saved, and following that determination, the person is sent to either heaven or hell. The Christian view is that a person's destiny is settled in God's mind *before* the judgment, for He knows who has and who has not trusted in Christ. (Scripture indicates that the spirits of believers go straight to heaven at death—see 2 Cor-inthians 5:8—while the spirits of nonbelievers go to a place of suffering—see Luke 16:19-31. Both await the future resurrection.) Further, the Bible teaches there are *two* judgments that will take place in the future—the judgment of believers at the judgment seat of Christ, and the judgment of nonbelievers at the Great White Throne judgment.

Another distinction relates to the God one will face at the judgment. In the Christian view, people will face a God whose attributes are absolutely consistent; that is to say, the Christian God is consistently holy (Leviticus 19:2). He is always pure in every way and is separate from all that is morally imperfect. He is also portrayed as *singularly* good, just, and righteous (1 John 1:5; Habakkuk 1:13; Matthew 5:48). The God of the Bible abhors evil, does not create moral evil, and does not lead men astray.

By contrast, the Muslim must face a God (Allah) who sometimes does good and other times evil, who sometimes shows mercy and other times cruelty. There is no absolute standard of righteousness to which Allah himself must adhere. As John Elder explains it, "Right is what Allah commands at a given time; wrong is that which He forbids at a given time. And what He commands at one time, He may forbid at another."[12] For example, as we saw earlier, Muhammad recorded certain revelations in the Quran from Allah which were considered final truth, only to have those revelations abrogated by other revelations from Allah later on.

The prospect of appearing before such an arbitrary God leaves one with a sense of profound uncertainty regarding one's future prospects. Indeed, as Elder notes, "if Allah is not bound to consistently act righteously, there can be no certainty as to what He may decide to do on the Judgment Day. Allah's sovereignty allows Him to make decisions that may seem inconsistent and arbitrary in man's view."[13]

## *Ask...*

- If Allah can sometimes do good and sometimes do evil, doesn't this mean there can be no certainty as to what he may decide to do with you on the Day of Judgment?

- Can I share with you my hope for the afterlife? *(Share material from below.)*

In what follows, I will briefly describe what the Bible says about both the judgment of Christians and the judgment of non-believers. If you share this information with your Muslim acquaintance—and he is an objective person—he will see that the Christian view involves a *righteous* and *just* judgment—one completely void of arbitrariness.

## The Judgment of Christians

All believers will one day stand before the judgment seat of Christ (Romans 14:8-12). At that time each believer's life will be examined in regard to deeds done while in the body. Personal motives and intents of the heart will also be weighed.

The idea of a "judgment seat" relates to the athletic games of Paul's day. When the races and games were over, a dignitary or perhaps the emperor himself would take a seat on an elevated throne in the arena. Then one by one the winning athletes would come up to the throne to receive a reward—usually a wreath of leaves, a victor's crown.[14]

In the case of Christians, each of us will stand before Christ the Judge and receive (or lose) rewards. Christ's judgment of us will not be in a corporate setting—like a big class being praised or scolded by a teacher. Rather it will be individual and personal. "We will all stand before God's judgment seat" (Romans 14:10). Each of us will be judged on an individual basis.

This judgment has nothing to do with whether or not the Christian will remain saved. Those who have placed faith in Christ are *saved*, and nothing threatens that. Believers are eternally secure in their salvation (Romans 8:30; Ephesians 4:30). This judgment rather has to do with the receiving or loss of rewards.

Scripture indicates that some believers at the judgment may have a sense of deprivation and suffer some degree of forfeiture and shame. Indeed, certain rewards may be forfeited that otherwise might have been received, and this will involve a sense of loss. The fact is, Christians differ radically in holiness of conduct and faithfulness in service. God in His justice and holiness takes all this into account. For this reason, 2 John 8 warns us, "Watch out that you do not lose what you have worked for, but that you may be rewarded fully." In 1 John 2:28 John wrote about the possibility of a believer actually being ashamed at Christ's coming.

We must keep all this in perspective, however. The prospect of living eternally with Christ in heaven is something that should give each of us joy. And our joy will last for all eternity. How, then, can we reconcile this eternal joy with the possible loss of reward and perhaps even some level of shame at the judgment seat of Christ? I think Herman Hoyt's explanation is the best I have seen:

> The Judgment Seat of Christ might be compared to a commencement ceremony. At graduation there is some measure of disappointment and remorse that one did not do better and work harder. However, at such an event the over-whelming emotion is joy, not remorse. The grad-uates do not leave the auditorium weeping because they did not earn better grades. Rather, they are thankful that they have been graduated, and they are grateful for what they did achieve. To overdo the sorrow aspect of the Judgment Seat of Christ is to make heaven hell. To underdo the sorrow aspect is to make faithfulness incon-sequential.[15]

## On What Basis Will Christians Be Judged?

First Corinthians 3:11-15 describes the believer's future judg-ment in terms of what kinds of "building materials" he has used throughout life:

> No one can lay any foundation other than the one already laid, which is Jesus Christ. If any man builds on this foundation using gold, silver, costly stones, wood, hay or straw, his work will be shown for what it is, because the Day will bring it to light. It will be revealed with fire, and the fire will test the quality of each man's work. If what he has built survives, he will receive his reward. If it is burned up, he will suffer loss; he himself will be saved, but only as one escaping through the flames.

Notice that the materials Paul mentions in this passage are combustible in increasing degrees. Obviously the hay and straw are the most combustible. Then comes wood. Precious metals and stones are not combustible.

It also seems clear that some of these materials are useful for building while others are not. If you construct a house made of hay or straw, it surely will not stand long. But a house constructed with solid materials such as stones and metals will stand and last a long time.

What do these building materials represent? Pastor Douglas Connelly insightfully suggests that "gold, silver, and costly stones refer to the fruit of the Spirit in our lives; they refer to Christ-honoring motives and godly obedience and transparent integrity. Wood, hay, and straw are perishable things—carnal attitudes, sinful motives, pride-filled actions, selfish ambition."[16]

It is noteworthy that fire in Scripture often symbolizes the holiness of God (Hebrews 12:29). And there are clear cases in the Bible in which fire portrays God's judgment upon that which His holiness has condemned (Genesis 19:24; Mark 9:43-48). God, then, will examine our works, and they will be tested against the fire of His holiness. If our works are built with good materials—like precious metals and stones—our works will stand. But if our works are built with less valuable materials—wood, hay, or straw—they will burn up.

***The scope of the judgment includes actions.*** The Christian's judgment will focus on his personal stewardship of the gifts, talents, opportunities, and responsibilities given to him in this life. The true character of each Christian's life and service will be utterly laid bare under the unerring and omniscient vision of Christ, whose "eyes [are] like a flame of fire" (Revelation 1:14 NASB).

Numerous Scripture verses reveal that each of our actions will be judged before the Lord. The psalmist said to the Lord, "Surely you will reward each person according to what he has done" (Psalm 62:12; compare with Matthew 16:27). In Ephesians 6:7-8 we read that the Lord "will reward everyone for whatever good he does, whether he is slave or free."

Christ's judgment of our actions will be infallible. There will be no confusion on His part. His understanding of the circumstances under which we committed acts on earth will be complete. As John Wesley once put it, "God will then bring to light every circumstance that accompanied each word and action. He will judge whether they lessened or increased the goodness or badness of them."[17]

***The scope of the judgment includes thoughts.*** At the judgment seat of Christ, it will not just be our actions that will come under scrutiny. Also scrutinized will be our thoughts. In Jeremiah 17:10 God said, "I the LORD search the heart and examine the mind, to reward a man according to his conduct, according to what his deeds deserve." The Lord "will bring to light what is hidden in darkness and will expose the motives of men's hearts" (1 Corinthians 4:5). The Lord is the One "who searches hearts and minds" (Revelation 2:23).

***The scope of the judgment includes words.*** Christ once said that "men will have to give account on the day of judgment for every careless word they have spoken" (Matthew 12:35-37). This is an important aspect of judgment, for tremendous damage can be done through the human tongue (see James 3:1-12).

John Blanchard reminds us that "if even our careless words are carefully recorded, how can we bear the thought that our calculated boastful claims, the cutting criticisms, the off-color jokes, and the unkind comments will also be taken into account. Even our whispered asides and words spoken in confidence or when we thought we were 'safe' will be heard again."[18]

## Rewards and Crowns

What kinds of rewards will believers receive at the judgment seat of Christ? Scripture often speaks of them in terms of crowns that we wear. In fact, there are a number of different crowns that

The Muslim View of the Afterlife • 265

symbolize the various spheres of achievement and award in the Christian life.

The crown of life is given to those who persevere under trial, and especially to those who suffer to the point of death (James 1:12; Revelation 2:10). The crown of glory is given to those who faithfully and sacrificially minister God's Word to the flock (1 Peter 5:4). The incorruptible crown is given to those who win the race of temperance and self-control (1 Corinthians 9:25). The crown of righteousness is given to those who long for the second coming of Christ (2 Timothy 4:8).

It is highly revealing that in Revelation 4:10 we find believers casting their crowns before the throne of God in an act of worship and adoration. This teaches us something very important. Clearly the crowns (as rewards) are bestowed on us not for our own glory but ultimately for the glory of God. We are told elsewhere in Scripture that believers are redeemed in order to bring glory to God (1 Corinthians 6:20). It seems that the act of placing our crowns before the throne of God is an illustration of this.

Here is something else to think about. The greater reward or crown one has received, the greater capacity one has to bring glory to the Creator. The lesser reward or crown one has received, the lesser is that person's capacity to bring glory to the Creator. Because of the different rewards handed out at the judgment seat of Christ, believers will have differing capacities to bring glory to God.

Still, we should not take this to mean that certain believers will have a sense of lack throughout eternity. After all, each believer will be glorifying God to the fullness of his capacity in the next life. Each one of us, then, will be able to "declare the praises of him who called [us] out of darkness into his wonderful light" (1 Peter 2:9).[19]

## _____ *Ask...* _____

- Doesn't Islam teach that a person goes to paradise if his good deeds outweigh his bad deeds on the scale of absolute justice?

- Are you sure your good deeds outweigh all your bad deeds?

- Would you be interested in hearing about a way you can be 100-percent good and be *assured* of heaven? *(Talk to them about how those who trust in Jesus have their "slate wiped clean" of all sins, and how Christ's own righteousness is imputed to them. See chapter 14.)*

---

### The Judgment of Nonbelievers

Unlike believers, whose judgment deals only with rewards and loss of rewards, nonbelievers face a horrific judgment that leads to their being cast into the Lake of Fire. The judgment that nonbelievers face is called the Great White Throne judgment (Revelation 20:11-15). Christ is the divine Judge, and those that are judged are the unsaved dead of all time. The judgment takes place at the end of the millennial kingdom, Christ's 1000-year reign on planet Earth.

Those who face Christ at this judgment will be judged on the basis of their works (Revelation 20:12-13). It is critical to understand that they actually get to this judgment because they are *already unsaved.* This judgment will not separate believers from unbelievers, for all who will experience it will have already made the choice during their lifetimes to reject salvation in Jesus Christ. Once they are before the divine Judge, they will be judged according to their works, not only to justify their condemnation, but also to determine the degree to which each person should be punished throughout eternity.

## Resurrected to Judgment

Those who participate in the Great White Throne judgment are resurrected to condemnation. Jesus Himself declared that "a time is coming when all who are in their graves will hear his voice and come out—those who have done good will rise to live, and those who have done evil will rise to be condemned" (John 5:28-29).

We need to emphasize, though, that Jesus is not teaching that there is just one general resurrection that will take place at the end of time. Contrary to this idea, the Scriptures indicate that there are two types of resurrection—respectively referred to as the "first resurrection" and the "second resurrection" (Revelation 20:5-6,11-15). The first resurrection is the resurrection of Christians, while the second resurrection is the resurrection of the wicked.

The second resurrection is an awful spectacle. Unsaved human beings will be given bodies that will last forever, which means they will be subject to pain and suffering forever.

## Degrees of Punishment

The Scriptures indicate that all those who are judged at the Great White Throne judgment have a horrible destiny ahead. Indeed, their common destiny will involve weeping and gnashing of teeth (Matthew 13:41-42), condemnation (Matthew 12:36-37), destruction (Philippians 1:28), eternal punishment (Matthew 25:46), separation from God's presence (2 Thessalonians 1:8-9), and trouble and distress (Romans 2:9).

Common observation shows that unsaved people vary as much in their quality of life as saved people do. Some saved people are spiritual and charitable (for example), and other saved people are carnal and unloving. Some unbelievers are terribly evil (like Hitler), while others—such as unbelieving moralists—are much less evil.

Just as believers differ in how they respond to God's law, and hence in their reward in heaven, so unbelievers differ in their response to God's law, and hence in their punishment in hell. Just as there are degrees of reward in heaven, so there are degrees of punishment in hell (see Luke 12:47-48; Matthew 10:15; 16:27; Revelation 20:12-13; 22:12). And these degrees of punishment will be determined at the Great White Throne judgment when Christ examines each person with His penetrating eyes.

## Judgment—A Final Comparison

What we can conclude, then, is that the Muslim view of judgment is wrong on three primary counts:

1. The Muslim view is incorrect in arguing that the purpose of the judgment is to determine whether or not one is saved.

2. The Muslim view is incorrect in arguing that there is only one general judgment, for Scripture indicates there is one judgment for Christians (the judgment seat of Christ) and another judgment for nonbelievers (the Great White Throne judgment).

3. The Muslim view is incorrect in that it declares that God (Allah) has no absolute standard of righteousness in judging, which means he may arbitrarily decide to save some and damn others.

## The Christian View of Heaven

The primary disagreement Christians have with the Muslim view of heaven is that it is portrayed as a sensual place of pleasure, where each faithful man can have 72 beautiful maidens at his disposal and eat and drink and enjoy full bodily satisfaction. Certainly heaven will *not* be a place where each man will have 72 beautiful maidens. Foundationally, such a view clearly goes against the entire thrust of Scripture, in which God reveals that His standard for the human race is and always has been monogamy (Genesis 1:27; 2:21-25; Deuteronomy 17:17; Matthew 19:4-5; 1 Corinthians 7:2; 1 Timothy 3:2,12).

Besides, in heaven this is not even an issue, for Jesus in Matthew 22:30 taught, "At the resurrection people will neither marry nor be given in marriage; they will be like the angels in heaven." The context here indicates that once believers receive their glorified resurrection bodies, the need for procreation (one of the fundamental purposes for marriage) will no longer exist. We will be "like" the angels in the sense that we will not be married and will not procreate any longer. (Angels do not procreate and reproduce.) The idea that the faithful will have sex in heaven for pure pleasure is not a view that is reflected in Scripture.

It is beyond the scope of this chapter to provide a full description of heaven and the many blessings that accompany life there. But a look at just a few key aspects of heaven is enough to show that it is not a place designed to provide sensual pleasure.

***Paradise.*** I purposefully begin my discussion with the fact that the Christian Bible sometimes uses the word "paradise" to describe heaven, though it does not mean what Muslims mean by the term. The word paradise literally means "garden of pleasure" or "garden of delight." Revelation 2:7 makes reference to heaven as the "paradise of God." The apostle Paul in 2 Corinthians 12:4 said he "was caught up to paradise" and "heard inexpressible things, things that man is not permitted to tell." Yet nowhere are we told that this "garden of delight" is a place where sensual pleasure abounds with 72 beautiful maidens at the disposal of each man. Biblically, the primary reason existence in heaven will be so delightful is that God Himself is there, Satan will be barred from there, and virtually no sin will be there. *Life will be perfect!* Who can deny that one reason for the pleasures of heaven is direct access to God? Psalm 16:11 says, "You will fill me with joy in your presence, with eternal pleasures at your right hand."

# _____ *Ask...* _____

- Did you know that the Bible teaches that a primary reason heaven is so delightful is that God will be there? Since the

Quran speaks approvingly of the psalms of David, can I read to you from Psalm 16:11?

• Can I talk to you about how you can be absolutely sure of going to this delightful place? *(Share the gospel of Jesus Christ.)*

---

***A holy city.*** In Revelation 21:1-2 we find heaven described as "the Holy City." This is a fitting description. Indeed, in this city there will be no sin or unrighteousness of any kind. Only the pure of heart will dwell there. This does not mean you and I must personally attain moral perfection in order to dwell there. Those of us who believe in Christ have been given the very righteousness of Christ. Because of what Christ accomplished for us at the cross (taking our sins upon Himself), we have been made holy (Hebrews 10:14). Hence, we will have the privilege of living for all eternity in the holy city.

***The home of righteousness.*** Second Peter 3:13 tells us that "in keeping with his promise we are looking forward to a new heaven and a new earth, the home of righteousness." Heaven will be the home of righteousness. It will therefore be a perfect living environment for those who have been made righteous by Christ. During our earthly lives, we have to lock up our houses; we fear the possibility of intruders breaking in. There is so much unrighteousness.

***The absence of death.*** The Old Testament promises that in the heavenly state death will be swallowed up forever (Isaiah 25:8). Paul speaks of this same reality as it relates to the future resurrection: "When the perishable has been clothed with the imperishable, and the mortal with immortality, then the saying that is written will come true: 'Death has been swallowed up in victory'" (1 Corinthians 15:54). Revelation 21:4 tells us that God "will wipe every tear from their eyes. There will be no more death or mourning or crying or pain, for the old order of things has passed away." Death will be gone and done away with, never again to be faced by those who dwell in heaven. Life in the eternal city will be painless, tearless, and deathless.

## _____ *Ask...* _____

- Do you ever fear death?

- Can I talk to you about how Jesus has forever taken the sting out of death for those who believe in Him? *(Share that the Bible promises eternal life in heaven for all who trust in Christ.)*

---

***Intimate fellowship with God and Christ.*** Can there be anything more sublime and more utterly satisfying for the Christian than to enjoy the sheer delight of unbroken fellowship with God, and have immediate and completely unobstructed access to the divine glory (John 14:3; 2 Corinthians 5:6-8; Philippians 1:23; 1 Thessalonians 4:17)? We shall see him "face to face," as it were, in all His splendor and glory. We will gaze upon His countenance, and behold His resplendent beauty forever.

Surely there can be no greater joy or exhilarating thrill for the creature than to look upon the face of the divine Creator and fellowship with Him forever. He "who alone possesses immortality and dwells in unapproachable light" (1 Timothy 6:16 NASB) will reside intimately among His own, and "they shall be His people, and God Himself will be among them" (Revelation 21:3 NASB).

In the afterlife there will no longer be intermittent fellowship with the Lord, blighted by sin and defeat. Instead, there will be continuous fellowship. Spiritual death will never again cause human beings to lose fellowship with God because, for believers, the sin problem will no longer exist.

*Reunion with Christian loved ones.* One of the most glorious aspects of our lives in heaven is that we will be reunited with Christian loved ones (see 1 Thessalonians 4:13-17). This is something to truly look forward to.

*Satisfaction of all needs.* In our present life on earth, there are times when we go hungry and thirsty. There are times when our needs are not met. But in the eternal state God will abundantly meet each and every need. As we read in Revelation 7:16-17, "Never again will they hunger; never again will they thirst. The sun will not beat upon them, nor any scorching heat. For the Lamb at the center of the throne will be their shepherd; he will lead them to springs of living water. And God will wipe away every tear from their eyes."

*Serene rest.* The Scriptures indicate that a key feature of heavenly life is rest (Revelation 14:13). No more deadlines to work toward. No more overtime work in order to make ends meet. No more breaking one's back. Just rest. Sweet serene rest. And our rest will be especially sweet since it is ultimately a rest in the very presence of God, who meets our every need.

*Sharing in Christ's glory.* The Scriptures indicate that in the heavenly state believers will actually share in the glory of Christ. Romans 8:17 tells us, "If we are children, then we are heirs—heirs of God and co-heirs with Christ, if indeed we share in his sufferings in order that we may also share in his glory." Likewise, Colossians 3:4 informs us that "when Christ, who is your life, appears, then you also will appear with him in glory." This, of course, does not mean that we become deity. But it does mean you and I as Christians will be in a state of glory, sharing in Christ's glory wholly because of what Christ has accomplished for us. We will have glorious resurrection bodies and be clothed with shining robes of immortality, incorruption, and splendor.

*Praise and worship of God and Christ.* The book of Revelation portrays believers in the eternal state as offering worship and praise before the throne of God and Christ. In Revelation 7:9-10, for example, we read of a great multitude of believers before God's throne crying out, "Salvation belongs to our God, who sits on the throne, and to the Lamb." Revelation 19:1-6 portrays a great multitude of believers shouting out "Hallelujah" before God's throne. This is one activity that redeemed human beings and angels will join together in doing. The worship that takes place in heaven will be ultimately fulfilling.

*The serving of God and Christ.* Another activity that will occupy us in the eternal state will be the perpetual serving of God and Christ. This will not be a tedious kind of service but a joyous one—fully meeting our heart's every desire (Revelation 1:5-6; see also 22:3). There will be no boredom in eternity. Because we will be servants of the Most High, and because there will be an endless variety of tasks to perform, the prospect of heaven is entrancingly attractive.

*The learning of more about our incomparable God.* Apparently we will be able to grow in knowledge in our heavenly existence. Throughout future ages believers will be shown "the incomparable riches of his grace" (Ephesians 2:7). Though our capacity for knowledge and our actual intelligence will be greatly increased, we will not be omniscient (all-knowing). Only God is omniscient. We will maintain our capacity to learn. This means that we will never get bored in heaven. God is so infinite—with matchless perfections that are beyond us in every way—that we will never come to the end of exploring Him and His marvelous riches.

## The Christian View of Hell

Hell is as awful as heaven is wonderful. The Scriptures assure us that hell is a real place. But hell was not part of God's original creation, which He called "good" (Genesis 1). Hell was created later to accommodate the banishment of Satan and his fallen angels, who rebelled against God (Matthew 25:41). Human beings who reject Christ will join Satan and his fallen angels in this infernal place of suffering.

One of the more important New Testament words for hell is "Gehenna" (Matthew 10:28). This word has an interesting history. For several generations in ancient Israel, atrocities were committed in the Valley of Ben Hinnom—atrocities that included human sacrifices, even the sacrifice of children (2 Chronicles 28:3; 33:6; Jeremiah 32:35). These unfortunate victims were sacrificed to the false Moabite god Molech. Jeremiah appropriately called this valley a "valley of slaughter" (Jeremiah 7:31-34).

Eventually the valley came to be used as a public rubbish dump into which all the filth of Jerusalem was poured. Not only garbage, but also the bodies of dead animals and the corpses of criminals were throne on the heap, where they—like everything else in the dump—would perpetually burn. The valley was a place where the fires never stopped burning. And there was always a good meal for a hungry worm.

This place was originally called (in the Hebrew) *Ge[gen] hinnom* (the valley of the sons of Hinnom). It was eventually shortened to the name *Ge-Hinnom*. The Greek transliteration of this Hebrew phrase is "Gehenna." It became an appropriate and graphic term for the reality of hell. Jesus Himself used the word 11 times as a metaphorical way of describing the eternal place of suffering of unredeemed humanity.

The Scriptures use a variety of words to describe the horrors of hell—including fire, fiery furnace, unquenchable fire, the lake of burning sulfur, the Lake of Fire, everlasting contempt, perdition, the place of weeping and gnashing of teeth, eternal punishment, darkness, the wrath to come, exclusion, torments, damnation, condemnation, retribution, woe, and the second death. Hell is a horrible destiny (see Matthew 13:42; 18:8; 25:41; Jude 7; Revelation 14:10; 19:20; 20:10).

One issue Christians take exception to in the Muslim view is the idea that people keep getting new skin so they can suffer the horrors of hell anew. Scripture is clear that unbelievers receive a permanent (nondissolving) resurrection body just as believers do, but they will spend eternity in their resurrection bodies suffering in hell (see Revelation 20:5-6,11-15). No "new skin" will be necessary.

But unquestionably the greatest pain suffered by those in hell is not the physical pain but the fact that they are forever excluded from the presence of God. If ecstatic joy is found in the presence of God (Psalm 16:11), then infinite heartache and utter disillusionment is found in the absence of His presence.

## _____ *Ask...* _____

- Do you know who has told us more about hell than anyone else in the Bible? *(It was Jesus!)*

- Can I talk to you about what Jesus said in regard to escaping a destiny in hell? *(Share the gospel.)*

### Conclusion

How heartbreaking it is that there are Muslims who die every day, hoping that Allah might have mercy on them and bring them to paradise. The reality is that to believe in Allah is to believe in a false god. To believe that submission to Allah brings salvation is to believe in a false gospel.

If we Christians really believe heaven is as wonderful as the Bible describes it, then shouldn't that be motivation enough for each of us to share this wonderful good news with our Muslim acquaintances?

# 16

## *Tips for Evangelizing Among Muslims*

In chapter 1 of this book, I provided some introductory tips on dialoguing with Muslims. In subsequent chapters I provided information about some of the key features of Islam, including Muhammad, the Quran, Allah, sin, salvation, and Jesus Christ. In this concluding chapter, I offer some witnessing tips to keep in mind as you share some of the information found in this book. You might consider this final chapter a list of do's and don'ts regarding witnessing to Muslims.

### Be Humble

First and foremost, be humble in your encounters with Muslims. Do not have a "spiritual chip" on your shoulder and talk down to a Muslim. This kind of attitude will erect an unnecessary barrier. Muslims will resent any kind of implied superiority. As Scripture says, we are to be clothed with humility (Colossians 3:12).

### Be Loving

In witnessing to Muslims, Christians should do all they can to let the love of Christ shine through them (see Ephesians 5:2;

1 Timothy 4:12; 1 Corinthians 16:14). William M. Miller, well experienced in witnessing to Muslims, observes that many Muslims who have converted to Christianity say the thing that got their attention is the Christlike love of Christians.[1] John Gilchrist, another man who has broad experience in witnessing to Muslims, provides a great illustration for the need for a loving approach:

> The sun and the wind were said to have had an argument one day. The wind mocked the sun for its inability to move around as and where it wished. The sun responded by pointing out a man who was dressed in a suit walking down a road and called on the wind, if it was so powerful, to get the jacket off the man. The more the wind blew on him, however, the more tightly the man pulled the jacket around himself. When the sun poured its warm rays upon the man, however, the man began to sweat and removed the jacket himself. I have no doubt that Muslims likewise will respond more readily to the warm rays of Christian love and compassion than the cold blasts of militancy.[2]

Do not consider the Muslim an enemy to be conquered, but rather a person to be loved. Let your love be genuine and embracing. People can sense if you truly care about them, as opposed to merely *acting* like you care only because you want to convert them. Pray that the Holy Spirit would fill your heart with love that shows itself in meaningful ways to your Muslim acquaintances. This kind of love is sacrificial and self-giving, and involves showing hospitality to people.

## Learn As Much As You Can About Islam

The Christian who seeks to witness to Muslims should learn as much about Islam as possible. He or she should learn something of the history of Muhammad, the doctrines taught in the Quran, and the practices Muslims engage in. (The book you are holding in your hands will help you here.) A Christian also ought to read at least the first two chapters of the Quran so he can honestly say he has read part of the Quran.

Only when a Christian understands some of these factors will he or she be able to intelligently share the gospel of Christ with a Muslim. Such an understanding of Islam will also help one avoid misunderstandings with a Muslim. For example, the informed Christian will not call Jesus the "Son of God" without making the qualification that this is not intended to be taken in the sense of the Father having a sexual partner, but rather is a figurative expression that describes the eternal relationship between the Father and Jesus. Another example relates to a question a Muslim might ask you: "Do you believe in the prophets?" If you simply say "yes" without qualifying your answer, he will think you believe in the 124,000 prophets who Muslims believe Allah sent into the world at different times in history.[3]

Muslims will respect you for going to the trouble of learning about Islam. They will take you much more seriously if you have done this.

## Avoid a Critical Approach

As I noted earlier in the book, it is not wise to start off your conversation with a Muslim by criticizing Muhammad, Allah, or the Quran. Coming right out and saying that Muhammad is a false prophet who spoke of a false God will only serve to close the Muslim's mind and create a huge barrier. Your conversation will essentially be over if you start out by saying bad things about someone (or something) they have revered their *entire life*. You may win an argument but lose a friend. Especially early on in your discussions, it is better to focus attention on a positive presentation of the Bible, Jesus, and His gospel of grace.[4] However, as your relationship develops and you grow to trust each other's motives, and as you become more comfortable with each other, *then* you can start to tactfully and gracefully focus attention on concerns you have about Muhammad, the Quran, and other Islamic distinctives.

## Quote from the Bible

Do not hesitate to quote from the Bible. Remember, "Faith comes from hearing, and hearing by the Word of Christ" (Romans 10:17 NASB). The psalmist affirmed, "The unfolding of your words gives light; it gives understanding to the simple" (Psalm 119:130). If you plant the seed of the Word of God in good soil (an open-minded Muslim), you may soon be seeing some fruit! (As a practical matter, I advise using an easy-to-understand Bible translation when witnessing.)

As you share from the Bible, pray that the Holy Spirit will bear witness to the truth of God's Word in your acquaintance's heart (1 Corinthians 2:9-12). It is likely that as you cite certain verses you will have to explain what the verses mean. *Be ready for this.* Also keep in mind that because of cultural differences, it is better for men to help men understand the Bible, and women to help women.

Be sure to show a high level of respect for your Bible. As I pointed out earlier in the book, Muslims show great respect for the Quran by not placing anything on top of it and by keeping it in the highest place in the house. So do not throw your Bible under your chair after you finish sharing. Also note that Muslims do not write in the Quran, so when you share from the Bible, you might want to use one you haven't written in. (They might consider writing in the Bible disrespectful.)

If they argue that the Bible has been corrupted, be ready to demonstrate why you trust the Bible's accuracy (see chapters 12 and 13).

## Ask Your Muslim Friend to Read One of the Gospels

If you can afford it, give your Muslim acquaintance a copy of the New Testament and ask him or her to read through one of the Gospels. Each of the Gospels is good for a different purpose. A great "first" Gospel for your Muslim friend to read is the Gospel of Luke. This Gospel already contains themes the Muslim is familiar with, such as the angel's announcement to Mary that she would bear Jesus and the birth of John the Baptist. Such familiar ground may help put the Muslim at ease.[5]

Another great thing about Luke's Gospel is that it contains many interesting stories and parables—*and Muslims love stories!* The story of Jesus calling Levi shows that Jesus accepts people who are considered the worst of sinners (Luke 5:27-31). The parable of the lost sheep shows how God rejoices when a sinner repents, and how God is the initiator in bringing lost people to Himself (Luke 15:1-7). The parable of the lost coin shows how God seeks sinners and rejoices when they turn to Him (Luke 15:8-10). The parable of the prodigal son demonstrates how wide open God's arms are to those who err and then come to Him (Luke 15:11-24).[6] Such stories will be highly meaningful to a Muslim.

Matthew's Gospel may also have a strong appeal to Muslims because of some of the themes it addresses—including ritual prayer, fasting, almsgiving, social justice, marriage, divorce, and the like. Understanding what Jesus says about these issues may strike a chord in their hearts.

The Gospel of John is great for focusing on Jesus' deity. After requesting your Muslim acquaintance to read this Gospel, tell him or her that you would be interested in meeting again to talk about what it says about Jesus. When you meet later to discuss the book, focus special attention on some of the "I am" statements of Jesus (see John 6:35; 8:12; 10:9,11; 11:25,26; 14:6; and 15:5). This will help your Muslim acquaintance see that Jesus was more than a prophet—that He was, in fact, God. Talk about the meaning of Jesus' words in John 8:58: "I tell you the truth…before Abraham was born, I am!" Share that Exodus 3:14 tells us that God's name is "I am."[7]

## Emphasize the Love of God

God is not just characterized *by* love. He is the very personi-fication of love (1 John 4:8). One of the wonderful teachings of the New Testament is that "God demonstrates his own love for us in this: While we were still sinners, Christ died for us" (Romans 5:8). "This is how we know what love is: Jesus Christ laid down his life for us" (1 John 3:16). Muslims desperately need to understand that God is not angry with them but is full of love for them. One Muslim who converted to Christianity writes,

> There is much fear in Islam because God is not recognized as a loving father. Once the Muslim has a real taste of the divine love of God the Father, all his fear will vanish, and he will be ready to be introduced to the salvation available for him through Jesus Christ—God the son.[8]

Understanding the true love of God will be quite a contrast for the Muslim, for he is used to a distant and transcendent deity known as Allah, who can arbitrarily show love and mercy to some and cruelty to others. You will especially want to emphasize that God loves us *while we are still sinners* (Romans 5:8), for the Quran teaches that Allah loves *only* those who are obedient to him.

## Emphasize God's Wonderful Grace

Since Muslims believe in a works-oriented salvation, share with them what the Bible says about this. Romans 3:20 tells us that "no one will be declared righteous in his [God's] sight by observing the law; rather, through the law we become conscious of sin." Emphasize the grace of God: "It is by grace you have been saved, through faith—and this not from yourselves, it is the gift of God—not by works, so that no one can boast" (Ephesians 2:8-9).

Try to show the futility of trying to live a life good enough to earn God's favor. According to the Bible, even the smallest failure brings condemnation ("Whoever keeps the whole law and yet stumbles in one point, he has become guilty of all"—James 2:10 NASB). This is why God's grace is so wonderful.

## Christianity Involves a Relationship, Not a Religion

Help your Muslim friend understand that Christianity is not just a religion but rather involves a personal relationship with Jesus Christ. This relationship begins the moment one places faith in Him for salvation (Acts 16:31). When one believes in Jesus (John 3:16), an *eternal* relationship with Him begins. (It is "eternal" because it lasts the rest of one's life on earth and then continues forever in heaven after one dies.) It is a blessed relationship in which the Christian has the profound privilege of spiritually walking with Jesus on a daily basis, trusting Him to meet each and every need.

## Give Your Testimony

Be sure to give your testimony about how Jesus has changed your life forever (see 1 John 1:3). Giving your personal story of what the Lord Jesus has done in your life is a very important component of any witnessing encounter (see 1 Chronicles 16:8,9; Matthew 10:32; Mark 5:19-20; John 4:28-30,39; 2 Timothy 1:8; 1 Peter 3:15).

Talk about the full assurance you have that your sins are forgiven and the joyful expectation of spending all eternity with Jesus. Speak with joy and enthusiasm about how God has changed your life, and that without His wonderful grace you would be lost forever and unable to manage by yourself. Remember, you may not be an expert on every verse in the Bible, but you are an expert on what Jesus has done in your life!

## Urge Consideration of Jesus' Truth-Claims

The Quran enjoins every true Muslim to believe in and honor all the prophets of God (Sura 2:136). Therefore, urge the Muslim to consider Jesus Christ. Focus on who Jesus is, what claims He made, and the significance of His death and resurrection from the dead (1 Corinthians 15:1-8).

Allow me to repeat again that one good way to talk about the sacrificial nature of Jesus' death on the cross is to talk about the story of Abraham and his sacrifice of his own son (Genesis 22:1-2). Right at the critical moment, God provided a ram to die as a substitute for Abraham's son. Use this story as a launch pad to show that Jesus died as a substitute for our sins. John the Baptist referred to Jesus as "the Lamb of God, who takes away the sin of the world" (John 1:29). Because Jesus took care of man's sin problem at the cross, help your Muslim friend see that the crucifixion was not a defeat (as Muslims often assume) but rather was a great victory. Sin and death were utterly defeated at the cross, after which Jesus resurrected from the dead.

Of course, not just any substitute or "lamb" will do. Jesus is the only substitute that can help us because He is the God-Man (God in human flesh). Jesus said, "I am the way and the truth and the life. No one comes to the Father except through me" (John 14:6). Peter said, "Salvation is found in no one else, for there is no other name under heaven given to men by which we must be saved" (Acts 4:12).

R. Max Kershaw suggests asking the Muslim, "Who is Jesus?" If he or she says Jesus was a very good man, perhaps the best who ever lived, you can ask, "How can a good man and a prophet like Jesus teach that He is the only way to God and even equal with God? How can a good man and prophet make such incredible statements if they are not true?"[9]

Beware that Muslims may try to argue that what is recorded in the New Testament is unreliable. If this issue comes up, see chapter 12 and 13 for information you can share in response. You can also share how the Quran holds to a high view of Scripture (Sura 4:47; 4:54) and that believers are exhorted to check the Quran against the Bible (Sura 5:44-49; 10:94).

## Gently Correct Quranic Misinterpretations About Jesus

The Quran speaks about Jesus' virgin birth, His miraculous ability to heal people and raise them from the dead, the fact that He is the Messiah, the fact that He is a word from God, that He is an "all-righteous" one, that He was sinless, and that He will one day return to the earth (for example, Suras 3:45; 4:158). The problem is, Muslims generally interpret these things much differently than do Christians. Use these statements from the Quran as a launchpad from which to correct their misconceptions about Jesus.

For example, you might point out that in the Gospel of John the miracles of Jesus are always called signs because *signs signify something*—in this case, that Jesus is the promised divine Messiah. In Isaiah 11 and 35, the prophets said that when the divine Messiah came, He would cause lame people to walk, deaf people to hear, and blind people to see. Jesus fulfilled these specific prophecies, thereby showing He truly is the divine Messiah.

You might also ask the Muslim about what he thinks the Quran means when Jesus is called a "word from God." Then you can show him what John's Gospel says about this (in its first chapter), where Jesus the Word is portrayed as God[10] (see chapter 9).

Further, you can point out that, whereas Muhammad was exhorted in the Quran to seek forgiveness for his faults (Suras 16:61; 40:55; 42:5,30; 47:19; 48:1-2), Jesus was sinless (Hebrews 5:14-15) and came to solve humankind's sin dilemma (2 Corinthians 5:19-21). You might acknowledge that since you are aware *you* are a sinner, you want to make sure that the person to whom you entrust your eternal destiny is sinless.

Finally, as noted earlier in the book, "Islam" literally means "submission." Emphasize that Jesus *submitted* in going to the cross for the sins of humankind, making possible the free gift of salvation for those who believe in Him (Hebrews 5:7ff.). Surely such submission is worthy of honor.

## Share the Gospel

You will obviously need to share the gospel in your discussions with Muslims. There are several effective ways of doing this. Harold J. Berry suggests focusing the attention on Jesus at first: "Tell them to compare the Christ of the Gospel to the Christ of the Quran. Never be afraid that the Christ of the Gospel will come up second best—He never will. There have been many conversions to Christ by using this very method."[11] Once Muslims see how wonderful the Christ of the Gospels is, you can share what He said about how to be saved (John 3:16-17).

Another good approach is to use biblical stories in communicating gospel truths. (I alluded to this earlier in the chapter.) It is well known that Muslims love to tell and to hear stories. Apologist Dean Halverson says that "Muslims are more influenced by stories and parables than they are by logical arguments."[12] John Haines says that "whole families have come to Christ in Muslim cultures through the use of 'The Storying Method.'"[13] Hence, I urge you to pick some good stories from the Gospels and share them with your Muslim acquaintance. Among excellent stories you can use are those of the wedding feast (Luke 14:7-14), the lost sheep, the lost coin, and the lost son (Luke 15), Lazarus and the rich man (Luke 16:19-31), the Pharisee and tax collector (Luke 18:9-14), the unmerciful servant (Matthew 18:21-35), the two sons (Matthew 21:28-32), and Jesus as the Good Shepherd (John 10:1-21). All of these stories could be used as launchpads from which to share the good news of the gospel.

## Distinguish Between Christianity and the United States

When speaking to Muslims—especially international Muslims—be sure to distinguish between Christianity and the United States. Many Muslims tend to think that everyone in the United States is a Christian, and hence, they naturally consider all the unflattering things about the United States as being related to Christianity. They see the low state of morality—high divorce rates, abortions, drinking and drugs, sex on TV, and the like—and think that Christianity must be a corrupt religion.[14]

Let your Muslim acquaintance know that you as a Christian are very concerned about these problems in the United States, and you—like other Christians—are doing everything you can to be salt and light in our society (Matthew 5:13-14).[15]

## A Committed Christian Lifestyle Is Important

It is not enough for you as a Christian to simply speak nice words about Christianity. Muslims must see that the life you live is a reflection of the beliefs you hold to. If they see an inconsistency between your mouth and your life, your words will ultimately mean nothing. One of the best ways to dispel the stereotypes many Muslims have about Christians is to truly "walk the walk" in a committed relationship with Jesus. A deeply committed Christian life will be like a fragrance that draws people to Christ. The way you live will either open the door for further discussions with a Muslim acquaintance, or it will close that door to further contact.

## Arguments Without Quarrels

In many Arab countries, a heated debate with someone is considered something that adds a little spice to life. Many times Muslims can become quite animated in such debates, and unless the more soft-spoken Westerner is aware that this is "common fare" among Muslims, he might feel uncomfortable continuing the discussion.[16] My point in bringing this up is that, should things shift into "debate mode" and your Muslim acquaintance gets animated, just keep your cool. If you sense it is fine to continue, keep making your points in a calm way, without succumbing to raising your voice. Your debate with the Muslim should be charitable, tactful, and friendly.

Be sure not to lose your temper. Scripture exhorts that the Lord's servant must not be quarrelsome (2 Timothy 2:24). Instead, we are to share the truth with gentleness and respect (1 Peter 3:15).

## Trust in the Work of the Holy Spirit

Remember that the Holy Spirit's role is central to effective evangelism with Muslims and everyone else. It is the Holy Spirit who touches their souls; it is He who convinces them of sin and of righteousness and of judgment (John 16:8). It is He who makes the Word of God come alive in their hearts. And in His hands we become effective instruments for the Master's use (see 1 Corinthians 6:19; 12:11; Ephesians 5:18).

Only God can lift the veil of darkness that Islam has cast over the hearts of individual Muslims. Our success in bringing a Muslim to Christ depends completely on the Holy Spirit's work in his or her life. For this reason, pray fervently for the Holy Spirit's involvement in all your witnessing encounters (Philippians 4:6; 1 Thessalonians 5:17).

## Do Not Pressure a Muslim to Become a Christian

Do not ever put pressure on a Muslim to become a Christian. After you have had some good discussions with a Muslim, it is fine to ask for a decision. But even when asking for a decision, do not use pressure tactics. This will not only cause discomfort, but will probably close the door to future discussions.

## Be Cautious About the First Church Invitation

It is important not to take Muslims to your church unless you know they are fully prepared for what they will experience. Muslims may well take offense at some of what they witness at a typical church service. They will see people putting Bibles under their chairs, right next to their feet; even when they are holding their Bibles, they write in them with pens. (Such things are considered disrespectful to the Word of God.) Sometimes they will witness a man putting his arm around his wife, or teenagers holding hands. Some people may dress more casually than seems appropriate for a church service.

Before going to a church service, a Muslim should be well-prepared in what to expect, or else it could catch him off guard.[17] For a first introduction to Christian fellowship, it is probably safer to bring him or her to a small Bible study.

## Some Practical Matters

***Wear appropriate clothes.*** If you have a Muslim over to your house, it is especially important that the women of the family dress modestly in clothing that does not draw too much attention to the female figure.

*Serve appropriate food.* Muslims do not eat foods that come from pigs (pork, ham, bacon, and so forth). If you invite Muslims over for a meal, it would be well to inform them up front that you will not serve foods that are inappropriate for them. You might even ask them what kind of food they would like to be served.

*Be cautious about eye contact.* Direct eye contact is not considered good manners among Muslims. If you are talking to a Muslim and he or she is constantly looking downward, understand that this is part of the culture.

*Don't be offended if they don't like your pets.* Muslims generally view dogs as unclean farm animals. Do not worry about it if they seem unimpressed with your dog.

## Sensitivity Is Important

I have included quite a few "witnessing tips" above. I know it's a lot of information to digest, but these items will make you a better witness to your Muslim friend. By being sensitive in these areas, your chances for successfully evangelizing among Muslims will be greatly increased.

# *Postscript*

I close this book with a gentle reminder. Never forget that if your Muslim acquaintance becomes a Christian, it will, in many cases, carry a great cost for him or her. Converting to Christ will at the very least put in jeopardy—and might possibly put an end to—his relationships with Muslim family members, friends, and possibly employers. A break in a relationship with parents can even cause the loss of inheritance. In certain parts of the world, the Muslim who converts to Christ may well find himself cast into prison, banished from his country, or in danger for his life.[1] We as Christians must be sensitive to these issues.

In the Muslim mind-set, the *individual* belongs to a *community* in which he functions as a member. Even if the Muslim lives in the United States, he is likely a part of a local Muslim community (members of his local mosque) that is foundational to his life. To suddenly be cut off from this community can be devastating. The Muslim who converts to Christ is well aware of the fact that he will break the hearts of his fellow Muslims, especially his parents, spouse, and children.[2]

In view of this, once a Muslim converts, *that* is the time you need to reach out to him and make sure he has a substitute family and network of friends. If the body of Christ is not there to help him absorb the shock wave of rejection from former significant Muslim relationships, he may well not be able to stand it and may renounce his conversion.[3] Make him a part of a caring Christian fellowship where he will receive support and much-needed fellowship. He needs to be nurtured by those more mature in the faith. If you know of other Muslims who have converted to Jesus Christ, then by all means introduce them and try to build those relationships.[4]

Beware that Satan, the enemy of our souls, will do all he can to discourage the new convert and make him wonder whether he has made the right decision. Satan will try to recapture those who have escaped from his power. For this reason, I recommend that you find a solid core of Christians that you respect and request that they pray daily for this individual for not less than a month. Pray specifically that he would grow in the knowledge of Scripture, that God would protect him from Satan, and that God would build new relationships for him among those in the body of Christ. Make sure the new convert knows that, if he runs into trouble—if he takes a spiritual or emotional nosedive—he has the phone numbers of some Christians who will be there for him. Your efforts will help ensure that he grows to maturity in Christ instead of falling by the wayside.

# Appendix A

## *The Two Major Sects of Islam*

Not all Muslims are the same. Though Muslims often criticize Christianity for having so many different groups within it, the reality is that there are also many sects within Islam, some estimates placing the figure around 150.[1] World religions scholar Lewis M. Hopfe is correct in saying that Islam is not a monolithic body. "Although most Muslims would agree on the basic principles of Islam, there are many variations in beliefs and practices."[2]

### The Sunnis

The two majors sects of Islam, the Sunnis and the Shiites, originally divided over a dispute as to who should serve as the first caliph (successor) to Muhammad, who had neglected to appoint one prior to his death. The Sunnis said Muhammad's successor should be elected. The Shiites believed the successor should come through Muhammad's bloodline. The Sunnis got their way. They accept the first four caliphs—Abu Bakr, Omar, Othman, and Ali—as the legitimate successors to Muhammad.

The Sunnis make up about 90 percent of all Muslims, and predominate in such countries as Egypt, Saudi Arabia, and Pakistan. Their name is derived from *Sunnah,* which refers to "the trodden path" or "tradition." Hence, the Sunnis are the traditionalists of Islam—they literally follow the traditions of Islam.

Toward this end, no matter where they live, Sunnis seek to live their lives according to the pattern set by Muhammad and to obey the Quran. Politically speaking, Sunnis believe their Muslim faith can be lived out in the context of various existing earthly governments.[3] Unlike their Shiite counterparts, Sunnis are generally more tolerant of diversity and hence adapt themselves more easily to divergent cultures around the world.

## The Shiites

While Shiites constitute only about 10 percent of the Muslim world, they are nevertheless the most visible and vocal of all the Muslim sects. The term "Shiite" is a corruption of *Shi'at Ali,* which means "partisans of Ali," and refers to the fact that they have rejected all subsequent caliphs who were not descendants of Ali (Muhammad's son-in-law).[4] The Shiites predominate in countries like Iran, Iraq, Lebanon, and in parts of Africa. They are much more literal in their interpretation and application of the Quran, and are much more militant than Sunnis. Politically speaking, the Shiites view government as being a divine institution of Allah, and they attempt to establish a theocracy (God-ruled nation) on earth.[5]

Shiites tend to view the present world order with great distrust. They favor the true believer in Allah, one who has clung to his faith and refused to sell out to the established order.[6]

Shiite leaders are known by the title *Imam,* and they wield extreme authority over their subjects. They are fiercely authoritarian in their interpretation of the Quran. It is believed that Allah speaks through them. World religions specialist Dean Halverson says the Imam is the Muslim counterpart to the Catholic pope.[7] Shiites believe that a divine spark and the "light of Muhammad" are passed from one Imam to the next.[8] An example of an Imam of recent times is Ayatollah Khomeini, who died in 1989.[9]

Shiites believe that the twelfth Imam—the "Lord of the Age"—did not die, but disappeared when he was only a child, in the year 873. They believe he will return at some point in the future and establish his rule. Some Shiites believe Jesus will return with him and lead in a conquest of the world for the Shiite version of Islam.

# Appendix B

## *Jihad—"Holy War"*

Jihad comes from the Arabic word *jahada,* which principally means "to struggle." For most Muslims, the term means "striving in the path of God." It is a term that has made the head-lines many times in recent years, especially as related to terrorist activities around the world. It seems that whenever the United States takes a stand against terrorist Muslims, a jihad, or "holy war," is declared.

The term is more generally taken among Muslims to refer to armed fighting and warfare in defending Islam and standing against evil. Some Muslims, however, have held to less dangerous forms of jihad. Indeed, some Muslims engage in a jihad of the *pen,* which involves engaging in a written defense of Islam.[1]

In keeping with this, scholar Frederick Denny notes that "holy war" doesn't fully capture the meaning of "jihad," although that is certainly part of it. Denny says that for Muslims there is a *greater* jihad and a *lesser* jihad. A person's struggle with his own vices, the evil tendencies in his soul, and his lack of faith is considered the greater jihad. Jihad in this sense is more of a spiritual struggle or striving. Engaging in armed struggle against the enemies of Islam is considered the lesser jihad.[2] Islam scholar Jamal J. Elias maintains that for most Muslims today, "any war that is viewed as a defense of one's own country, home, or community is called a Jihad. This understanding is very similar to what is called 'just war' in Western society."[3]

Radical Islamic fundamentalists are well known for their use of arms in defending their version of Islam. Jihad in this sense has the goal of terrorizing perceived enemies of Islam into submission and retreat. They justify their acts by their belief in jihad, even though the majority of Muslims would disagree that their actions are justifiable. Though most Muslims abhor terrorism, those who advocate it do so by appealing to a literal interpretation of the Quran.[4]

This radical form of jihad is taken much more seriously today than it used to be, if only because of the sheer numbers of radical Muslims threatening it against various countries, and because of the growing availability of weapons of mass destruction. Though radical Islamic fundamentalists constitute a relatively small minority of Muslims, even a minority can be a substantial threat. John Ankerberg and John Weldon explain that "since we are talking about 1.3 billion adherents to Islam, even a 'very small minority' can involve tens of millions of people who have the potential to cause a great deal of trouble in the world, not only for America, but for moderate Muslim governments as well."[5]

Islamic fundamentalists often cite verses from the Quran to support their view that arms are permissible and even *compulsory* in the defense of Islam. We read, "Fighting is prescribed for you, and ye dislike it. But it is possible that ye dislike a thing which is good for you" (Sura 2:216). In Sura 47:4 we read, "Therefore, when ye meet the unbelievers (in fight), smite at their necks: At length, when ye have thoroughly subdued them, bind a bond firmly (on them)." Sura 9:5 says, "But when the forbidden months are past, then fight and slay the pagans wherever ye find them, and seize them, beleaguer them, and lie in wait for them in every stratagem (of war)."

# Appendix C

## *Resources Dealing with Bible Difficulties*

I believe that the following books will help you answer the great majority of alleged Bible contradictions brought up by Muslims.

Ron Rhodes, *The Complete Book of Bible Answers* (Harvest House Publishers).

Norman Geisler and Thomas Howe, *When Critics Ask: A Popular Handbook on Bible Difficulties* (Baker Book House).

Gleason Archer, *An Encyclopedia of Bible Difficulties* (Zondervan).

Walter C. Kaiser, *Hard Sayings of the Old Testament* (InterVarsity Press).

Walter C. Kaiser, *More Hard Sayings of the Old Testament* (InterVarsity Press).

Larry Richards, *Bible Difficulties Solved* (Fleming H. Revell).

Robert H. Stein, *Difficult Passages in the New Testament* (Baker Book House).

William Arndt, *Bible Difficulties and Seeming Contradictions* (Concordia).

Manfred T. Brauch, *Hard Sayings of Paul* (InterVarsity Press).

F.F. Bruce, *The Hard Sayings of Jesus* (InterVarsity Press).

John W. Haley, *Alleged Discrepancies of the Bible* (Baker Book House).

# Notes

## The Phenomenal Growth of Islam

1. These statistics are listed in Ron Rhodes, *Islam: What You Need to Know* (Eugene, OR: Harvest House Publishers, 2000).
2. Richard Bernstein, "A Growing Islamic Presence," *New York Times*, 2 May 1993, p. 1. See also John Ankerberg and John Weldon, *Fast Facts on Islam* (Eugene, OR: Harvest House Publishers, 2001), p. 13.
3. Bruce A. McDowell and Anees Zaka, *Muslims and Christians at the Table* (Phillipsburg, NJ: Presbyterian and Reformed, 1999), p. 8.
4. Harold J. Berry, *Islam: What They Believe* (Lincoln, NE: Back to the Bible, 1992), p. 4.
5. Reza F. Safa, *Inside Islam: Exposing and Reaching the World of Islam* (Lake Mary, FL: Charisma House, 1996), p. 34.
6. Safa, p. 34.
7. Berry, p. 5.
8. Russell Chandler, *Racing Toward 2001* (Grand Rapids, MI: Zondervan, 1992), p. 184.
9. Daniel Pipes, "How Many Muslims Live in the United States?" *New York Post*, 29 October 2001, downloaded from <www.gc.cuny.edu/studies/aris_part_two.htm>.
10. Pipes.
11. William M. Miller, *A Christian's Response to Islam* (Phillipsburg, NJ: Presbyterian and Reformed, 1976), p. 94.
12. Kenneth Boa, *Cults, World Religions, and You* (Wheaton, IL: Victor Books, 1979), p. 52.
13. Lewis M. Hopfe, *Religions of the World* (New York: Macmillan, 1991), p. 420.
14. Donald S. Tingle, *Islam & Christianity* (Downers Grove, IL: InterVarsity Press, 1985), p. 5.
15. Geoffrey Parrinder, *World Religions: From Ancient History to the Present* (New York: Facts on File Publications, 1971), p. 462.
16. Charles J. Adams, ed., *A Reader's Guide to the Great Religions* (New York: The Free Press, 1965), p. 287.
17. The Institute for the Study of Islam and Christianity, *Survey of Islam*, Section Six: "Islam—The Practice," in *The World of Islam* CD-ROM, © 2000 Global Mapping International, from <http://answering-islam.org>.
18. Jamal J. Elias, *Islam* (Upper Saddle River, NJ: Prentice Hall, 1999), p. 66.
19. Elias, p. 66.

20. See *Beliefs of Other Kinds: A Guide to Interfaith Witness in the United States* (Atlanta: Baptist Home Mission Board, 1984), p. 121.
21. Hopfe, p. 415.
22. Winfried Corduan, *Islam: A Christian Introduction* (Downers Grove, IL: Inter-Varsity Press, 1998), p. 17.
23. Dean Halverson, *The Compact Guide to World Religions* (Minneapolis: Bethany House Publishers, 1996), p. 107.
24. Elias, p. 67.
25. Frederick Mathewson Denny, *An Introduction to Islam* (New York: Macmillan, 1985), p. 120.
26. Hopfe, p. 416.
27. Miller, p. 59.
28. McDowell and Zaka, p. 60.
29. George A. Mather and Larry A. Nichols, *Dictionary of Cults, Sects, Religions and the Occult* (Grand Rapids, MI: Zondervan Publishing House, 1993), p. 142.
30. Miller, p. 59.
31. Denny, p. 126.
32. Ravi Zacharias, *Jesus Among Other Gods: The Absolute Claims of the Christian Message* (Nashville, TN: Word Publishing, 2000), p. 98.
33. Mather and Nichols, p. 142.
34. Abdulkader Tayob, *Islam: A Short Introduction* (Oxford: Oneworld, 1999), p. 99.
35. Denny, p. 132.
36. Denny, p. 132.
37. John B. Noss, *Man's Religions* (New York: Macmillan Publishing Company, 1974), p. 524.
38. Noss, p. 510.
39. Halverson, p. 107.
40. McDowell and Zaka, p. 58.
41. Elias, p. 73.
42. McDowell and Zaka, p. 26.
43. Miller, p. 102.

### Chapter 1—Dialoguing with Muslims

1. R. Max Kershaw, *How to Share the Good News with Your Muslim Friend* (Colorado Springs, CO: International Students Inc., 2000), p. 3.
2. Phil Parshall, *The Fortress and the Fire* (India: Gospel Literature Service, 1975), p. 104.
3. John Gilchrist, *The Christian Witness to the Muslim;* in *The World of Islam* CD-ROM, © 2000 Global Mapping International, originally posted at http://answering-islam.org.
4. Dean Halverson, *The Compact Guide to World Religions* (Minneapolis: Bethany House Publishers, 1996), p. 109.
5. William M. Miller, *A Christian's Response to Islam* (Phillipsburg, NJ: Presbyterian and Reformed, 1976), pp. 94-95.
6. Reza F. Safa, *Inside Islam* (Lake Mary, FL: Charisma House, 1996), p. 18.

7. Phil Parshall, *The Cross and the Crescent: Understanding the Muslim Mind and Heart* (Wheaton, IL: Tyndale House Publishers, 1989); in *The World of Islam* CD-ROM.

8. Kershaw, p. 9. See also Frederick Mathewson Denny, *An Introduction to Islam* (New York: Macmillan Publishing Company, 1985), p. 269.

9. Bruce A. McDowell and Anees Zaka, *Muslims and Christians at the Table* (Phillipsburg, NJ: Presbyterian and Reformed, 1999), pp. 62-63.

10. Colin Chapman, *Cross and Crescent: Responding to the Challenge of Islam* (Leicester, England: Inter-Varsity Press, 1995); in *The World of Islam* CD-ROM.

11. Sobhi Malek, *Islam: Challenge and Mandate;* in *The World of Islam* CD-ROM.

12. Malek.

13. See Walter Martin, "The Do's and Don'ts of Witnessing to Cultists," *Christian Research Newsletter,* January-February 1992, p. 4.

14. Safa, p. 9.

15. Safa, pp. 82-83.

16. Safa, pp. 82-83.

17. Jamal J. Elias, *Islam* (Upper Saddle River, NJ: Prentice-Hall, (1999), p. 15.

18. Donald S. Tingle, *Islam & Christianity* (Downers Grove, IL: InterVarsity Press, 1985), p. 3.

19. David Reed, *Jehovah's Witnesses: Answered Verse by Verse* (Grand Rapids, MI: Baker Book House, 1992), p. 115.

20. Miller, p. 105.

21. John Ankerberg and John Weldon, *The Facts on Islam* (Eugene, OR: Harvest House Publishers, 1991), p. 17.

*Chapter 2—Muhammad and the Emergence of Islam*

1. William M. Miller, *A Christian's Response to Islam* (Phillipsburg, NJ: Presbyterian and Reformed, 1976), p. 51.

2. Badru D. Kateregga and David W. Shenk, *A Muslim and a Christian in Dialogue* (Scottdale, PA: Herald Press, 1997); in *The World of Islam* CD-ROM, © 2000 Global Mapping International, from <http://answering-islam.org>.

3. Bruce A. McDowell and Anees Zaka, *Muslims and Christians at the Table* (Phillipsburg, NJ: Presbyterian and Reformed, 1999), p. 127.

4. John B. Noss, *Man's Religions* (New York: Macmillan, 1974), p. 518.

5. Kateregga and Shenk.

6. Norman Geisler and Abdul Saleeb, *Answering Islam: The Crescent in the Light of the Cross* (Grand Rapids, MI: Baker Book House, 1993), p. 52.

7. Geoffrey Parrinder, *World Religions: From Ancient History to the Present* (New York: Facts on File Publications, 1971), p. 463.

8. Noss, p. 511.

9. Noss, p. 509.

10. Gerald L. Berry, *Religions of the World* (Lincoln, NE: Back to the Bible Publishing, 1992), p. 60.

11. Berry, p. 80; Josh McDowell and Don Stewart, *Handbook of Today's Religions* (San Bernardino, CA: Here's Life Publishers, 1989), p. 379.

12. Kenneth Boa, *Cults, World Religions, and You* (Wheaton, IL: Victor Books, 1979), p. 49.
13. George A. Mather and Larry A. Nichols, *Dictionary of Cults, Sects, Religions and the Occult* (Grand Rapids, MI: Zondervan Publishing House, 1993), p. 139; Lewis M. Hopfe, *Religions of the World* (New York: Macmillan Publishing Company, 1991), p. 402.
14. Berry, p. 28.
15. David G. Bradley, *A Guide to the World's Religions* (Englewood Cliffs, NJ: Prentice-Hall, 1963), p. 68.
16. McDowell and Zaka, p. 32.
17. Parrinder, p. 466.
18. Hopfe, p. 403.
19. Parrinder, p. 472.
20. Miller, p. 20.
21. McDowell and Stewart, p. 389.
22. Hopfe, p. 404.
23. Dean Halverson, *The Compact Guide to World Religions* (Minneapolis: Bethany House Publishers, 1996), p. 104.
24. Reza F. Safa, *Inside Islam: Exposing and Reaching the World of Islam* (Lake Mary, FL: Charisma House, 1996), p. 27.
25. Boa, p. 51.
26. Miller, p. 28.
27. Jamal J. Elias, *Islam* (Upper Saddle River, NJ: Prentice-Hall, 1999), p. 35.
28. William J. Saal, *Reaching Muslims for Christ: A Handbook for Christian Outreach Among Muslims* (Chicago: Moody Press, 1993); in *The World of Islam* CD-ROM.
29. Samuel M. Zwemer, *The Muslim Christ: An Essay on the Life, Character, and Teachings of Jesus Christ According to the Quran and Orthodox Traditions* (New York: American Tract Society, 1912); in *The World of Islam* CD-ROM.
30. Geisler and Saleeb, p. 86.
31. Frederick Mathewson Denny, *An Introduction to Islam* (New York: Macmillan, 1985), p. 159.
32. Elias, p. 26.

### Chapter 3—A Christian Critique of Muhammad

1. Bruce A. McDowell and Anees Zaka, *Muslims and Christians at the Table* (Phillipsburg, NJ: Presbyterian and Reformed, 1999), p. 37.
2. William J. Saal, *Reaching Muslims for Christ: A Handbook for Christian Outreach Among Muslims* (Chicago: Moody Press, 1993); in *The World of Islam* CD-ROM, © 2000 Global Mapping International, from <http://answering-islam.org>.
3. William M. Miller, *A Christian's Response to Islam* (Phillipsburg, NJ: Presbyterian and Reformed, 1976), p. 48.
4. See, for example, Norman Geisler and Abdul Saleeb, *Answering Islam: The Crescent in the Light of the Cross* (Grand Rapids, MI: Baker Book House, 1993), p. 171.

5. Robert Morey, "Common Logical Fallacies Made by Muslims," Research Education Foundation, downloaded from the Internet, 1998.
6. W. St. Clair Tisdall, *Christian Reply to Muslim Objections* (London: Society for Promoting Christian Knowledge, 1904); in *The World of Islam* CD-ROM.
7. Tisdall.
8. Geisler and Saleeb, p. 203.
9. I am here indebted to Geisler and Saleeb, pp. 164-65.
10. Gerhard Nehls, *Christians Ask Muslims;* in *The World of Islam* CD-ROM.
11. McDowell and Zaka, p. 36.
12. W. Montgomery Watt and Richard Bell, *Bell's Introduction to the Quran* (Edinburgh: Edinburgh University Press, 1970); in *The World of Islam* CD-ROM.
13. Norman L. Geisler and Ron Rhodes, *When Cultists Ask* (Grand Rapids, MI: Baker Book House, 1996), p. 43. Norman Geisler is especially acknowledged for his contribution here.
14. *Keil and Delitzsch Commentary on the Old Testament,* ©1996 by Hendrickson Publishers; in PC Study Bible, BibleSoft Company, insert added.
15. Geisler and Rhodes, p. 43.
16. Geisler and Rhodes, p. 45.
17. Nehls.
18. "Paran," in *Nelson's Illustrated Bible Dictionary,* © 1986 Thomas Nelson Publishers; in PC Study Bible, BibleSoft Company.
19. *Keil and Delitzsch,* "Deuteronomy 33:2."
20. Geisler and Rhodes, p. 45.
21. Geisler and Rhodes, pp. 45-46. See also *Keil and Delitzsch,* "Deuteronomy 34:10."
22. *Barnes' Notes,* "Psalm 45:3"; in PC Study Bible, BibleSoft Company; see also *Adam Clarke's Commentary,* "Psalm 45:3"; in PC Study Bible, BibleSoft Company.
23. Geisler and Rhodes, p. 64. See also *Jamieson, Fausset, and Brown Commentary,* "Psalm 45:3"; in PC Study Bible, BibleSoft Company.
24. *The Zondervan NIV Commentary,* Kenneth Barker and John Kohlenberger III, eds. (Grand Rapids, MI: Zondervan, 1994), p. 1079; see also Geisler and Rhodes, p. 79.
25. *Nelson's Illustrated Bible Dictionary.*
26. Geisler and Rhodes, p. 89.
27. Geisler and Rhodes, p. 182.
28. Nehls.
29. John Ankerberg and John Weldon, *The Facts on Islam* (Eugene, OR: Harvest House Publishers, 1991), p. 13.
30. Ankerberg and Weldon, p. 10.

### Chapter 4—The Quran—The Scriptures of Islam

1. Winfried Corduan, *Islam: A Christian Introduction* (Downers Grove, IL: InterVarsity Press, 1998), p. 11.
2. Jamal J. Elias, *Islam* (Upper Saddle River, NJ: Prentice Hall, 1999), p. 21.
3. Elias, p. 21.

4. Geoffrey Parrinder, *World Religions: From Ancient History to the Present* (New York: Facts on File Publications, 1971), p. 473.

5. Mishkat III, p. 664; in *The World of Islam* CD-ROM, © 2000 Global Mapping International, from <http://answering-islam.org>.

6. Elias, p. 21.

7. William M. Miller, *A Christian's Response to Islam* (Phillipsburg, NJ: Presbyterian and Reformed, 1976), p. 53.

8. Bruce A. McDowell and Anees Zaka, *Muslims and Christians at the Table* (Phillipsburg, NJ: Presbyterian and Reformed, 1999), p. 72.

9. John Gilchrist, *Quran: The Scripture of Islam* (Muslim Evangelicalism Resource Center, 1995); in *The World of Islam* CD-ROM.

10. Elias, p. 19.

11. J. Christy Wilson, *Introducing Islam* (New York: Friendship Press, 1958), p. 30; insert added.

12. Badru D. Kateregga and David W. Shenk, *A Muslim and a Christian in Dialogue* (Scottdale, PA: Herald Press, 1997); in *The World of Islam* CD-ROM.

13. Lewis M. Hopfe, *Religions of the World* (New York: Macmillan, 1991), p. 408.

14. Harold J. Berry, *Islam: What They Believe* (Lincoln, NE: Back to the Bible, 1992), p. 18.

15. Parrinder, p. 473.

16. Elias, p. 20.

17. H.U.W. Stanton, *The Teaching of the Quran* (New York: Bible and Tannen, 1969), pp. 10-11.

18. See Norman Geisler and Abdul Saleeb, *Answering Islam: The Crescent in the Light of the Cross* (Grand Rapids, MI: Baker Book House, 1993), p. 91.

19. McDowell and Zaka, pp. 74-75.

20. Maului Muhammad Ali, *Muhammad and Christ* (Lahore, India: The Ahmadiyya Anjuman-i-Ishaat-i-Islam, 1921), p. 7.

21. Susanne Haneef, *What Everyone Should Know About Islam and Muslims* (Chicago: Kazi Publications, 1979), pp. 18-19.

22. Kateregga and Shenk.

23. McDowell and Zaka, p. 84.

24. See Geisler and Saleeb, p. 96.

25. Elias, p. 25.

26. Gerhard Nehls, *Christians Ask Muslims;* in *The World of Islam* CD-ROM.

27. Wilson, p. 30.

28. Kateregga and Shenk.

29. Seyyed Nasr, *Ideals and Realities of Islam* (Boston: Beacon Press, 1972), pp. 82-83.

### Chapter 5—A Christian Critique of the Quran

1. A. Guillaume, pp. 57-58, cited in Gerhard Nehls, *Christians Ask Muslims;* in *The World of Islam* CD-ROM, © 2000 Global Mapping International, from <http://answering-islam.org>.

2. Data derived from Answering Islam Web site, at <http://answering-islam .org/Quran/Text/warsh.html>. See also Adrian Brockett, "The Value of the Hafs

and Warsh Transmissions for the Textual History of the Quran," in *Approaches to the History of the Interpretation of the Quran*, Andrew Rippin, ed. (Oxford: Clarendon Press, 1988), pp. 34, 37.

3. Norman Geisler and Abdul Saleeb, *Answering Islam: The Crescent in the Light of the Cross* (Grand Rapids, MI: Baker Book House, 1993), p. 194.

4. John Gilchrist, "The Textual History of the Qur'an and the Bible: A Study of the Qur'an and the Bible," The Good Way, P.O. Box 66, CH-8486 Rikon, Switzerland.

5. Geisler and Saleeb, p. 187.

6. Ravi Zacharias, *Jesus Among Other Gods: The Absolute Claims of the Christian Message* (Nashville, TN: Word Publishing, 2000), pp. 159-60.

7. Ali Dashti, *Twenty-Three Years: A Study of the Prophetic Career of Mohammad* (London: Allen and Unwin, 1985), pp. 48, 50.

8. Nehls.

9. Nehls.

10. Walter Martin, *The Kingdom of the Cults* (Minneapolis: Bethany House Publishers, 1999), Quickverse software.

11. Gleason Archer, "Confronting the Challenge of Islam in the 21st Century," *Contend for the Faith* (Chicago: EMNR, 1992), p. 106.

12. Robert Morey, "Common Logical Fallacies Made by Muslims," Research Education Foundation, downloaded from the Internet, 1998.

13. Frederick Mathewson Denny, *An Introduction to Islam* (New York: Macmillan, 1994), p. 159.

14. William J. Saal, *Reaching Muslims for Christ: A Handbook for Christian Outreach Among Muslims* (Chicago: Moody Press, 1993); in *The World of Islam* CD-ROM.

### Chapter 6—Allah—The God of Islam

1. Note that the term "Allah" is also the Arabic word for "God." So, among Arabs, "Allah" and "God" are synonymous. However, this should not be taken to mean that the Allah of the Quran and the Yahweh of the Christian Bible are revealed to have the same nature and character, for they are different in numerous ways.

2. Lewis M. Hopfe, *Religions of the World* (New York: Macmillan, 1991), p. 401.

3. George A. Mather and Larry A. Nichols, *Dictionary of Cults, Sects, Religions and the Occult* (Grand Rapids, MI: Zondervan Publishing House, 1993), p. 140.

4. Frederick Mathewson Denny, *An Introduction to Islam* (New York: Macmillan, 1985), p. 52.

5. William M. Miller, *A Christian's Response to Islam* (Phillipsburg, NJ: Presbyterian and Reformed, 1976), p. 45.

6. Bruce A. McDowell and Anees Zaka, *Muslims and Christians at the Table* (Phillipsburg, NJ: Presbyterian and Reformed, 1999), p. 94.

7. Donald S. Tingle, *Islam & Christianity* (Downers Grove, IL: InterVarsity Press, 1985), p. 8.

8. Jamal J. Elias, *Islam* (Upper Saddle River, NJ: Prentice Hall, 1999), p. 62.

9. Dean Halverson, *The Compact Guide to World Religions* (Minneapolis: Bethany House Publishers, 1996), p. 113.

10. See McDowell and Zaka, pp. 93-94.

11. Abdiyah Akbar Abdul-Haqq, *Sharing Your Faith with a Muslim* (Minneapolis: Bethany, 1980), p. 159.

12. Kenneth Cragg, *The Call of the Minaret* (New York: Oxford, 1964), pp. 42-43.

13. Al-Ghazali; quoted in Abdul-Haqq, p. 152.

14. Risaleh-i-Barkhawi, quoted in Gerhard Nehls, *Christians Ask Muslims* (Bellville, IL: SIM International Life Challenge, 1987), p. 21.

15. Hopfe, p. 410.

16. McDowell and Zaka, p. 124.

17. John Gilchrist, *Quran: The Scripture of Islam* (Muslim Evangelicalism Resource Center, 1995); in *The World of Islam* CD-ROM, © 2000 Global Mapping International, from <http://answering-islam.org>, insert added.

18. Norman Geisler and Abdul Saleeb, *Answering Islam: The Crescent in the Light of the Cross* (Grand Rapids, MI: Baker Book House, 1993), pp. 141-42.

19. Al-Ghazali, quoted in John Elder, *The Biblical Approach to the Muslim* (Madison, GA: Source of Light Ministries International, 2000); in *The World of Islam* CD-ROM.

### *Chapter 7—The Biblical View of God*

1. J.I. Packer, *Knowing God* (Downers Grove, IL: InterVarsity Press, 1979), p. 29.

2. J.I. Packer, *Knowing Christianity* (Wheaton, IL: Harold Shaw Publishers, 1995), p. 10.

3. Sobhi Malek, *Islam: Challenge and Mandate;* in *The World of Islam* CD-ROM, © 2000 Global Mapping International, from <http://answering-islam.org>.

4. William J. Saal, *Reaching Muslims for Christ: A Handbook for Christian Outreach Among Muslims* (Chicago: Moody Press, 1993); in *The World of Islam* CD-ROM.

5. W. St. Clair Tisdall, *Christian Reply to Muslim Objections* (London: Society for Promoting Christian Knowledge, 1904); in *The World of Islam* CD-ROM.

6. Benjamin B. Warfield, *The Person and Work of Christ* (Philadelphia: Presbyterian and Reformed Publishing Co., 1950), p. 66.

7. Robert L. Reymond, *Jesus, Divine Messiah: The New Testament Witness* (Phillipsburg, NJ: Presbyterian and Reformed Publishing Co., 1990), p. 84, insert added.

8. *Bible Illustrations*, electronic media (Hypercard stack for Macintosh).

9. Dean Halverson, *The Compact Guide to World Religions* (Minneapolis: Bethany House Publishers, 1996), p. 113.

10. C.S. Lewis, *Mere Christianity* (New York: Macmillan, 1943), p. 145.

11. John Gilchrist, "The Love of God in the Qur'an and the Bible," from the Answering Islam home page, <http://answering-islam.org>.

12. Norman Geisler and Abdul Saleeb, *Answering Islam: The Crescent in the Light of the Cross* (Grand Rapids, MI: Baker Book House, 1993), pp. 137-38.

13. Norman Geisler, *Thomas Aquinas: An Evangelical Appraisal* (Grand Rapids, MI: Baker Book House, 1991), chapter 10.

14. Cited in Packer, *Knowing Christianity*, p. 94.

15. Gleason Archer, "Confronting the Challenge of Islam in the 21st Century," *Contend for the Faith* (Chicago: EMNR, 1992), p. 99.

## Chapter 8—Jesus—A Prophet of Islam

1. Donald S. Tingle, *Islam & Christianity* (Downers Grove, IL: InterVarsity Press, 1985), p. 26.
2. Bruce A. McDowell and Anees Zaka, *Muslims and Christians at the Table* (Phillipsburg, NJ: Presbyterian and Reformed, 1999), p. 108.
3. See *Ministry in Islamic Contexts* (Lausanne Committee for World Evangelization and Institute for the Study of Islam and Christianity); in *The World of Islam* CD-ROM, © 2000 Global Imaging International, from <http://answering-islam.org>.
4. William Miller, *A Christian's Response to Islam* (Phillipsburg, NJ: Presbyterian and Reformed, 1976), p. 77.
5. Ahmed Deedat, *Christ in Islam* (Islamic Propagation Center International, South Africa), downloaded from the Internet at <http://jamaat.net/deedat.htm>.
6. W. St. Clair Tisdall, *Christian Reply to Muslim Objections* (London: Society for Promoting Christian Knowledge, 1904); in *The World of Islam* CD-ROM.
7. Deedat, *Christ in Islam*.
8. Deedat, *Christ in Islam*.
9. Norman Geisler and Abdul Saleeb, *Answering Islam: The Crescent in the Light of the Cross* (Grand Rapids, MI: Baker Book House, 1993), p. 259.
10. Anis A. Shorrosh, *Islam Revealed* (Nashville, TN: Thomas Nelson Publishers, 1988), p. 278.
11. Tisdall.
12. Ahmed Deedat, *Resurrection or Resuscitation?* (The Islamic Propagation Center, South Africa), downloaded from the Internet at <http://jamaat.net/deedat.htm>.
13. Tisdall.
14. Larry A. Poston with Carl F. Ellis Jr., *The Changing Face of Islam in America* (Camp Hill, PA: Horizon Books, 2000), p. 188.
15. Abdiyah Akbar Abdul-Haqq, *Sharing Your Faith with a Muslim* (Minneapolis: Bethany, 1980); cited in *The World of Islam* CD-ROM.
16. David Sox, *The Gospel of Barnabas* (London: George Allen & Unwin, 1984), p. 96.
17. McDowell and Zaka, pp. 117-18.
18. McDowell and Zaka, p. 118.
19. Norman Anderson, *Islam in the Modern World* (Leicester: Apollos, 1990), p. 219.
20. Ahmed Deedat, *Crucifixion or Cruci-fiction?* downloaded from Deedat Web site at <http://jamaat.net/deedat.htm>.
21. Debate between Josh McDowell and Ahmed Deedat, August 1981, Durban, South Africa. Transcript downloaded from Internet.
22. Quoted in McDowell and Zaka, p. 126.
23. Deedat, *Resurrection or Resuscitation?*
24. See John Gilchrist, "The Textual History of the Qur'an and the Bible: A Study of the Qur'an and the Bible," The Good Way, P.O. Box 66, CH-8486 Rikon, Switzerland.

## Chapter 9—The Biblical View of Jesus, Part One

1. Dean Halverson, *The Compact Guide to World Religions* (Minneapolis: Bethany House Publishers, 1996), p. 114.
2. Benjamin B. Warfield, *The Person and Work of Christ* (Philadelphia: Presbyterian and Reformed Publishing Co., 1950), p. 62.
3. S.E. Johnson, "Lord (Christ)," *The Interpreter's Dictionary of the Bible* (New York: Abingdon, 1976), 3:151.
4. William G.T. Shedd, *Romans* (New York: Scribner, 1879), p. 318.
5. Quoted in Donald S. Tingle, *Islam & Christianity* (Downers Grove, IL: InterVarsity Press, 1985), pp. 20-21.
6. Leon Morris, *The Gospel According to John,* from *The New International Commentary on the New Testament* (Grand Rapids, MI: Wm. B. Eerdmans Publishing Co., 1987), p. 119.
7. R.C.H. Lenski, *The Interpretation of St. John's Gospel* (Minneapolis: Augsburg Publishing House, 1961), p. 27.
8. Morris, p. 73.
9. Morris, p. 77.
10. Lenski, p. 103.
11. F.F. Bruce, *The Gospel of John* (Grand Rapids, MI: Eerdmans, 1984), p. 40.
12. *New Bible Dictionary*, J.D. Douglas, ed. (Wheaton, IL: Tyndale, 1982), p. 1101.
13. Warfield, p. 55.
14. J. Dwight Pentecost, *The Words and Works of Jesus Christ* (Grand Rapids, MI: Zondervan Publishing House, 1982), p. 29.
15. Warfield, p. 55.

## Chapter 10—The Biblical View of Jesus, Part Two

1. Norman L. Geisler; cited in *Miracles Are Heaven Sent* (Tulsa, OK: Honor Books, 1995), p. 10.
2. John Ankerberg, John Weldon, and Walter C. Kaiser, *The Case for Jesus the Messiah* (Chattanooga, TN: The John Ankerberg Evangelistic Association, 1989), p. 16.
3. Ankerberg, Weldon, and Kaiser, p. 91.
4. I acknowledge credit here to Norman Geisler and Abdul Saleeb, *Answering Islam: The Crescent in the Light of the Cross* (Grand Rapids, MI: Baker Book House, 1993), pp. 228-30.
5. John Haines, *Good News for Muslims* (Philadelphia: Middle East Resources, 1998), p. 66.
6. Geisler and Saleeb, p. 277.
7. William J. Saal, *Reaching Muslims for Christ: A Handbook for Christian Outreach Among Muslims* (Chicago: Moody Press, 1993); in *The World of Islam* CD-ROM, © 2000 Global Mapping International, from <http://answering-islam.org>.
8. Harold J. Berry, *Islam: What They Believe* (Lincoln, NE: Back to the Bible, 1992), p. 33.

*Chapter 11—The Muslim View of the Bible*

1. Gleason Archer, "Confronting the Challenge of Islam in the 21st Century," *Contend for the Faith* (Chicago: EMNR, 1992), p. 97.
2. Stephen Neill, as cited in Josh McDowell and Don Stewart, *Handbook of Today's Religions* (San Bernardino, CA: Here's Life Publishers, 1989), p. 387.
3. Alhaj Ajijola, *The Essence of Faith in Islam* (Lahore, Pakistan: Islamic Publications, 1978), p. 79.
4. Gerhard Nehls, *Christians Answer Muslims;* in *The World of Islam* CD-ROM, © 1988, compiled from <http://answering-islam.org>, insert added.
5. Maurice Bucaille, *The Bible, The Quran, and Science: The Holy Scriptures Examined in the Light of Modern Knowledge* (Pakistan: Darulfikr, 1977), p. 9.
6. Larry A. Poston with Carl F. Ellis, Jr., *The Changing Face of Islam in America* (Camp Hill, PA: Horizon Books, 2000), p. 183.
7. Martin Goldsmith, *Islam and Christian Witness* (Carlisle, Cumbria, Great Britain: OM Publishing, 1998); in *The World of Islam* CD-ROM, © 2000 Global Imaging International from <http://answering-islam.org>.
8. John Gilchrist, "The Textual History of the Qur'an and the Bible: A Study of the Qur'an and the Bible," The Good Way, P.O. Box 66, CH-8486 Rikon, Switzerland.
9. Bucaille, p. vi.
10. Quoted in Nehls.
11. W. St. Clair Tisdall, *Christian Reply to Muslim Objections* (London: Society for Promoting Christian Knowledge, 1904); in *The World of Islam* CD-ROM.
12. Tisdall.
13. Bucaille, p. 43.
14. Bucaille, p. 22.
15. Bucaille, p. 33.
16. Nehls.
17. Ahmed Deedat, *Is the Bible God's Word?* (Durban, RSA: IPCI), p. 35.
18. Bucaille, pp. 58, 94.
19. Bucaille, p. 83.
20. This alleged contradiction sometimes surfaces in online debates on the Internet between Muslims and Christians.
21. Ahmed Deedat, *What Was the Sign of Jonah?* Downloaded from Ahmed Deedat Web site (<http://jamaat.net/deedat.htm>).
22. Nehls.
23. Tisdall.
24. Nehls.
25. Tisdall
26. Nehls.
27. M.A. Yusseff, *The Dead Sea Scrolls, the Gospel of Barnabas, and the New Testament* (Indianapolis, IN: American Trust Publication, 1985), p. 5.
28. Deedat, *Is the Bible God's Word?* p. 2.

*Chapter 12—A Defense of the Bible, Part One*

1. W. St. Clair Tisdall, *Christian Reply to Muslim Objections* (London: Society for Promoting Christian Knowledge, 1904); in *The World of Islam* CD-ROM, © 2000 Global Mapping International, from <http://answering-islam.org>.

2. William J. Saal, *Reaching Muslims for Christ: A Handbook for Christian Outreach Among Muslims* (Chicago: Moody Press, 1993); in *The World of Islam* CD-ROM.

3. L. Bevan Jones, *Christianity Explained to Muslims: A Manual for Christian Workers* (Calcutta: YMCA Publishing House, 1938); in *The World of Islam* CD-ROM.

4. Norman Geisler and Abdul Saleeb, *Answering Islam: The Crescent in the Light of the Cross* (Grand Rapids, MI: Baker Book House, 1993), p. 212.

5. Greg L. Bahnsen, "The Inerrancy of the Autographa," in *Inerrancy*, Norman L. Geisler, ed. (Grand Rapids, MI: Zondervan Publishing House, 1980), p. 161.

6. See B.M. Metzger, *The Text of the New Testament*, 3rd ed. (New York: Oxford University Press, 1992); B.M. Metzger, *The Early Versions of the New Testament* (Oxford: Clarendon, 1977); B.D. Ehrman and M.W. Holmes, eds., *The Text of the New Testament in Contemporary Research: Essays on the* Status Quaestionis (Grand Rapids, MI: Eerdmans, 1995).

7. Norman Geisler and William Nix, *A General Introduction to the Bible* (Chicago: Moody Press, 1978), p. 357.

8. Winfried Corduan, *Islam: A Christian Introduction* (Downers Grove, IL: InterVarsity Press 1998), p. 29.

9. Gleason Archer, *A Survey of Old Testament Introduction* (Chicago: Moody Press, 1964), p. 19, emphasis added.

10. Dan Story, *Defending Your Faith: How to Answer the Tough Questions* (Nashville, TN: Thomas Nelson Publishers, 1992), p. 35.

11. Gary R. Habermas, *Ancient Evidence for the Life of Jesus* (Nashville, TN: Thomas Nelson Publishers, 1984), p. 65.

12. Habermas, p. 66.

13. Geisler and Nix, p. 186.

14. Geisler and Nix, p. 190.

15. Geisler and Nix, p. 190.

16. Geisler and Nix, p. 190.

17. Story, p. 45.

18. See Archer, p. 98.

19. Though there is some debate among Christians as to which manuscripts are the most reliable. (King James Version proponents argue that the manuscripts upon which the KJV is based are the most accurate, whereas most others believe significant manuscripts predate those used for the KJV and are more accurate.) See John Gilchrist, "The Textual History of the Qur'an and the Bible: A Study of the Qur'an and the Bible," The Good Way, P.O. Box 66, CH-8486 Rikon, Switzerland.

20. Quoted in Gilchrist, "The Textual History of the Qur'an and the Bible."

21. Maurice Bucaille, *The Bible, the Quran, and Science: The Holy Scriptures Examined in the Light of Modern Knowledge* (Pakistan: Darulfikr, 1977), p. vi.

*Chapter 13—A Defense of the Bible, Part Two*

1. Maurice Bucaille, *The Bible, the Quran, and Science: The Holy Scriptures Examined in the Light of Modern Knowledge* (Pakistan: Darulfikr, 1977), p. 43.
2. Norman Geisler and Abdul Saleeb, *Answering Islam: The Crescent in the Light of the Cross* (Grand Rapids, MI: Baker Book House, 1993), p. 220.
3. Bucaille, p. 22.
4. Bucaille, p. 33.
5. See Geisler and Saleeb, p. 222.
6. Ahmed Deedat, *Is the Bible God's Word?* (Durban, RSA: IPCI), p. 35.
7. Bucaille, p. 83.
8. Ahmed Deedat, *What Was the Sign of Jonah?* Downloaded from Ahmed Deedat Web site (<http://jamaat.net/deedat.htm>).
9. Gerhard Nehls, *Christians Ask Muslims* (Bellville: SIM International Life Challenge, 1987); in *The World of Islam* CD-ROM.
10. W. St. Clair Tisdall, *Christian Reply to Muslim Objections* (London: Society for Promoting Christian Knowledge, 1904); in *The World of Islam* CD-ROM, © 2000 Global Mapping International, from <http://answering-islam.org>.
11. Nehls, *Christians Answer Muslims*, from <http://answering-islam.org>.
12. William J. Saal, *Reaching Muslims for Christ: A Handbook for Christian Outreach Among Muslims* (Chicago: Moody Press, 1993); in *The World of Islam* CD-ROM.
13. Anne Cooper, compiler, *In the Family of Abraham: Christians and Muslims Reasoning Together;* in *The World of Islam* CD-ROM.
14. Cooper.
15. Cooper.
16. See Geisler and Saleeb, pp. 297-99.
17. Norman Geisler, class notes for Bibliology, Dallas Theological Seminary.
18. Geisler, class notes for Bibliology.

*Chapter 14—Sin and Salvation in Islam*

1. Badru D. Kateregga and David W. Shenk, *A Muslim and a Christian in Dialogue* (Scottdale, PA: Herald Press, 1997), p. 18.
2. J. Dudley Woodberry, *Dimensions of Witness Among Muslims* (Seoul, Korea: Chongshin University, 1997); in *The World of Islam* CD-ROM, © 2000 Global Mapping International, from <http://answering-islam.org>.
3. Isma'il R. Al Faruqi, *Islam* (Niles, IL: Argus Communications, 1984), p. 9.
4. Norman Geisler and Abdul Saleeb, *Answering Islam: The Crescent in the Light of the Cross* (Grand Rapids, MI: Baker Book House, 1993), p. 122.
5. Reza F. Safa, *Inside Islam: Exposing and Reaching the World of Islam* (Lake Mary, FL: Charisma House, 1996), p. 80.
6. E.K. Simpson and F.F. Bruce, *Commentary on the Epistles to the Ephesians and Colossians* (Grand Rapids, MI: Eerdmans, 1975), p. 50.
7. John Ankerberg and John Weldon, *Encyclopedia of Cults and New Religions* (Eugene, OR: Harvest House, 1999), p. 517.
8. David Shenk, *The People of God,* Part 1 (Nairobi, Kenya: Evangel Publishing House, 1982); in *The World of Islam* CD-ROM.

9. Billy Graham, *How to be Born Again* (Dallas, TX: Word Publishing, 1989), p. 118.
10. William J. Saal, *Reaching Muslims for Christ: A Handbook for Christian Outreach Among Muslims* (Chicago: Moody Press, 1993); in *The World of Islam* CD-ROM.
11. Gleason Archer, "Confronting the Challenge of Islam in the 21st Century," *Contend for the Faith* (Chicago: EMNR, 1992), p. 99.

### Chapter 15—The Muslim View of the Afterlife

1. William M. Miller, *A Christian's Response to Islam* (Phillipsburg, NJ: Presbyterian and Reformed, 1976), p. 56.
2. Miller, p. 82.
3. Quoted in Harold J. Berry, *Islam: What They Believe* (Lincoln, NE: Back to the Bible, 1992), p. 42.
4. Phil Parshall, *The Cross and the Crescent: Understanding the Muslim Mind and Heart* (Wheaton, IL: Tyndale House Publishers, 1989); in *The World of Islam* CD-ROM, © 2000 Global Mapping International, from <http://answering-islam.org>.
5. Parshall, *The Cross and the Crescent*.
6. Lewis M. Hopfe, *Religions of the World* (New York: Prentice Hall, 2000), p. 412.
7. Gerald L. Berry, *Religions of the World* (New York: Harper Collins, 1956), p. 64.
8. Miller, p. 56.
9. Jamal J. Elias, *Islam* (Upper Saddle River, NJ: Prentice Hall, 1999), p. 65.
10. Phil Parshall, *Inside the Community: Understanding Muslims through Their Traditions* (Grand Rapids, MI: Baker Book House, 1994); in *The World of Islam* CD-ROM.
11. Parshall, *Inside the Community*.
12. John Elder, *The Biblical Approach to the Muslim* (Madison, GA: Source of Light Ministries International, 2000); in *The World of Islam* CD-ROM.
13. Elder.
14. Douglas Connelly, *What the Bible Really Says: After Life* (Downers Grove, IL: InterVarsity Press, 1995), p. 119.
15. Cited in Charles C. Ryrie, *Basic Theology* (Wheaton, IL: Victor Books, 1986), p. 513.
16. Connelly, p. 118.
17. John Wesley, *The Nature of Salvation* (Minneapolis: Bethany House Publishers, 1987), p. 135.
18. John Blanchard, *Whatever Happened to Hell?* (Durham, England: Evangelical Press, 1993), p. 116.
19. J. Dwight Pentecost, *Things to Come* (Grand Rapids, MI: Zondervan, 1974), p. 226.

### Chapter 16—Tips for Evangelizing Among Muslims

1. William M. Miller, *A Christian's Response to Islam* (Phillipsburg, NJ: Presbyterian and Reformed, 1976), p. 134.

2. John Gilchrist, "Our Approach To Islam: Charity Or Militancy?" John Gilchrist's books, <http://answering-islam.org>.

3. Miller, p. 132.

4. Larry A. Poston with Carl F. Ellis Jr., *The Changing Face of Islam in America* (Camp Hill, PA: Horizon Books, 2000), p. 238.

5. William J. Saal, *Reaching Muslims for Christ: A Handbook for Christian Outreach Among Muslims* (Chicago: Moody Press, 1993); in *The World of Islam* CD-ROM, © 2000 Global Mapping International, from <http://answering-islam.org>.

6. Saal.

7. R. Max Kershaw, *How to Share the Good News with Your Muslim Friend* (Colorado Springs, CO: International Students Inc., 2000), p. 15.

8. Reza F. Safa, *Inside Islam: Exposing and Reaching the World of Islam* (Lake Mary, FL: Charisma House, 1996), p. 94.

9. Kershaw, p. 15.

10. Kershaw, p. 12.

11. Harold J. Berry, *Islam: What They Believe* (Lincoln, NE: Back to the Bible, 1992), p. 46.

12. Dean Halverson, *The Compact Guide to World Religions* (Minneapolis: Bethany House Publishers, 1996), p. 109.

13. John Haines, *Good News for Muslims* (Philadelphia: Middle East Resources, 1998), p. 29.

14. Gleason Archer, "Confronting the Challenge of Islam in the 21st Century," *Contend for the Faith* (Chicago: EMNR, 1992), p. 93.

15. See Bruce A. McDowell and Anees Zaka, *Muslims and Christians at the Table* (Phillipsburg, NJ: Presbyterian and Reformed, 1999), p. 202.

16. Poston, p. 221.

17. Halverson, p. 109.

## *Postscript*

1. R. Max Kershaw, *How to Share the Good News with Your Muslim Friend* (Colorado Springs, CO: International Students Inc., 2000), p. 23. See also Donald S. Tingle, *Islam & Christianity* (Downers Grove, IL: InterVarsity Press, 1985), p. 25.

2. William M. Miller, *A Christian's Response to Islam* (Phillipsburg, NJ: Presbyterian and Reformed, 1976), p. 95.

3. Larry A. Poston with Carl F. Ellis Jr., *The Changing Face of Islam in America* (Camp Hill, PA: Horizon Books, 2000), p. 243.

4. Kershaw, p. 25.

## *Appendix A—The Two Major Sects of Islam*

1. Harold J. Berry, *Islam: What They Believe* (Lincoln, NE: Back to the Bible, 1992), p. 15.

2. Lewis M. Hopfe, *Religions of the World* (New York: Macmillan Publishing Company, 1991), p. 422.

3. George A. Mather and Larry A. Nichols, *Dictionary of Cults, Sects, Religions and the Occult* (Grand Rapids, MI: Zondervan Publishing House, 1993), p. 141.
4. Walter Martin, *The Kingdom of the Cults* (Minneapolis: Bethany House Publishers, 1999), QuickVerse software.
5. Mather and Nichols, p. 141.
6. Hopfe, p. 425.
7. Dean Halverson, *The Compact Guide to World Religions* (Minneapolis: Bethany House Publishers, 1996), p. 105.
8. Bruce A. McDowell and Anees Zaka, *Muslims and Christians at the Table* (Phillipsburg, NJ: Presbyterian and Reformed, 1999), p. 45.
9. Mather and Nichols, p. 141.

*Appendix B—Jihad—"Holy War"*

1. Jamal J. Elias, *Islam* (Upper Saddle River, NJ: Prentice Hall, 1999), p. 73.
2. Frederick Mathewson Denny, *An Introduction to Islam* (New York: Macmillan, 1985), p. 136.
3. Elias, p. 73.
4. John Ankerberg and John Weldon, *Fast Facts on Islam* (Eugene, OR: Harvest House Publishers, 2001), p. 105.
5. Ankerberg and Weldon, p. 19.

# Bibliography

Anderson, Sir Norman. *Islam in the Modern World*. Leicester, England: Inter-Varsity Press, 1990.

Ankerberg, John, and John Weldon. *Fast Facts on Islam*. Eugene, OR: Harvest House, 2001.

*Beliefs of Other Kinds: A Guide to Interfaith Witness in the United States*. Atlanta, GA: Baptist Home Mission Board, 1984.

Berry, Gerald L. *Religions of the World*. New York: Harper Collins, 1956.

Berry, Harold J. *Islam: What They Believe*. Lincoln, NE: Back to the Bible Publishing, 1992.

Boa, Kenneth. *Cults, World Religions, and You*. Wheaton, IL: Victor Books, 1979.

Bradley, David G. *A Guide to the World's Religions*. Englewood Cliffs, NJ: Prentice-Hall, 1963.

Bucaille, Maurice. *The Bible, the Quran, and Science*. Pakistan: Darulfikr, 1977.

Chapman, Colin. *Cross and Crescent: Responding to the Challenge of Islam*. Leicester, England: Inter-Varsity Press, 1995.

———. *Going Soft on Islam? Reflections on Some Evangelical Responses to Islam*. London: London Bible College, 1989.

Cooper, Anne, compiler. *Ishmael My Brother: A Biblical Course on Islam*. Tunbridge Wells, England: Evangelical Missionary Alliance, 1993.

Corduan, Winfried. *Islam: A Christian Introduction*. Downers Grove, IL: InterVarsity, 1998.

Denny, Frederick Mathewson. *An Introduction to Islam*. New York: Macmillan, 1994.

Elder, John. *The Biblical Approach to the Muslim*. Madison, GA: Source of Light Ministries International, 2000.

Elias, Jamal J. *Islam*. Upper Saddle River, NJ: Prentice Hall, 1999.

Geisler, Norman, and Abdul Saleeb. *Answering Islam: The Crescent in the Light of the Cross*. Grand Rapids, MI: Baker Book House, 1993.

Geisler, Norman, and Ron Rhodes. *When Cultists Ask*. Grand Rapids, MI: Baker, 1997.

Goldsmith, Martin. *Islam and Christian Witness*. Carlisle, Cumbria, England: OM Publishing, 1998.

Haines, John. *Good News for Muslims*. Philadelphia: Middle East Resources, 1998.

Halverson, Dean C., ed. *The Compact Guide to World Religions*. Minneapolis: Bethany, 1996.

Hopfe, Lewis M. *Religions of the World*. New York: Prentice Hall, 2000.

Jones, Bevan. *Christianity Explained to Muslims: A Manual for Christian Workers*. Calcutta: YMCA Publishing House, 1938.

Kateregga, Badru D., and David W. Shenk. *A Muslim and a Christian in Dialogue*. Scottdale, PA: Herald Press, 1997.

Kershaw, R. Max. *How to Share the Good News with Your Muslim Friend*. Colorado Springs, CO: International Students, 2000.

Martin, Walter. *The Kingdom of the Cults*. Minneapolis: Bethany House Publishers, 1999.

Mather, George A., and Larry A. Nichols. *Dictionary of Cults, Sects, Religions and the Occult*. Grand Rapids, MI: Zondervan Publishing House, 1993.

McDowell, Bruce A., and Anees Zaka. *Muslims and Christians at the Table*. Phillipsburg, NJ: Presbyterian and Reformed, 1999.

McDowell, Josh, and Don Stewart. *Handbook of Today's Religions*. San Bernardino, CA: Here's Life Publishers, 1989.

Miller, William M. *A Christian's Response to Islam*. Phillipsburg, NJ: Presbyterian and Reformed, 1976.

Morey, Robert. *The Islamic Invasion*. Eugene, OR: Harvest House Publishers, 1992.

Noss, John B. *Man's Religions*. New York: Macmillan Publishing Company, 1974.

Parrinder, Geoffrey, ed. *World Religions: From Ancient History to the Present*. New York: Facts on File Publications, 1971.

Parshall, Phil. *Inside the Community: Understanding Muslims Through Their Traditions*. Grand Rapids, MI: Baker Book House, 1994.

———. *The Cross and the Crescent: Understanding the Muslim Mind and Heart*. Wheaton, IL: Tyndale House Publishers, 1989.

Pement, Eric, ed. *Contend for the Faith*. Chicago: EMNR, 1992.

Poston, Larry A., and Carl F. Ellis. *The Changing Face of Islam in America*. Camp Hill, PA: Horizon Books, 2000.

Rhodes, Ron. *Islam: What You Need to Know*. Eugene, OR: Harvest House Publishers, 2000.

Saal, William J. *Reaching Muslims for Christ*. Chicago: Moody Press, 1993.

Safa, Reza F. *Inside Islam*. Lake Mary, FL: Charisma House, 1996.

Shenk, David. *The People of God*, Part 2. Nairobi, Kenya: Evangel Publishing House, 1982.

Tayob, Abdulkader. *Islam: A Short Introduction*. Oxford, England: Oneworld, 1999.

Tingle, Donald S. *Islam & Christianity*. Downers Grove, IL: InterVarsity Press, 1985.

Tisdall, W. St. Clair. *Christian Reply to Muslim Objections*. London: Society for Promoting Christian Knowledge, 1904.

Watt, W. Montgomery, and Richard Bell, *Bell's Introduction to the Quran*. Edinburgh: Edinburgh University Press, 1970.

Woodberry, J. Dudley. *Dimensions of Witness Among Muslims*. Seoul, Korea: Chongshin University, 1997.

Zacharias, Ravi. *Jesus Among Other Gods*. Nashville, TN: Word Publishing, 2000.

Zwemer, Samuel M. *The Muslim Christ*. New York: American Tract Society, 1912.

# Index to Subjects

Abrogation and the Quran — 75-76, 87-89
Adoption into God's family — 252-53
Afterlife
    Christian view — 259-75
    Muslim view — 255-59
Allah — 95-103
    Does good and evil — 99-102
    Love of — 102-103
    Many names — 96
    Meaning of the name — 95
    Not a Trinity — 98-99
    Not truly God — 129-30
    Singularly one — 97-98
Almsgiving — 14-15
Angels — 12
Atonement
    Necessity of, according to Bible — 248-52
    Unnecessary, according to Islam — 138, 235
Barnabas, Gospel of —
    Muslim use of — 192-93
    Unreliability of — 227-29
Beauty of the Quran — 82-84
Bible
    Alleged contradictions in — 189-92
    Christian view of — 195-231
    Claims of corruption — 185-88
    Claims of defectiveness — 188
    Contradictions, easily explained — 215-27

    Impossibility of changes — 196-200
    Manuscript evidence — 202-205
    Muslim view of — 185-93
    Not corrupted — 200-202
    Variants in — 206-210
    Versions of — 212-13
Birth of Muhammad — 35-36
Canonicity, tests of — 229-31
Circular reasoning by Muslims — 91-92
Compilation of the Quran — 73-74
Conflict in Muslim families — 30
Creedal recitation — 13
Crucifixion
    Denied by Muslims — 136-38
    Historical proof for — 173-74
Dead Sea scrolls — 208-209
Death of Jesus, explaining to a Muslim — 176-78
Death of Muhammad — 44
Deity of Jesus — 145-50
Demonic source of Muhammad's revelations — 64-66
Dialoguing with Muslims — 21-31
Evangelism among Muslims — 19-20, 277-89
Fasting — 15-16
Fate — 12
Finality of Quran — 71-72
Five Doctrines of Islam — 11-12
Five Pillars of the Faith — 13-19
Forgiveness, objective basis in Christianity — 127-29
Free will and God's sovereignty — 125-27
Giving alms — 14-15
God
    Biblical view — 105-30
    Good, just, and righteous — 123-25
    Holiness of — 122-23
    Love of — 121-22
    Muslim view — 11
    Reveals Himself — 110-13
    Sovereign — 125-27

Spirit — 108-109

Transcendent and immanent — 109-110

Trinity — 113-20

Gospel of Barnabas

Muslim use of — 192-93

Unreliability of — 227-29

Growth of Islam — 7-8

Hadith — 76-78

*Hajj* — 17-19

Heaven

Christian view — 268-73

Muslim view — 257

Hell

Christian view — 273-75

Muslim view — 258

Holy books — 12

Holy war — 297-98

Illiteracy of Muhammad — 56-57

Islam

Brotherhood religion — 10

Comprehensive religion — 9

Easy-to-obey religion — 9

Growth of — 7-8

Meaning of the term — 11

Rational religion — 10

Reasons for growth — 9-10

Simple religion — 9

Universal religion — 9

Way of life — 23

Islamic fundamentalism — 27-28

Jesus

Apostle of Allah — 132

Bible verses and deity — 153-59

Biblical view of — 141-84

Crucifixion denied — 136-38

Crucifixion proved — 173-74

Deity denied — 134-36

Deity proved — 145-50

324 • Index to Subjects

    Divine Messiah — 165-69

    Miracle worker — 133, 161-63

    More than a prophet — 169-73

    Not the Son of God (Muslim view) — 133-34

    Prophesied in Old Testament — 165-69

    "Prophet," the — 58-61

    Resurrection and ascension of — 179-84

    Resurrection denied — 139

    Second coming — 139

    Son of God — 141-44

    Son of Man — 144-45

    Word of God — 150-53

Jihad — 297-98

Judgment

    Christian view — 259-67

    Muslim view — 12, 256-57

Justification — 247-48

Manuscript evidence for Bible — 202-205

Mecca

    Conquered by Muhammad — 43-44

    Culture of — 35

    Resisted Muhammad — 41-42

Medina, migration to — 42-43

Militancy — 27-28

Miracles

    Of Jesus — 133

    Of Muhammad — 55-56

Muhammad — 33-47

    Birth of — 35-36

    Christian critique of — 49-67

    Death of — 44

    Illiteracy of — 56-57

    Influenced by demons — 64-66

    Knew little of true Christianity — 50

    Lacking as moral example — 51-52

    Merchant — 36-38

    Miracles of — 55-56

    Misunderstood Bible — 211-12

Not "the prophet" of Deuteronomy — 58-61
Not prophesied in Old Testament — 57-63
Not the Paraclete — 63-64
Resisted by Meccans — 41-42
Revelation of — 38-41
Superior prophet (according to Muslims) — 44-46
Veneration of — 46-47
Muslim evangelism, tips — 277-89
Muslims, divergence of beliefs — 26-27
New Testament
Early support for — 210-11
Eyewitness testimony — 213-14
Patristic quotations — 205-206
Old Testament, no references to Muhammad — 57-63
Original sin — 237-40
Paraclete not Muhammad — 63-64
Personal relationships with Muslims — 22-23
Pilgrimage to Mecca — 17-19
Prayer for Muslims — 21-22
Prayer, in Muslim practice — 13-14
Prophecy in the Quran — 75, 84-86
Prophecies of Jesus in Old Testament — 165-69
Prophets — 12, 33-35
Proselytizing, Muslim practice of — 10
Questions for Muslims — 28-29
Quran — 69-94
Abrogation — 75-76
Arrangement of — 72
Beauty of — 82-84
Changed lives — 90-91
Compilation of — 73-74
Copy of heavenly document — 72-73
Divine nature of — 74-75
Finality of — 71-72
Highly respected — 70
Meaning of — 11
a Miracle — 70
Modern science, proves reliability — 86-87

Not eternal — 89-90
Not God's Word — 92-93
Prophecy in — 75
Variants in — 80
Veneration of — 69
Ramadan, month of — 15-16
Rapid growth of Islam, divine blessing? — 53-55
Reciting the creed — 13
Recommended reading — 299-300
Resurrection
Muslim view — 139, 256-57
Proof of — 179-84
Revelation of Muhammad — 38
Salvation
Assurance of in Christianity — 253-54
Good works — 235-36
No assurance of in Islam — 236
Satanic miracles — 163-65
Satanic resistance to Muslim evangelism — 29-30
Science and the Quran — 86-87
Second coming of Jesus — 139
Sects of Islam — 293-95
Shiites — 294-95
Sin
According to Jesus — 242-44
Inner reality — 244-45
Muslim view — 233-35
Not just feebleness and forgetfulness — 240-42
Universality of — 237-40
Sin and salvation, Christian view of — 237-54
Son of God, Jesus
Christian view — 141-44
Muslim view — 133-34
Son of Man, Jesus — 144-45
Sovereignty of God — 125-27
Stereotypes of Muslims — 24
Sunnah — 76-78
Sunnis — 293-94

Tradition in Islam — 76-78
Tradition, unreliable — 93-94
Trinity
    Christian view — 113-20
    Muslim view — 98-99
Variants in Quran — 80
Veneration of Muhammad — 46-47
Versions of Bible — 212-13
Works cannot save — 245-47

# Index to Bible Quotations

Genesis 1:1,21 — 163

Genesis 1:2 — 118

Genesis 1:26 — 106

Genesis 1:27 — 268

Genesis 2–3 — 189, 216

Genesis 2:7 — 118

Genesis 2:17 — 189, 216

Genesis 2:18 — 106

Genesis 2:21-25 — 268

Genesis 3 — 112

Genesis 3:1-7 — 126

Genesis 3:8 — 107

Genesis 3:13 — 127

Genesis 5:5 — 189, 216

Genesis 5:24 — 107

Genesis 6–8 — 189, 218

Genesis 6:3 — 189, 217

Genesis 6:6 — 188, 217

Genesis 6:9 — 107

Genesis 6:13 — 107

Genesis 7:4 — 189-190, 218

Genesis 7:4,12,17,24 — 218

Genesis 7:12 — 219

Genesis 7:24 — 190, 219

Genesis 8:2 — 189, 218

Genesis 8:3 — 219

Genesis 8:4 — 92

Genesis 8:21 — 237

Genesis 11:10-32 — 189

Genesis 11:27 — 92

Genesis 12:1 — 107

Genesis 12:2 — 168

Genesis 14:6 — 61

Genesis 17:18 — 58

Genesis 18:25 — 125

Genesis 19:24 — 263

Genesis 21:12 — 58

Genesis 22 — 177

Genesis 22:1-2 — 284

Genesis 26:24 — 107

Genesis 28:13 — 107

Exodus 1:15-16,22 — 59

Exodus 2:2-10 — 59

Exodus 2:5 — 92

Exodus 3:4 — 107

Exodus 3:5 — 102

Exodus 3:7-8 — 108

Exodus 3:14 — 281

Exodus 7:10 — 164

Exodus 7:10,19,20 — 59

Exodus 8–12 — 59

Exodus 8:18-19 — 165

Exodus 8:19 — 163-164

Exodus 15:11 — 123

Exodus 19–20 — 59

Exodus 19:17 — 151

Exodus 20:7 — 150
Exodus 25:8 — 152
Exodus 29:45-46 — 110
Exodus 33:11 — 59, 188, 190, 219
Exodus 34:14 — 150
Exodus 40:34-38 — 152
Leviticus 1:8 — 263
Leviticus 19:2 — 122, 259
Leviticus 25:11 — 228
Numbers 10:12 — 61
Numbers 12:16–13:3 — 61
Deuteronomy 4:2 — 201
Deuteronomy 4:7 — 110
Deuteronomy 4:39 — 110, 129
Deuteronomy 6:4 — 115
Deuteronomy 6:13 — 150
Deuteronomy 12:32 — 201
Deuteronomy 17:15 — 58
Deuteronomy 17:17 — 268
Deuteronomy 18 — 202
Deuteronomy 18:1-2 — 58
Deuteronomy 18:15 — 60
Deuteronomy 18:15,18 — 44, 57-58, 60-61, 168
Deuteronomy 18:18 — 59, 229
Deuteronomy 25:4 — 230
Deuteronomy 31:24-26 — 230
Deuteronomy 32:39 — 115, 163
Deuteronomy 33:2 — 45, 61
Deuteronomy 34:10 — 45, 61
Deuteronomy 34:10-11 — 62
Joshua 1:1 — 107
Joshua 24:26 — 230
Judges 6:25 — 107
1 Samuel 2:2 — 123
1 Samuel 3:4 — 107
1 Samuel 23:9-12 — 107
1 Samuel 25:6 — 179
2 Samuel 7:12-16 — 116, 168

2 Samuel 7:22 — 116
2 Samuel 24:1 — 190, 219-220
1 Kings 8:10-11 — 153
1 Kings 8:27 — 109
1 Kings 17:2-4 — 107
1 Kings 18 — 165
1 Kings 20:35 — 141
2 Kings 23:10 — 274
1 Chronicles 16:8,9 — 283
1 Chronicles 21:1 — 190, 219
2 Chronicles 28:3 — 274
2 Chronicles 33:6 — 274
Ezra 9:15 — 125
Nehemiah 12:28 — 141
Job 1:10-12 — 164
Job 15:14-16 — 238
Job 33:4 — 118
Job 34:28 — 108
Psalm 2:6 — 168
Psalm 2:6-9 — 169
Psalm 11:7 — 125
Psalm 16:10 — 168, 173-174
Psalm 16:11 — 269, 275
Psalm 19 — 111
Psalm 22:1 — 168
Psalm 22:16 — 168, 173-174
Psalm 22:17 — 168
Psalm 22:22 — 168
Psalm 25:8 — 124
Psalm 31:19 — 124
Psalm 32:1-2 — 252
Psalm 33:5 — 125
Psalm 34:8 — 124
Psalm 41:13 — 109
Psalm 45:3-5 — 45, 62
Psalm 45:6-7 — 62
Psalm 48:10 — 63
Psalm 50:1 — 126

Psalm 51:5 — 237-238, 240

Psalm 53:8 — 237

Psalm 62:12 — 244, 263

Psalm 66:7 — 126

Psalm 68:18 — 168

Psalm 81:10 — 108

Psalm 86:10 — 116

Psalm 89:14 — 125

Psalm 90:2 — 109

Psalm 91:14-15 — 108

Psalm 93:1 — 126

Psalm 99:9 — 123

Psalm 100:5 — 124

Psalm 102:25 — 118

Psalm 103:11-12 — 252

Psalm 104:30 — 118

Psalm 106:1 — 125

Psalm 110:1 — 168-169

Psalm 110:4 — 168-169

Psalm 111:9 — 123

Psalm 113:5-6 — 109

Psalm 119 — 147

Psalm 119:130 — 280

Psalm 135:6 — 126

Psalm 139:7 — 117

Proverbs 30:5-6 — 201

Ecclesiastes 3:1 — 66

Ecclesiastes 7:20 — 238, 240

Isaiah 5:20 — 124

Isaiah 6:1-5 — 146

Isaiah 6:3 — 123

Isaiah 6:5 — 241

Isaiah 6:8 — 107

Isaiah 7:3 — 84

Isaiah 7:14 — 85, 168

Isaiah 9:6-7 — 169

Isaiah 11:2 — 168

Isaiah 21:7 — 45, 62

Isaiah 25:8 — 270

Isaiah 26:19 — 173-174

Isaiah 29:18-21 — 162, 165

Isaiah 31:3 — 108

Isaiah 33:22 — 168

Isaiah 35:5-6 — 162, 165, 168

Isaiah 37:20 — 116

Isaiah 40:3 — 146, 168

Isaiah 40:15 — 126

Isaiah 40:17 — 126

Isaiah 42:8 — 146

Isaiah 43:10 — 116

Isaiah 43:11 — 145-146

Isaiah 43:13 — 109

Isaiah 43:25 — 144

Isaiah 44:6 — 109, 116

Isaiah 44:7 — 166

Isaiah 44:24 — 145-146

Isaiah 45:5,14,21-22 — 116

Isaiah 45:21 — 166

Isaiah 45:22-24 — 148

Isaiah 46:8-10 — 116

Isaiah 46:9 — 116

Isaiah 48:3,5 — 166

Isaiah 48:12 — 109

Isaiah 51:16 — 64

Isaiah 53 — 59

Isaiah 53:3 — 168

Isaiah 53:5 — 168

Isaiah 53:5-10 — 173-174

Isaiah 53:7 — 168, 250

Isaiah 53:12 — 168

Isaiah 57:15 — 109-110, 129

Isaiah 59:21 — 64

Isaiah 61:1-2 — 162, 165

Isaiah 64:6 — 238, 240, 246

Jeremiah 1:9 — 65

Jeremiah 7:31-34 — 274

Jeremiah 9:23-24 — 106
Jeremiah 12:1 — 125
Jeremiah 17:10 — 264
Jeremiah 18:7-10 — 217
Jeremiah 23:23-24 — 110, 129
Jeremiah 32:35 — 274
Ezekiel 43:2 — 147
Daniel 7:9 — 144
Daniel 7:13 — 144
Daniel 9:26 — 173-174
Daniel 9:27 — 224
Daniel 12:2 — 173-174
Hosea 11:1 — 168
Micah 5:2 — 84-85, 118, 168
Micah 7:19 — 252
Nahum 1:7 — 125
Habakkuk 1:13 — 124, 259
Habakkuk 3:3 — 45, 62
Zephaniah 3:5 — 125
Zechariah 11:12 — 168
Zechariah 12:10 — 84, 173-174
Zechariah 13:7 — 168
Malachi 3:1 — 168
Matthew 1:1 — 168
Matthew 1:1-17 — 190, 220
Matthew 1:23 — 168
Matthew 2:6 — 168
Matthew 2:11 — 149
Matthew 2:13ff. — 59
Matthew 2:14 — 168
Matthew 3:3 — 168
Matthew 3:16-17 — 168
Matthew 4:10 — 150
Matthew 4:23-24 — 162
Matthew 5:13-14 — 286
Matthew 5:17 — 166
Matthew 5:17-18 — 172
Matthew 5:44 — 51

Matthew 5:48 — 124, 259
Matthew 6:9 — 129
Matthew 6:9,26,32 — 108
Matthew 7:7-12 — 21
Matthew 7:15-23 — 246
Matthew 7:28-29 — 170
Matthew 8:2 — 149
Matthew 8:3 — 163
Matthew 8:14ff — 59
Matthew 8:15 — 163
Matthew 8:23-27 — 171
Matthew 8:26 — 163
Matthew 9:2 — 163
Matthew 9:4 — 118
Matthew 9:12 — 243
Matthew 9:18 — 149
Matthew 9:35 — 168
Matthew 9:37-38 — 20
Matthew 10:15 — 268
Matthew 10:28 — 249, 274
Matthew 10:32 — 283
Matthew 10:36-39 — 30
Matthew 11:4-5 — 162
Matthew 11:14 — 190, 221
Matthew 11:23 — 161, 249
Matthew 11:27 — 157
Matthew 11:28 — 171
Matthew 12:34 — 243
Matthew 12:35-37 — 264
Matthew 12:36-37 — 267
Matthew 12:40 — 173-174, 191, 221-222
Matthew 13:41-42 — 267
Matthew 13:42 — 274
Matthew 13:53-57 — 169
Matthew 14:13 — 59
Matthew 14:19 — 163
Matthew 14:25 — 163
Matthew 15:25 — 149

Matthew 15:36 — 163
Matthew 16:16 — 169
Matthew 16:16,17 — 144
Matthew 16:20 — 136, 158
Matthew 16:25 — 249
Matthew 16:27 — 244, 263, 268
Matthew 16:28 — 191, 222
Matthew 17:1-13 — 222
Matthew 17:2 — 153
Matthew 17:3 — 59
Matthew 17:18 — 163
Matthew 17:22-23 — 173-174
Matthew 17:27 — 157, 163
Matthew 18:8 — 274
Matthew 18:21-35 — 286
Matthew 19:4 — 268
Matthew 19:26 — 117
Matthew 20:18 — 144
Matthew 20:28 — 174, 177-178,
    249-251
Matthew 20:29-34 — 191
Matthew 20:30 — 223
Matthew 21:5 — 168
Matthew 21:11 — 59
Matthew 21:14 — 162
Matthew 21:28-32 — 286
Matthew 22:18 — 244-245
Matthew 22:30 — 269
Matthew 23:16-26 — 243
Matthew 23:33 — 249
Matthew 23:37 — 126
Matthew 24:14 — 20
Matthew 24:24 — 133
Matthew 24:24-25 — 50
Matthew 24:30 — 144, 223
Matthew 24:34 — 191, 223
Matthew 24:35 — 172, 200
Matthew 25:31 — 223
Matthew 25:41 — 249, 274

Matthew 25:46 — 267
Matthew 26:15 — 168
Matthew 26:26-28 — 249
Matthew 26:52 — 52
Matthew 26:53 — 249
Matthew 26:56 — 166
Matthew 26:63-64 — 144
Matthew 27:5 — 191, 224
Matthew 27:12-19 — 168
Matthew 27:35 — 92
Matthew 27:38 — 168
Matthew 27:46 — 168
Matthew 28:6 — 168
Matthew 28:9 — 149
Matthew 28:17 — 149
Matthew 28:18 — 117-118
Matthew 28:18-20 — 172
Matthew 28:19 — 20, 118, 129
Mark 1:2-4 — 146
Mark 1:15 — 243
Mark 1:22 — 229
Mark 1:31 — 163
Mark 1:41 — 163
Mark 2:1-12 — 171
Mark 2:5 — 163
Mark 2:7-10 — 144
Mark 4:39 — 163
Mark 5:19-20 — 283
Mark 6:41 — 163
Mark 6:48 — 163
Mark 7:20-23 — 243
Mark 7:21-23 — 244-245
Mark 8:6 — 163
Mark 8:25 — 163
Mark 8:31 — 173
Mark 9:7 — 107
Mark 9:25 — 163
Mark 9:43-48 — 263

Mark 10:18 — 135, 155, 245
Mark 10:46-52 — 191, 223
Mark 13:31 — 170
Mark 13:32 — 135, 156-157
Mark 14:50 — 135, 158, 168
Mark 14:51-54 — 158
Mark 14:61-62 — 169
Mark 15:44-45 — 174
Mark 16:9-20 — 225
Mark 16:15 — 20
Mark 16:17-18 — 192, 224
Luke 1:20 — 92
Luke 1:23-38 — 190, 220
Luke 2:6-7 — 93
Luke 2:11 — 145-146, 168
Luke 4:20-21 — 167
Luke 4:32 — 170
Luke 4:39 — 163
Luke 5:4,6 — 157
Luke 5:5,6 — 163
Luke 5:20 — 163
Luke 5:27-31 — 281
Luke 6:8 — 244-245
Luke 7:11 — 59
Luke 7:16 — 59
Luke 7:20 — 162
Luke 7:22 — 162
Luke 7:37-48 — 243
Luke 8:24 — 163
Luke 9:16 — 163
Luke 9:20 — 28
Luke 9:22 — 182
Luke 9:42 — 163
Luke 10:7 — 230
Luke 12:47-48 — 268
Luke 13:33 — 59, 61
Luke 14:7-14 — 286
Luke 15:1-7 — 281

Luke 15:8-10 — 281
Luke 15:10 — 243
Luke 15:11-24 — 129, 281
Luke 16:19-31 — 259, 286
Luke 16:22-28 — 249
Luke 17:11-19 — 163
Luke 18:1-8 — 21
Luke 18:35-43 — 191, 223
Luke 19:10 — 243, 249
Luke 23:34 — 148
Luke 23:43 — 246
Luke 23:46-49 — 173
Luke 23:49 — 158
Luke 24 — 136
Luke 24:19 — 59
Luke 24:27 — 167
Luke 24:39 — 139, 182
Luke 24:44 — 167
Luke 24:46 — 183
Luke 24:46-47 — 182
Luke 24:47 — 20
Luke 24:50-53 — 168
John 1:1 — 132, 151, 156
John 1:2 — 118
John 1:3 — 118, 146, 150-151
John 1:12 — 253
John 1:12-13 — 107
John 1:14 — 152-153
John 1:14,18 — 133, 143
John 1:14-18 — 169
John 1:18 — 109, 112, 190, 219
John 1:19-21 — 190, 221
John 1:29 — 249, 284
John 1:29,36 — 178, 250
John 2:7,8 — 163
John 2:19 — 153
John 2:19-21 — 173-174
John 2:25 — 157

John 3:1-5,16-17 — 246

John 3:2 — 112

John 3:16 — 93, 121-122, 129, 133, 249, 281

John 3:16-17 — 142, 286

John 3:17 — 249

John 4:17-19 — 244-245

John 4:19 — 59

John 4:24 — 108, 129

John 4:25-26 — 169

John 4:26 — 62

John 4:28-30,39 — 283

John 4:54 — 161

John 5:8 — 163

John 5:18 — 142, 144

John 5:21 — 147

John 5:28-29 — 267, 275

John 5:30 — 168

John 5:37 — 219

John 5:39-40 — 167

John 5:44 — 116

John 5:46 — 60

John 5:46-47 — 167

John 6:11 — 163

John 6:14 — 59, 161

John 6:19 — 163

John 6:35 — 171, 281

John 7:5,48 — 168

John 7:29 — 157

John 7:33 — 183

John 7:37-38 — 171

John 7:40 — 59

John 7:46 — 170

John 8:12 — 243, 281

John 8:28 — 59, 61

John 8:32 — 21

John 8:32-36 — 59

John 8:34 — 243

John 8:54-56 — 142

John 8:55 — 157

John 8:58 — 62, 144, 156, 281

John 9:7 — 163

John 9:16 — 161

John 9:17 — 59

John 9:38 — 149

John 10:1-21 — 286

John 10:9 — 281

John 10:10 — 171

John 10:10-11 — 173

John 10:11 — 249

John 10:15 — 157

John 10:18 — 163, 249

John 10:28 — 29

John 10:28-30 — 254

John 10:30 — 62, 135, 144, 153-154, 156

John 10:33 — 154

John 11:25 — 281

John 11:25-27 — 169

John 11:43,44 — 163

John 12:27 — 249

John 12:35-46 — 243

John 12:41 — 146

John 12:44 — 113

John 12:49 — 59

John 13:1 — 254

John 14 — 202

John 14:3 — 271

John 14:6 — 281

John 14:9 — 113

John 14:10 — 169

John 14:16 — 45, 63-64

John 14:17 — 63

John 14:26 — 63-64

John 14:27 — 171

John 14:28 — 135, 154-155

John 15:5 — 281

John 15:20 — 179

John 15:27 — 63
John 16:5 — 183
John 16:7-14 — 118
John 16:10 — 183
John 16:14 — 63-64
John 16:30 — 157
John 17:3 — 116, 169
John 17:25 — 125, 157
John 18:15-16 — 158
John 18:19 — 179
John 19:1,18 — 168
John 19:7 — 142
John 19:16-17 — 158, 173, 214
John 19:33-36 — 168
John 19:34 — 173-174
John 20:17 — 183
John 20:19 — 179
John 20:20 — 180
John 20:25 — 168
John 20:28 — 135, 149, 156
John 20:29 — 156
John 20:30 — 162, 188, 226
John 20:31 — 162
John 21:6-11 — 157
John 21:17 — 157
John 21:25 — 163, 188, 226
Acts 1:3 — 180
Acts 1:4-5 — 64
Acts 1:9 — 183
Acts 1:9-11 — 137
Acts 1:18 — 191, 224
Acts 2:4-11 — 225
Acts 2:22 — 163
Acts 2:23 — 126
Acts 2:32 — 26
Acts 3:14 — 118
Acts 3:15 — 26
Acts 3:19-23 — 59, 61

Acts 3:22-23 — 168
Acts 4:12 — 284
Acts 4:33 — 26
Acts 5:3-4 — 117
Acts 5:29 — 30
Acts 8:7 — 225
Acts 8:9-11 — 164
Acts 8:13 — 164
Acts 8:29 — 107
Acts 9:4-6 — 107
Acts 9:10 — 107
Acts 10:46 — 225
Acts 13:30-31 — 26
Acts 13:48 — 126
Acts 15:18 — 126
Acts 16:14 — 21
Acts 16:16 — 164
Acts 16:18 — 225
Acts 16:31 — 283
Acts 17:11 — 49, 230
Acts 17:26 — 26
Acts 19:6 — 225
Acts 19:15-16 — 225
Acts 28:3-5 — 225
Romans 1:18 — 250
Romans 2:5,8 — 250
Romans 2:9 — 267
Romans 3:5 — 250
Romans 3:20 — 192, 226, 282
Romans 3:23 — 127, 241, 247
Romans 3:24 — 127, 247
Romans 3:25 — 250
Romans 3:25,28,30 — 247
Romans 3:26 — 125
Romans 3:28 — 245
Romans 3:29-30 — 116
Romans 4:1-25 — 246
Romans 5:1 — 128, 248

Romans 5:1-10 — 121
Romans 5:8 — 93, 121, 282
Romans 5:12 — 237
Romans 5:12,19 — 238, 240
Romans 5:19 — 237
Romans 6:18-22 — 59
Romans 8:1 — 248
Romans 8:2 — 59
Romans 8:3-4 — 175
Romans 8:14 — 107
Romans 8:15 — 108, 252-253
Romans 8:16 — 253
Romans 8:17 — 253
Romans 8:30 — 254, 261
Romans 8:33-34 — 247
Romans 10:9 — 148
Romans 10:14 — 20
Romans 10:17 — 280
Romans 11:11-26 — 224
Romans 11:29 — 254
Romans 11:33 — 118
Romans 14:8-10 — 261
Romans 15:19 — 118
Romans 16:27 — 116
1 Corinthians 1:24 — 112
1 Corinthians 2:9-12 — 280
1 Corinthians 2:10 — 118
1 Corinthians 3:11-15 — 262
1 Corinthians 3:21-23 — 253
1 Corinthians 4:5 — 244, 264
1 Corinthians 5:7 — 177-178, 250-251
1 Corinthians 6:19 — 288
1 Corinthians 6:20 — 265
1 Corinthians 7:2 — 268
1 Corinthians 7:5 — 288
1 Corinthians 8:4 — 116
1 Corinthians 9:25 — 265
1 Corinthians 12:3 — 148
1 Corinthians 12:10 — 225
1 Corinthians 12:11 — 288
1 Corinthians 13:12 — 127
1 Corinthians 14:1-24 — 225
1 Corinthians 14:37 — 231
1 Corinthians 15:1-8 — 283
1 Corinthians 15:6 — 180-181
1 Corinthians 15:21-22 — 237
1 Corinthians 15:25,28 — 62
1 Corinthians 15:54 — 270
1 Corinthians 16:14 — 278
2 Corinthians 1:3-4 — 108
2 Corinthians 3:17 — 21
2 Corinthians 4:4 — 21
2 Corinthians 5:6-8 — 271
2 Corinthians 5:8 — 259
2 Corinthians 5:19-21 — 285
2 Corinthians 5:21 — 249
2 Corinthians 11:14 — 65
2 Corinthians 12:4 — 269
2 Corinthians 13:14 — 119
Galatians 1:1-24 — 229
Galatians 1:8 — 49-50, 230
Galatians 2:16 — 192, 226, 245
Galatians 3:6-14 — 246
Galatians 3:20 — 116
Galatians 3:26 — 107
Galatians 4:4 — 59, 60
Galatians 4:7 — 253
Galatians 4:21–5:12 — 247
Galatians 5:1 — 59
Ephesians 1:3 — 253
Ephesians 1:7 — 252
Ephesians 1:11 — 126
Ephesians 1:13 — 254
Ephesians 2:1-3 — 217, 237
Ephesians 2:3 — 237
Ephesians 2:7 — 273

Ephesians 2:8-9 — 30, 245, 282
Ephesians 4:6 — 116
Ephesians 4:30 — 254, 261
Ephesians 5:2 — 277
Ephesians 5:18 — 288
Ephesians 5:25-28 — 93
Ephesians 6:7-8 — 244, 263
Ephesians 6:10-20 — 29
Philippians 1:23 — 271
Philippians 1:28 — 267
Philippians 2:5-11 — 157
Philippians 2:6-8 — 144
Philippians 2:11 — 148
Philippians 3:7-8 — 106
Philippians 4:6 — 288
Philippians 4:6-7 — 108
Colossians 1:15 — 108, 219
Colossians 1:16 — 118, 146
Colossians 1:17 — 142
Colossians 2:9 — 169
Colossians 3:4 — 272
Colossians 3:12 — 277
Colossians 3:22 — 147
Colossians 4:6 — 25
Colossians 4:16 — 230
1 Thessalonians 1:9 — 116
1 Thessalonians 2:13 — 230-231
1 Thessalonians 4:13-17 — 272
1 Thessalonians 4:17 — 271
1 Thessalonians 5:17 — 288
1 Thessalonians 5:27 — 230
2 Thessalonians 1:8-9 — 267
2 Thessalonians 1:12 — 112
2 Thessalonians 2:9 — 164
1 Timothy 1:17 — 108-109, 116, 219
1 Timothy 2:5 — 116
1 Timothy 2:5-6 — 177-178, 250-251
1 Timothy 3:2,12 — 268

1 Timothy 4:12 — 278
1 Timothy 5:10,25 — 246
1 Timothy 5:18 — 230
1 Timothy 6:15 — 126
1 Timothy 6:16 — 109, 219, 271
2 Timothy 1:8 — 283
2 Timothy 1:9 — 245
2 Timothy 2:24 — 287
2 Timothy 2:24-25 — 25
2 Timothy 3:16 — 215
2 Timothy 3:16-17 — 230
2 Timothy 4:8 — 265
Hebrews 1:1-3 — 93
Hebrews 1:2 — 118, 142, 146
Hebrews 1:2-3 — 112-113
Hebrews 1:3 — 168
Hebrews 1:6 — 149
Hebrews 1:8 — 117
Hebrews 1:8-9 — 62
Hebrews 4:12 — 230
Hebrews 5:6-10 — 168
Hebrews 5:7ff — 175-176, 285
Hebrews 5:14 — 285
Hebrews 6:10 — 125
Hebrews 7–10 — 59
Hebrews 7:17-28 — 169
Hebrews 7:25 — 254
Hebrews 7:27 — 178, 250-251
Hebrews 9:14 — 118
Hebrews 9:15 — 177
Hebrews 9:15,28 — 178, 250-251
Hebrews 9:28 — 178
Hebrews 10:14 — 270
Hebrews 10:17-18 — 252
Hebrews 12:24 — 59
Hebrews 12:29 — 263
James 1:12 — 265
James 2:10 — 282

James 2:14-26 — 192, 226
James 2:19 — 116
James 3:1-12 — 264
James 5:16 — 21
1 Peter 1:2 — 117
1 Peter 1:5 — 118
1 Peter 1:16 — 102
1 Peter 1:18-20 — 175
1 Peter 2:9 — 265
1 Peter 3:15 — 25, 283, 287
1 Peter 5:4 — 265
2 Peter 1:16 — 214
2 Peter 1:16-18 — 153
2 Peter 1:20-21 — 229
2 Peter 3:9 — 130
2 Peter 3:13 — 270
2 Peter 3:16 — 231
1 John 1:1 — 213
1 John 1:3 — 283
1 John 1:5 — 124, 129, 259
1 John 1:7–2:2 — 247
1 John 1:8 — 238
1 John 2:28 — 261
1 John 3:1-2 — 253
1 John 3:16 — 112, 282
1 John 4:1 — 65
1 John 4:7-11 — 122
1 John 4:8 — 121, 281
1 John 4:16 — 102
1 John 5:11-13 — 254
1 John 5:20-21 — 116
2 John 8 — 261
Jude 7 — 274
Jude 25 — 116
Revelation 1:5-6 — 273
Revelation 1:8 — 109
Revelation 1:8, 17 — 118
Revelation 1:14 — 263

Revelation 1:15 — 147
Revelation 1:18 — 163, 183
Revelation 2:7 — 269
Revelation 2:10 — 265
Revelation 2:23 — 244, 264
Revelation 4:10 — 149, 265
Revelation 5:11-14 — 149
Revelation 7:9-10 — 273
Revelation 7:16-17 — 272
Revelation 11:2 — 224
Revelation 12:9 — 164
Revelation 13:13-14 — 164
Revelation 13:15 — 164
Revelation 14:10 — 274
Revelation 14:13 — 272
Revelation 15:4 — 118, 123
Revelation 19–20 — 59
Revelation 19:1-6 — 273
Revelation 19:11-16 — 62
Revelation 19:20 — 274
Revelation 20:5-6,11-15 — 267, 275
Revelation 20:10 — 274
Revelation 20:11-15 — 266
Revelation 20:12-13 — 268
Revelation 21:3 — 271
Revelation 21:4 — 270
Revelation 21:1-2 — 270
Revelation 22:3 — 273
Revelation 22:12 — 268
Revelation 22:18-19 — 201

# Index to Quran Quotations

2:75 — 199
2:97 — 12
2:106 — 76, 89
2:125 — 76
2:132 — 80
2:135 — 102
2:136 — 283
2:140 — 80
2:150 — 76
2:190 — 93
2:216 — 298
2:256 — 53
3:31 — 102
3:32 — 57, 93
3:41 — 93
3:45 — 132, 285
3:49 — 133
3:140 — 121
3:165 — 99
3:181-84 — 55-56, 94
3:185 — 255-256
4:3 — 42, 51, 53
4:28 — 34, 235, 240
4:34 — 93
4:47 — 284
4:54 — 284
4:136 — 185
4:153 — 55, 94

4:157 — 92, 132, 136
4:158 — 285
4:171 — 98, 132
5:17 — 134
5:44-49 — 284
5:49 — 130
5:54 — 80
5:69 — 196, 202, 212, 231
5:73 — 134
5:75 — 93, 228
5:110 — 133
5:116 — 98-99, 117
5:116-17 — 134
6:8-9 — 55-56
6:34 — 198
6:74 — 92
6:93 — 255
6:101 — 133
6:115 — 199
7:11-27 — 34
7:20 — 243-244
8:50 — 255
9:5 — 298
9:30 — 133
9:74 — 43
10:64 — 89
10:94 — 185, 187, 193, 196, 202, 212, 231, 284

341

11:44 — 92
11:90 — 102
11:118-19 — 101
12:53 — 240
14:34 — 240
16:4 — 240
16:61 — 240, 285
16:101 — 75
16:125 — 10
17:80-81 — 18
18:86 — 86
19:23 — 93
19:88-92 — 129
20:63 — 80
23:14 — 86
23:102-103 — 235, 257
24:56 — 14
25:2 — 133
25:13 — 258
28:8-9 — 92
28:16 — 34
29:27 — 60
29:48-50 — 56
30:1-5 — 84
33 — 89-90
33:40 — 34
37:45-47 — 257
37:102-7 — 177-178, 250-251
38:18-25 — 34
38:31-36 — 34
39:7 — 138, 176
40:55 — 51, 53, 285
42:5 — 285
42:30 — 285
46:33 — 256
47:4 — 298
47:19 — 34, 285
48:1-2 — 285

48:2 — 51, 53
50:16 — 97
50:17 — 12
56:42-43 — 258
57:18 — 14
59 — 135
59:22-24 — 96
61:6 — 45, 63
70:19-21 — 240
85:14 — 102
93:6f. — 36
96:6 — 240
105 — 89
111 — 89-90
112:3 — 129, 133

# Harvest House Books by Ron Rhodes

*Angels Among Us*
*The Complete Book of Bible Answers*
*Find It Fast in the Bible*
*Reasoning from the Scriptures with Catholics*
*Reasoning from the Scriptures with Masons*
*Reasoning from the Scriptures with Muslims*
*Reasoning from the Scriptures with the Jehovah's Witnesses*
*Reasoning from the Scriptures with the Mormons*

## The 10 Most Important Things Series

*The 10 Most Important Things You Can Say to a Catholic*
*The 10 Most Important Things You Can Say to a Jehovah's Witness*
*The 10 Most Important Things You Can Say to a Mason*
*The 10 Most Important Things You Can Say to a Mormon*

## Quick Reference Guides

*Angels: What You Need to Know*
*Believing in Jesus: What You Need to Know*
*Bible Translations: What You Need to Know*
*Islam: What You Need to Know*
*Jehovah's Witnesses: What You Need to Know*